POSTULATING CHRIST – 1
DEFAULT

By Robert Mullen

Acknowledgments:

A special thanks to Dr. Kent Hovind for sacrificing his career in public education to gather information to bolster and teach what the Bible records as the Christian creation model. Dr. Hovind has also compiled evidence concerning the conflicts surrounding evolution based upon the unethical and immoral practices of it's proponents as they support and teach it. Dr. Hovind presented many falsehoods and inaccuracies concerning evolution and has discovered many admissions by leading evolutionists that evolution as a science is not the 'fact' that they would have their students believe but rather an unproven and unprovable religion and in certain instances, proven deceit. Dr. Hovind has spent years researching, traveling and speaking out against the failings of evolution through presentations at churches, public debates at leading universities and through his 16 hour Creation seminars. Part of Dr. Hovinds evidence is recorded in this book and we are grateful to Dr. Hovinds ministry for allowing us to include and expound upon portions of his discoveries. It was through Dr. Hovinds discoveries combined with the divine guidance of the Holy Spirit and Gods gift of discernment that this book was written.

TABLE OF CONTENTS

Postulating Christ – The Evolutionary Default

Chapter 1
1   The Scientific Method – An attempt to apply it to the evolution theory (for illustrative purposes)
10   'Hitlers Evolutionary Progression of Man'– Hitlers favored races
12   The Nazi Party is the Evolution Party
14   The Nuremberg Trials, AKA – The Nazi War Crimes Trials
15   The Nazis may have killed up to 20,000,00 people in more concentration camps than previously thought: Study
16   Mans Internal Moral Law
19   The Destroyer of Souls

Chapter 2
23   You are a spirit – Right now: Even as you walk on the earth in a flesh and blood body
25   What does your spirit, the real you look like?
28   Offense; a mans heart and soul will phase it out
30   Gods two definitions of death
35   God treats our reborn spirits differently than he treats our flesh bodies
37   Mans internal struggle
40   God's capabilities
41   Spirit, Soul and Body and others within
44   "The Holy Spirit; Presence, Manifestation and Indwelling …….verses ……..
Satanic or demonic; Infestation, Oppression and Possession"
49   God gives gifts unto men
50   Satanic Spirits sent to indwell men
54   Quotes from Godly intellectual men who have made great contributions to humanity

Chapter 3

59	Gods Big Bang or Big Stretch
62	The Biblical age of the earth
63	The Epistle of Barnabus- Gods 7000 year plan
68	The Jewish Talmud, from about 70 A.D., also speaks about the age of the earth
70	The Launch of the Messiahs ministry in Israel
75	Old Testament prophesies about the Messiah (Jesus) and the corresponding New Testament fulfillment of those prophecies
79	Evolutions age of the earth and the reason homosexuality exists
83	Quotes about the shortcomings of evolution as a science

Chapter 4

93	God uses men to do his will on the earth
93	Nicola Tesla – Science
95	Dr. Johannes Brahms – Music
98	Srinivas Ramanujan – Mathematics
100	God is an alien or 'extraterrestrial'... by mans definition!
101	Every man, woman and child on the planet are, in part, extraterrestrial
102	Biblical UFO's
111	Today's Chariots of Fire, aka ; UFO's
114	The Clouds of God
118	Binary Code from a Chariot of Fire
128	The Extra-Dimensional Spirit World
129	God knows your DNA sequence
131	If we were "created" would we be robots or machines- or something altogether different?
132	DNA researchers have discovered that DNA itself excludes the possibility that evolution could happen - Gods 'fail-safe'

Chapter 5

134	Is the Spirit world powered by electricity and electromagnetism?
137	Are the Spirits of men electric?

137   Low light imaging technologies
145   Evidence that Gods word is true
146   The Angkor Wat Temple Stegosaurus
146   Dinosaurs depicted on the Ica Stones in Peru
148   Dinosaurs depicted on Moche pottery
149   The Acambaro Statues- Dinosaurs, mixed species of animals

Chapter 6
153   The Anunnaki, Big Foot [Hairy Men] and the book of Jasher
157   Are Big Foot in the "Man" class?
161   Noah's Ark and the Flood of the Judgment of Men

Chapter 7
168   The "Device" that floated stones.
        The Sapphire Stick- God used it, Abraham used it, Moses and others used it
169   Ed Leedskalnin's Coral Castle
171   Ed Leedskalnin's book- "Electric Current"
179   The Hidden Code within the Bible

Chapter 8
186   Science in the Bible: Some modern scientific discoveries were recorded within the pages of the Bible centuries ago.
193   God knows all about men – Past, Present, and Future- that includes you!

Chapter 9
195   Evidence that provides overwhelming "Reasonable Doubt" about the evolution religion
196   The Shrinking Sun
200   Super Nova
202   Evolutionists devour their own!
204   Potassium Argon dating with known eruption dates – the numbers don't match
204   Ontogeny Recapitulates Phylogeny- Proven to be false in 1875

209	NC State Paleontologist Discovers Soft Tissue in Dinosaur Bones
212	Ancient T.Rex and Mastodon Protein Fragments Discovered, Sequenced
215	Carbon 14 is still measurable in coal, diamonds and fossils – it' everywhere
220	Why are there only 7 billion people on the earth today?
222	Noah's flood was not the only flood that God used
223	Pharaohs war machines
224	Do all Scholars, Professors, Doctors, Politicians and Governments always have your best interest in mind as they are living their own personal lives and following their own beliefs?
225	Radioactive products for everyday household use
227	Phrenology
227	"Death by Medicine" A research paper done by 5 doctors
231	The numbers don't lie – The statistics of evolution

Chapter 10

237	Satan at work to destroy men
237	The Church of Satan – Opposites don't attract!
242	The Bible compared to evolutionary science – Direct opposition, by design!
245	Satan's false religions; his rulership over the earth to destroy the souls of men
247	A Course in Miracles – Written by Satan
272	Bible – A.C.I.M. comparison

Chapter 11

273	Is the God of the Christian Bible also the God of the Koran of Islam?
276	As in "A Course in Miracles" Satan wrote the Koran specifically to drive men away from Jesus Christ
277	The Madrases – Islamic Schools of Intolerance
286	Is it acceptable to lie in the Muslim faith?...Yes!
288	The Morality of Islam
289	The God of the Christian Bible and the God of the Koran both claim that created the heavens, the earth and men.

293	'Son of Hamas' warns Islamic group can't be appeased

Chapter 12

294	Israel does own the land they live on today!
295	Gods land contract with Israel- A record in Jacobs "Book of Purchase" that Israel owns the land of Israel

Chapter 13

301	The Muslim Mahdi – Mohammed's successor
302	A Muslim would tell you the 'Gods' of Christianity and Islam are not the same God.
303	The Falling Away
304	Chrislam
307	A significant Islamic community in the U.S.A.? (article)
307	The rise of the Islamic No-Go Zones (article)
308	Muslim Enclaves U.S.A. (article)
311	List of cities with Islamic No-Go Zones in America
313	Background on the Prophet Mohammed
314	The Bible Koran Comparison
318	The Satanic Verses
320	Islamic Jihadist Organizations declared to be terrorist organizations by the United States and others.
327	Islamic Attacks perpetrated against the United States
330	Islam's Conquering of the World
339	With all of the checks and balances in Washington, what real effect would an Islamic President have during his Presidency.
345	All men have eternal consciousness in heaven or hell
346	Satan and Israel

Chapter 14

351	The testimony of a believer My witness that Gods word is true
356	The downloads from heaven
357	There is nothing to small for the Lord

Chapter 15

361 Speaking in an unknown language or tongues
363 Are there contradictions in the Bible or is it a comprehension issue?

BONUS:

Chapter 16

365 **THE HEALING SCRIPTURES AND HINDRANCES TO SCRIPTURAL HEALING**

370 Healing scriptures confession... to be read out-loud

378 **CONCLUSION**

381- 389 **(References in line) Alphabetical reference pages**

POSTULATING CHRIST – THE EVOLUTIONARY DEFAULT

By Robert Mullen

Copyright Robert Mullen – December 2013
Cover art - "The Icon Graft" – Robert Mullen
Publisher – Robert Mullen through CreateSpace
1st Revision - September 2014

PREFACE

"A long habit of not thinking a thing wrong gives it a superficial appearance of being right...Time makes more converts than reason."
...Thomas Payne, Common Sense, January 10, 1776

"I was a young man with unformed ideas. I threw out queries, suggestions, wondering all the time over everything; and to my astonishment the ideas took like wildfire. People made a religion out of them.!"
.....Charles Darwin on his own theory of evolution

Merriam–Webster defines **"Postulate"** as: "A proposal taken for granted as true and made the starting point in a chain of **reasoning**."

This book was written from a Christian perspective by an ex-evolutionist who is today, in part due to Dr. Hovinds evidence of a young earth creation model, once again totally adherent to the Christian creation world view. There are numerous religions in the world today that compete to influence your world view- they are not all created equal nor do they serve the same God. During my research, I have found no other religious work comparable to the continuation of theme, syntax, historical and ideational completeness and accuracy of the Christian Bible via the earlier Masoretic texts (you will see why in chapter 7) and other equivalent original Hebrew and Greek manuscripts of the New

Testament and their early translations. The closer you get to the original manuscripts the more divinely inspired, authoritative and significant the text becomes. The Bible is spiritual, religion is intellectual; the Bible is designed to be spiritually discerned or understood – not for mans **intellect. Most Universities (not all) hire "Religious Educators" that only have an intellectual understanding of the Bible because they are not connected to the Spirit of the Bible- the Holy Spirit, the Bible can only be spiritually discerned.** Not only did I discover the truth about evolution but also the truth about Islam and Anton Lavey's Church of Satan, they all serve and obey the same God. This book is not meant to offend those of other religions but rather to give the reader an understanding, by comparisons, of the way the spirit world operates through men and to bring the truth of what the Bible teaches to those of Christianity and other religions. In this book Christianity, Islam, Darwin , Hitler and evolution are all on trial and the testimony of witnesses, including the God of Christianity, will expose the truth about each of them. My research began with a question; What is the truth?

Merriam–Webster defines "Default", in part, as "failure to do something required by duty or law: Failure to compete in or finish an appointed contest."
A victory can be obtained by the failure of the opposition to perform, act or prove something that is required of them.

Merriam–Webster defines "**Religion**" as:
1 -The service and worship of God or the supernatural.
2 - Devotion to a religious faith.
3* – <u>**An organized system of faith**</u> **and worship, A personal set of religious beliefs and practices. 4* –** <u>**A cause, principle or belief**</u> **held to with faith and ardor(Zeal).**
*Special emphasis on definitions 3 and 4 above!

Merriam–Webster defines "**Axiom**" as: A proposal deemed to be self-evident and assumed without proof."

What a "religion" boils down to is a person's core beliefs based upon the doctrinal teachings of the religion he or she is in. **There is no need for a divine God in religion, you only need a system of faith, principle or a cause**; see definitions 3 and 4 above. Generally speaking, there are no tangible proofs of or for a religion but there are proofs against certain false religions when some of their beliefs are based upon physical attributes. Case in point, "Evolution" - evolution is a religion yet taught in schools as a scientific fact. Evolution has always been unproven and unprovable and that fact alone excludes it from being accepted as a true discipline of science. Since evolution is taught as a proven fact in science classes, to the exclusion of all other models (Christianity), it should first be proven as "science" and not just believed and forced upon students as an axiom. The better half of this book is devoted to disproving evolution as a science by offering dozens of articles and quotes from scientific leaders and others from around the globe. If you were to try to prove evolution you would need to apply all of the scientific "Proof of Concept" parameters to Darwins theory in order to make it a theorem or a 'proven theory', this detail about Darwin's theory has never been done and with good reason as mentioned above, it can't be done, how can one observe anything about Darwin's theory? How can a researcher reproduce any part of it? The hope has always been that it would become an 'unproven' axiom and just believed by blind faith. All that is required to defend evolution is time - enormous amounts of time which cannot be challenged because no one can go back in time to observe the beginning. However, there are other evidences that render evolution 'much less' than factual and need to be seriously addressed prior to it's blind acceptance as true only because the public school systems have adopted it in their curriculum. For the sake of time I am using only the major personalities involved in bringing evolution to the for-front in our educational systems. There were many other men involved in forming the concept of "Evolution" but Darwin was the one that attempted to unify everything into one hypothesis.

Chapter 1

Let's begin with what all true science begins with, "The Scientific Method", there are strict guidelines that must be adhered to in order to make an unproven hypothesis a proven theory:

THE SCIENTIFIC METHOD – An attempt to apply it to evolution (for illustrative purposes)

Steps:
1...Make observations
2...Form a testable, unifying hypothesis to explain the observations.
3...Deduce predictions from the hypothesis
4...Search for confirmation of the predictions; **if the predictions are contradicted by empirical evidence (evidence derived from experience or observation), go back to step 2.**

Rules:
1...Scientific explanations must make predictions.
2...Predictions should prove to be necessary to prove the hypothesis.
3...**Predictions must be validated by independent observers.**
4...**The validity of a hypothesis must stand on the totality of the evidence.**
5...**If there is one shred of evidence that falsifies the hypothesis then the hypothesis is false, form another hypothesis.**
6...If the hypothesis is proven, it becomes a theory.

Science claims that life on earth is 3.8 billion years old. **(using today's numbers)**
The universe is 20 + billion years old.
Q. Can a scientist observe evolution or the Big Bang occurring from the beginning? No
Q. Can a scientist reproduce evolution, transformation or the Big Bang? No

Q. Can a scientist create life? No
Q. Has a scientist ever observed life instantaneously begin? No
Q. Can an independent observer reproduce or observe the beginning of life or the universe? No
Q. Why do evolutionarily writers use "terms of faith" such as; "... and these early life forms **'must have emerged'** from this primordial soup?
They don't know it did – they believe and hope it did yet they still force it upon students as a fact. This is the greatest objection from Christianity, the way evolution is taught, it is not a scientific fact. Evolution will always be an unproven hypothesis and it's support is based solely upon the faith that the observer has in it. Not one shred of the theory has ever been proven since its inception over 150 years ago.

In 1830, Sir Charles Lyell, an ex-lawyer turned geologist, wrote a book called "Principles of Geology". In his book he claimed the earth was 300,000 million years old. Sir Lyell had no rock dating technology available at the time to prove his hypothesis since the first dating technology of any type, Carbon 14 dating, was not invented until 1949, 119 years after his book was published. He could not have used this first technology on rock since rock has no Carbon 14 in it. So 180 plus years ago the age of the earth **and** the geologic column were a "guess" introduced with absolutely nothing in the form of a "dating technology" or other "scientific methodology", these technologies would not exist for another 119 + years. Beyond that, Lyells guesswork continues in the way we date index fossils within the rock layers to this day. "We date the index fossils by the rock layers they are found in" **and** "we date the rock layers by the index fossils found in them. " Circular Reasoning! The ages Lyell gave for rock strata and fossils had nothing to do with science but rather what an amateur geologist that clearly despised everything associated with God guessed at 180+ years ago.

Would you go to a doctor today that earned his Medical degree from a university that taught medicine from the early 1800's? Unfortunately we have allowed ourselves to be "locked into" this antiquated guesswork by a man that claimed to be superior to God! Lyell, as most evolutionists today, was a humanist- he relied only upon his own capability and intellect, in his book he spoke about the Bible. He says the Bible is outdated and cannot be used to reference the age of the earth (even though the Bible records - "from the beginning"). Lyell says the Bible is a book of futile reasoning with false conclusions – he has the right to his opinion but he and Darwin both expressed their opinions and their opinions became unsubstantiated scientific facts and they are still to this day expressed as facts.

"Men of superior talent, who thought for themselves, and were not blinded by authority"
.... Charles Lyell

The "Authority" Lyell was referring to was the Catholic church's position on the age of the earth, Lyell is saying he is not blinded by Gods word and that he is 'essentially' of a higher intellect than the men that believed in God. Could it be that Lyell came up with 300 million years for the earths age because God records about 6000 years in the Bible and he didn't want to appear to be agreeing with God. After all, how could Lyell be superior to men that believed there was a God and also agree with what God is saying. Lyell is by no means the only scientist to overtly oppose Gods word!

Carbon dating cannot be used to date rock since rock has no carbon in it. Carbon dating is limited to once living and living organisms. Throughout the lifetime of a living organism they would breathe in Carbon 14 and consume food that has an accumulation of Carbon 14 in it. Upon the death of the organism, the C-14 radiation collected would decay out and that decay is assumed to be measurable which will give a date of existence based on Carbon 14's half- life every 5770 years. This technique is only viable out to 50,000 years max until it dissipates out of the bones, fossils or other organic matter. Again, Lyell was only

4.

guessing at an inflated age of the earth because he had no room for God in his intellect.
Charles Darwin read Lyells book and told a friend, Russell Wallace, that Lyells book had changed his life forever and went on to say;

"Disbelief [in God] crept over me on a very slow rate, but at last complete. The rate was so slow that I felt no distress"
..... Charles Darwin.

Charles Darwin wrote "The Origin of Species" partly based on what Charles Lyell had written, Darwin had Lyells book with him on the 'Beagle'. Darwins book was originally titled- **"The Origin Of Species by Means of Natural Selection, or, The Preservation of Favored Races in the Struggle for Life"**. This was the entire original title but today its been reduced to "The Origin of Species" to take the racist overtones out and to make it sound more "Scientifically" palatable. Charles was born the same day as Abraham Lincoln, 2/12/1809, ironically one went on to do an enormous amount of good in the world and the other an enormous amount of injury to the world as you will see later. Today's evolutionary religion began from men which had no true means to measure the age of anything and they both admittedly did not believe in God and were just making guesses probably to disprove the authority of the Bible and bolster their own authority. Darwin claimed that he had researched the historical record and that he and Aristotle both believed the earth to be of great age (intellectual support). Darwin cited Lyells book and agreed with Lyell that the age of the earth was 300 million years (academic support). Neither Lyell or Darwin saw any proofs of their hypothesis and Darwin, hopefully, may have recanted his theory of evolution on his deathbed. Darwin published with no evidence for the validity of his theory, he was expecting other researchers to find his proofs for him. To date, in the last 150+ years since Darwin's book came out no intermediate fossils linking any supposedly early stage species with a supposedly later stage species have been found.

5.

There have been no technical, social, moral or ethical advancements that can be attributed to the evolution 'science' or religion. On the contrary, there have been several anti-social, immoral and unethical practices directly related to the evolution religion.
In 1859 when Darwin's book first hit the bookstores he originally thought the earth to be 300,000,000 years old as Lyell had suggested.

For illustrative purposes, per the evolutionists claim, we are using today's ages of when life and the earth began to apply the 'Scientific methodology' to his hypothesis. Granted, its not going to fit into a testable and predictable model but I do have the benefit of hindsight and my predictions are derived from the historical record which will show the true effect that evolution had on humanity. This exercise is designed to show you the inherent flaws of evolution especially at it's inception and is intended to show you the "Rest of the Story"of what Darwinian evolution did for the world... and continues to do.

1.Make observations; (using today's values for the ages of the earth and life)
a... The earth is billions of years old ... Darwin agreed with Lyell on 300 million
b... Life on earth is billions of years old ... Darwin suggested millions
c... Life forms change over time.
d... Life began as single celled organisms and evolved to multi-cellular organisms
e... A more powerful organism can dominate or eradicate a less powerful organism to survive, the survival of the fittest!

2. Form a testable , unifying hypothesis to explain the observations

a... **The earth is millions or billions of years old!**
Not testable, as of 1859 , there are no methods to measure the

age of rock, including fossils and bones. We can only guess as of now.
The first dating technique will be developed 90 years in the future in 1949 but useless on rock

b... Life on earth is millions or billions of years old!
Not testable, this will not be tenable for 90 more years until 1949 yet Carbon 14 dating has an outside parameter of only 50,000 years.

c... Life forms change over time!
Darwin witnessed a slight variation in the beaks of finches on Galapagos Island during drought and non-drought periods. In the overall scheme of things, as we are talking about millions of years for changes to occur, the results are insignificant and inconclusive. The finches, as birds, remained finches, as birds.

d... Life began as a single cell organism and evolved to multi-cellular organisms!
Darwin, as stated in his book had no proof of this claim but was relying upon the research of others in their respective fields to prove his hypothesis. He was looking for a missing link between apes and chimps and men. None have been found nor have any other links between any other life forms to date.

e... A more powerful organism can dominate or eradicate a less powerful organism to survive!
The survival of the fittest! We expect to see large predators devouring smaller prey animals. We expect predator populations to keep prey populations in check. We expect to see overpopulation genocide since some species are competing for limited resources. We expect to see more advanced men rule over less advanced or evolved men.

3. Deduce predictions from the hypothesis.

a... The earth is millions of years old!
We are hoping for a future technology that will be able to answer this question. As for now, it remains only a guess. (Today, in 2013 there are no accurate means to measure anything, rock or biological as you will see in later chapters)

b... Life on earth is millions of years old!
Again, we are hoping that future technology will answer this question and prove the hypothesis.
c... Lifeforms change over time!
We believe that if a certain group of collaborators study the Galapagos Island finches for several thousand generations, approximately 5 – 10 million years then a change might happen that renders them a higher species, maybe a chimp or apelike creature, time will tell.
d... Life began as a single celled organism and evolved to a multi-cellular organism!
If we take a large group of single cell organisms and apply the same research model in prediction "C" above then after several million years we should see multi-cellular organisms emerge. This will take the collaborative efforts of several hundred university professors to watch over and pass down the experiment. Critical thinkers and precise record keeping will be required and absolutely essential to prove the hypothesis.
e... A more powerful organism can dominate or eradicate a less powerful organism to survive!
The survival of the fittest. We predict the wild animal populations will continue to fight for survival. They will fight over resources, food, water, land and mating ability. Men of favored races will exercise dominance over 'less evolved' races of men. Men will struggle to obtain the limited resources necessary to survive and the less favored races of men will be dominated over by higher races of men and the less evolved men will eventually diminish in numbers over time and some races will die out.

4. Search for confirmation of the predictions; if the predictions are contradicted by empirical observation, go back to step 2.

The 'Evolution Hypothesis' (religion) is in direct violation of steps 2 and 4 and Rules 3, 4 and 5 of the Scientific Method. It is not confirm-able with or without our current capabilities of empirical observation concerning animals changing species or the millions or billions of years that it takes for evolution to occur. It cannot be weighed, tested, confirmed or reproduced in any way, shape, form or fashion by an independent observer. The requirement of millions of years for species transformation has not been observed in action nor has it be verified as having happened in the fossil record. Rule number 5 states that if there is one shred of evidence that falsifies the hypothesis then the hypothesis is false, form another hypothesis. Since nothing about evolution can be verified as fact, then it remains an unproven hypothesis and should not be taught in the public schools as scientific fact to the exclusion of all other 'Models'. The U.S. government and each of the 50 independent states are teaching a state sponsored religion. If taught at all, it should be taught as a religion and not mixed into the science curriculum as science.

a.... The earth is billions of years old?

In 1905, the scientific community agreed the earth was 2 billion years old.
In 1969, the scientific community agreed the earth was 3.5 billion years old.
In 2005, the scientific community agreed the earth was 4.8 billion years old.
Science more than doubled the age of the earth in just 100 years. That's more than a 100% error in one life-time. If they all agree that they got that wrong what else did they get wrong?

Lyell wrote his book in 1830 based on a hope and a guess and Darwin wrote his book partly based on Lyell.
Today we have Carbon 14 , Potassium Argon, Lead 208, Lead 206, Rubidium Strontium, Uranium
205, Uranium 238 dating and, with the exception of C-14, they all have "millions of years" as a baseline for the results they obtain and none have been 'Proven' (As you will see later). They don't have to use millions as a baseline for their results for earths history but that's what their religion calls for. These measurements can be scaled at 100's of years or 1000's of years

but they need millions of years. That is the only reason they get the huge numbers they get. Lunch time will be 12,000,000 o'clock.

b. c.... Is life on earth millions of years old? Do life forms change over time?
The evolution hypothesis was formed over 150 years ago and no change has ever been observed. No missing links have ever been discovered save a few bird and supposed early man hoaxes. Only variation and adaptation have been observed.

d... Did life begin as a single cell organism and evolve to multi-cellular?
In 150 years, this has never been observed or documented. As you will see later, DNA itself limits an organism from changing to the point where it is impossible for evolution to happen. Very small DNA changes result in the death of the organism. Any change to an organism would have to take place at the DNA level for evolution to happen and the chances that an organism can change and survive through the Darwinian evolutionary process is zero.

e.... Can a more powerful organism dominate or eradicate a less powerful organism to survive, the survival of the fittest! Can one race of man dominate another, 'lesser' race of man?

This part of Darwin's theory is both true and immoral. It is true that all living things are competing for the earths natural resources and some living creatures do perish in the struggle for life because the stronger do survive one on one. However, superimposing the natural order of predator and prey over mans dominion of man was just wrong to suggest and that led to the deaths of millions of men and women. Darwin planted the 'seeds of racism' into men- and how one race of man could possibly dominate another race of man. Darwin's book was the trigger in Stalin and Hitlers mind that led to the holocaust in Germany.

10.

Joseph Stalin went to a Christian school as a young man but then read Charles Darwin's book and became an atheist. Stalin murdered between 60-100 million of his own people.

Adolf Hitler read Darwin's book and the second half of the title really stuck in his mind, "The Preservation of Favored Races [of Men] in **the struggle for life**". Hitler concluded that he was favored through natural selection and should be preserved and all unfavorable's should be destroyed for the good of Germany. Hitler wrote his own book called "Mien Komfe" which translates to "**My Struggle**". Hitler wrote about developing a "Master Race" of men which were blonde haired blue eyed white skinned Nordics. All others, (including himself), were inferior human beings because they had not evolved as much as the Nordics.

" The German Fuhrer...has consistently sought to make the practice of Germany conform to the theory of evolution."
...Sir Arthur Keith, Evolution and Ethics, 1947

"**Evolution** is unproven and unprovable. We believe it because the only alternative is special creation, and that is unthinkable."
...Sir Arthur Keith

In other words, Sir Keith is saying Christianity would be the default if the evolution religion fails! If an educator (Darwin, Lyell and others) hates God or feels he is intellectually beyond what the inferior people believe and does not wish to teach "Gods Creation Model" in their classroom then they have a dilemma. They needed to think of something to replace God with in the school system. Satan stepped in and gave them a hand.

"Hitlers Evolutionary Progression of Man"

Hitler penned his own list of favored races of men that would live in his new world that he was creating. At the top of Hitlers list are the most evolved humans - as you descend down the list Hitler 'supposed' that the races of men were less and less evolved and hence, less favorable.

"Species" ....**"Blood Mix"**

Nordic -
white skin blonde hair blue eyes .... Close to   pure Aryan

Germanic -
white skin brown hair .... Predominately Aryan
blue or brown eyes

Mediterranean .... Slightly Aryan

Slavic .... Close to ½ Aryan ½ Ape

Oriental .... Slight Ape preponderance

Black African .... Predominately Ape

Jewish (Fiendish Skull) .... Close to pure Ape

... The Hitler Movement, a Millenarian Revolution, James Rhodes, 1980, pg. 107

"I regard Christianity as one of the most fatal, seductive lies that ever existed"
... Adolf Hitler, 20th Century in Crisis, Larry Azar, 1990, pg. 180

Adolf Hitler spelled out the holocaust in his book and then proceeded to execute his plan to rid the world of the "inferior species" of men by extermination. Darwin, Stalin and Hitler caused the deaths of millions because they believed they were more highly evolved and since they were of superior stock it was their duty to eradicate the inferior races to purify Germany.

In 1935, Hitler instituted his "Blood Law" that made it unlawful for anyone in Germany to marry a Jewish person or have sexual relations with a Jewish person. Hitler also launched his "Preferred Stock" program which caused 400,000 people to be sterilized because they did not qualify as "fit" or they did not have the qualities Hitler wanted for his 'Master Race' and he did not want their "Inferior Blood" mixing with his the new Nordic/Germanic population.

Hitler convinced his Law Branch to change the law and declare Jewish people non-humans so Hitlers regime would not be guilty of murder when they slaughtered the Jews at the death camps. In 1936, the German Supreme Court passed the law that stated that Germany did not recognize Jews as persons in the legal sense. Adolf was later asked about the slaughter of the Jews and he replied:
"I have the right to exterminate an inferior race that breed like the vermin"
.... Adolf Hitler

THE NAZI PARTY IS THE EVOLUTION PARTY

Today's evolutionists don't realize that **the exact same spirits and ideologies** that divide Christianity and evolution were shared with Christianity and the Nazi Party. Evolutionists believe that science explains the reason that the earth exists and that God had nothing to do with it. Evolutionists believe that science and technology are the main reasons people get healed in hospitals and God is not involved. Science and, specifically, the men of science have all the answers to almost every question in the universe or will have if they put their intellects to the task. Christianity and religion in general, according to evolutionists are useless constructs from a by-gone era to control the ignorant masses of men on the earth. In 1981, George Mosse wrote a book called "Nazi Culture": Intellectual, Cultural and Social Life in the 3rd Reich". The following is an **excerpt from his book that was written by the** head of the Nazi Party Chancellery:

"National Socialist [Nazi] and Christian concepts are incompatible. The Christian churches build upon the ignorance of men and strive to keep large portions of the people in ignorance... On the other hand, National Socialism is based on scientific foundations. Christianities immutable principles, which were laid down almost 2000 years ago, have increasingly stiffened into life-alien dogmas. National Socialism, however, if it wants to fulfill its task further, must always guide itself according to the newest data of scientific researches... The Christian churches have long been aware that **exact** scientific knowledge poses a threat to their existence. Therefore, by means of such pseudo-science as theology, they take great pains to suppress or falsify scientific research. Our National Socialist world view stands on a much higher level than the concepts of Christianity, **which in** the essentials **were** taken over from Judaism. For this reason, too, we can do without Christianity.
... Martin Bormann, head of the Nazi Party Chancellery and Hitlers Private Secretary

Today's pro-evolution **University** professors that are against everything the Bible stands for are telling their students something very similar to what's recorded in this letter by Bormann. I have replaced "National Socialist" and added "evolution" in its place and re-wrote it below:

Evolution and Christian concepts are **incompatible**. The Christian churches build upon the ignorance of men and strive to keep large portions of the people in ignorance...On the other hand, **evolution** is based on scientific foundations. Christianities immutable principles, which were laid down almost 2000 years ago, have increasingly stiffened into life-alien dogmas. **Evolution**, however, if it wants to fulfill its task further, must always guide itself according to the newest data of scientific researches... The Christian churches have long been aware that exact scientific knowledge poses a threat to their existence. Therefore, by means of such pseudo-science as theology, they take great pains to suppress or falsify scientific research. **Our evolution world view** stands on a much higher level than the concepts of Christianity, which in their essentials were taken over from Judaism. For this reason, too, we can do without Christianity.

Satan used Darwin to plant the "inferiority of races" seed into Hitlers thoughts and Hitler thought he had the right to murder the Jewish people solely upon his superiority to them by his own 'highly evolved' status. Hitler believed he would not have to fear legal retribution since the Jews were non-persons in the courts of Germany. Hitler was Wrong!

THE NUREMBERG TRIALS

Aka; The Nazi War Crimes Trials

The Nuremberg trials were post war trials to bring to justice everyone involved in the planning and execution of Hitlers plan to exterminate those whom Hitler tagged as 'inferior races' which included the German Jews, the Polish Jews and others. For decades after the war these "War criminals" were hunted worldwide in an attempt to bring them to justice. Until recently the estimated death toll of civilian Jews through Hitlers extermination plan was thought to be approximately 6,000,000 people. New research increases the toll closer to potentially 20,000,000 people who were murdered by Hitlers regime.

15.

The following is an excerpt from an article written for the "Global Post" News agency by Freya Petersen;

"NAZIS MAY HAVE KILLED UP TO 20,000,000 PEOPLE IN MORE CONCENTRATION CAMPS THAN PREVIOUSLY THOUGHT: STUDY"

"The Nazis …. may have killed up to 20 million people, operating more than 6 times the number of concentration camps as previously thought, according to new research. Researchers at the U.S. Holocaust Memorial Museum spent 13 years analyzing evidence and cataloged some 42,500 ghettos and forced labor camps run by Hitlers regime.
That number includes "Killing Centers" as well as "Care Centers" where pregnant women were forced to have abortions or their babies were killed after birth, and about 500 brothels.

The New York Times reported in an article titled:
"The Holocaust Just Got More Shocking."
Conventional wisdom on the Holocaust suggests that the Nazis killed 6,000,000 Jewish people in Europe. According to researchers [at] the United States Holocaust Memorial Museum in Washington D.C., construction of the camps began as early as 1933, with facilities purpose built to imprison political opponents of Adolf Hitler...The largest of the camps, the Warsaw Ghetto, held around 500,000 people.
One of the lead editors of the project, called the Encyclopedia of Camps and Ghettos. Geoffrey Megargee said when the study began in 2000, he had assumed they would find about 7,000 camps and ghettos. But as their work continued and they discovered more and more camps, "The numbers skyrocketed to 11,500, then 20,000, then 30,000, and now 42,500. " "The independent" quoted Megargee as saying: "The results of our research are shocking, we are putting together numbers that no one ever compiled before, even for camp systems that have been fairly well researched – and many of them have not been."

The Holocaust Museum created maps of the sites, which were scattered across Europe from France to Russia, and which imprisoned or killed between 15 and 20 million people..."
.... Freya Petersen, Global Post, March 4, 2013

Defendants on trial plead "Not guilty" and claimed they had not broken the laws of Germany. The defendants claimed they were only obeying the orders of their superiors. They were correct, they did not break a single German law and they were obeying orders. They were all found guilty as charged based upon man's internal moral law.

"MAN'S INTERNAL MORAL LAW"

The internal moral law that's written upon each mans heart (by God) lead to the conviction of each defendant. By mans free will he can choose to ignore his "internal moral law" but by doing so - God calls him a "carnally minded" man and as such, is made a servant of Satan;

"Because the carnal mind is enmity [made and enemy] against God"
.... Romans 8:7

The 'Law' was written by the God that created the heavens and earth and no law written by a man takes precedence over it. God has given the earth to men to rule over using his internal law.

" The heavens are the Lords, the earth has he given to the children of men"
.... Psalms 115

17.

The following is what God says about his application of his law in mankind:

"For when the Gentiles [non-Jews] which have not the law [of Moses], do by nature the things contained in the law, these, having not the law, are a law unto themselves: Which show the work of the law written in their hearts, their conscience also bearing witness, and their thoughts the mean while accusing or else excusing one another. In the day when God shall judge the secrets of men by Jesus Christ according to my gospel"
...... Roman 2: 14-16

For a better understanding I have included the Amplified version; a more modern English version of the same verses;

"When Gentiles who have not the [Mosaic] law do instinctively what the law requires they are a law unto themselves [since they do not have an understanding based upon instruction in the law]. They show that the essential requirements of the law are written in their hearts and are operating there. With which their consciences [sense of right and wrong] also **bear** witness; and their [moral] decisions [the argument of reason, their condemning or approving thoughts] will accuse or perhaps defend and excuse them. On that day when, as my gospel [Mathew, Mark, Luke, John] proclaims, God by Jesus Christ will judge men in regard to the things which they conceal [their hidden thoughts]."
... Romans 2: 14-16 Amp

Even though every man on earth has this law inside his soul - it is either agreed with or disagreed with by each mans "free will". **There are two choices**, you either serve the God of the 'law' or the God of lawlessness which is Satan, the latter was Hitlers **choice**.

18.

Men such as Darwin and Hitler are spoken of in the Bible, the same scriptures that apply to Hitler also apply to evolutionists that teach their students to disregard God, read them very carefully if you are one of those evolutionists;

"And even though they did not like to retain God in their knowledge, God gave them over to a reprobate mind, to do those things which are not convenient; being filled with all unrighteousness, fornication, wickedness, covetousness, maliciousness; full of envy, murder, debate, deceit, malignity, whisperers, back biters, haters of God, despiteful, proud, boasters. Inventors of evil things, disobedient to parents, without understanding, covenant–breakers, without natural affection, implacable, unmerciful: who knowing the judgment of God, they that commit such things are worthy of death, not only do the same, but have pleasure in them that do them."
.... Romans 1: 28-32

"Having the understanding darkened, being alienated from the life of God through the ignorance that is in them, because of the blindness of their heart: who being past feeling have given themselves over to lasciviousness [immorality], to work all uncleanness with greediness."
.... Ephesians 4: 18-19

"See to it that no one carries you off as spoil or makes you yourselves captive by his so called philosophy and intellectualism and vain deceit (plain nonsense). Following human tradition [mans ideas of the material world rather than the spiritual world]. Just crude notions following the rudimentary and elemental teachings of the universe and disregarding [the teachings of] Christ [the Messiah]"
..... Colossians 2: 8 AMP

Hitler, through Darwin's book, envisioned a 'Master race' of humans in his ever-expanding 3rd Reich Empire that he proclaimed would last 1000 years, he made it to 12 years. While attempting to exercise his "right" to destroy inferior races in order to create his Master Race he shared in the responsibility of the deaths of an estimated *70 million people.
*Up recently from the previous estimate of 56 million and possibly still rising.
Let's apply the outcome of Hitlers attempt to create a Master Race to Darwin's scientific method.

Part 4; e... Can one race of man dominate another race of man? Survival of the fittest
Yes, he can, for a season, but morality and love intervened. God used the combined might of all the Allied forces to share in the destruction of Adolf Hitlers 3rd Reich.

"THE DESTROYER OF SOULS"

As devastated as the world was at the close of World War II most of the world did not understand the underlying "cause and effect" which was Satan's use of men like Darwin, Hitler and Stalin for his own purposes- the destruction of man. Satan's plan was to plant the seeds of superiority in their minds which exalted one race of men over another. Darwin's evolution led to the removal of God from the world equation which led to Adolf Hitlers attempt to exercise what he thought was his right to destroy inferior races of men. Satan is still using Darwin's ideology today in his evolution religion to destroy mans faith in God and in the end, destroying the souls of men. Evolution as a science has been proven bogus as you will see in later chapters yet evolution as a religion lives on. When 'Evolution' became an axiom they didn't have to prove anything, it was just added as a requirement in the curriculum and taught and received as a "Fact" and in a religion you are not required to provide proof, just believe by faith.

By taking a young persons faith in the Lord Jesus away by teaching **'evolution replaces creation'** and that Christianity is "useless" then our children are not brought up in the admonition of Lord. They do not surrender their lives to Jesus, they are having their relationship with God stripped from them and heaven will be forfeited. It seems so innocent since it is being taught to our children by people that we know and should trust – teachers, this is the greatest harm any man could perpetrate on another man (or child); causing the destruction of their spirits and souls in hell.

Today's evolution student will become tomorrows evolution teacher, the pattern is already in place and has been for decades. The blind are leading the blind and they are both headed for the ditch. Evolution as a religion that's taught in science classes has been carefully guarded to the point that some meaningful 'scientific discoveries' that do not fit into the 'evolution religious dogma' have been and will continue to be covered up and the world will suffer from their lack of disclosure (some of these are recorded in future chapters). Evolution is not 'Science', it's a religion and not a very moral or meaningful religion, it's a false destructive religion sponsored by the U.S. Government and other governments around the world with tax dollars that should not be spent on Satan's agenda. I'm not saying the government knows they are supporting a false religion, but they are forcing taxpayers to financially back a religion that they incorrectly believe is science. God has a message for 'evolution' teachers that know they are teaching a falsehood;

"But whoso shall offend one of these little ones which believe in me, it were better for him that a millstone were hanged about his neck, and that he were drowned in the depth of the sea."
… Mathew 18: 6

Notice that God makes a distinction in which little ones that harm is done to, **the little ones that believe in him**, meaning they already have a relationship with him. God calls us his children and as a human father would take a dim view of a person that had a part in his child's death. So does God.

"75% of children raised in Christian homes reject their Christian faith in their first year of College"
… Carol Matritiano, Let My Children Go.

I myself was one of those children brought up in church and Sunday school. I remember thinking about the things that I was taught in Sunday school about God creating the earth while sitting in a public school classroom and listening to a teacher talk about evolution. I was, to say the least, confused about the mixed messages that I was hearing but never questioned anyone about the disappointment that I was experiencing. I believed the creation story of the Bible 100% back then and over the years- the public school system replaced Gods creation with Satan's evolution and I quit going to church and Sunday school and spent the next 26 years away from church because I believed a lie. Even though I wasn't in church, I still remembered the things I had been taught when I was a child in church and still felt like I had a connection to God. Back at that time in my life I didn't dare question authority and I viewed school teachers as being certified, state sponsored experts with the utmost authority, equal to the law and the courts. I thought they had to be experts in everything and if they were sanctioned by the State they must be teaching on a subject that absolutely had to be the truth – I was wrong! They were not teaching pure science, they were teaching science mixed with religion, a "state sponsored religion" at that. To be fair to most of the 'Science' teachers out there, they may have been like myself and they also 'bought into' evolution as I did in my early life. All I ask of them is to teach science, not religion, pure science, not evolution. If you want to teach 'evolution', make it an elective course under "World Religions" along with Islam, Buddhism, Hinduism- call it Evolutionism.

God records his thoughts about what we teach our children:

"Train up a child in the way he should go: And when he is old, he will not depart from it."
... Proverbs 22:6

"And you fathers, provoke not your children to wrath: but bring them up in the nurture and admonition of the Lord."
... Ephesians 6:14

God said he created the heavens and the earth and all they that dwell therein - he breathed the breathe of life into every one of us. God never said he created anything over millions of years, he said he created all things in 6 days beginning on "The First Day" ["The", definite article, and there is only one] and rested from all of his work on the 7th day.

"Why do the heathen [the ungodly] rage, and the people imagine a vain thing? The Kings [Presidents and Prime Ministers] of the earth set themselves, and the rulers take council together [The United Nations – The World Bank], against the Lord, and against his anointed [Pastors, Prophets, Preachers, Teachers of Christ, Christian's and Evangelists], saying "Let us break their bands [the Godly laws that restrain them], and cast away their cords [of control, like the bridal of a horse] from us." He that sitteth in the heavens shall laugh: the Lord shall have them in derision....."
.... Psalms 2: 1-4

Chapter 2

YOU ARE A SPIRIT------RIGHT NOW: Even as you walk on the earth in a flesh and blood body

The Bible records that every man that ever lived on the earth is a spirit being and God created our spirits and our bodies separately.

Human beings are a conglomeration of three parts; We are a spirit with a soul and we live inside of a body. You are first and foremost a spirit- the eternal 'you'. The body you live in is just a vessel that you have been given to live here on planet earth. Like a hand in a glove, you are a spirit in a body. Its a temporary relationship between you and your body, the body will eventually wear out and you will leave your body behind. You will retain what you learned and experienced here on the earth and go on to greater or lesser things depending upon which Lord you claimed or claimed you while on the earth.

Paul writes in Thessalonians:
"And the very God of peace sanctify you wholly; and I pray God your whole spirit and soul and body be preserved blameless unto the coming of our Lord Jesus Christ."
.... 1 Thessalonians 5:23

GOD CREATED THE SPIRITS OF ADAM AND EVE – Genesis 1: 27

In Genesis 1:27 **God created** Adam and Eves spirits before he created their bodies to place their spirits inside of:
"So God created man in his own image, in the image of God created he him; male and female created he them."
.... Genesis 1:27

24.

God is a Spirit, he is not a man, what God created in his own image were the spirits of Adam and Eve.

"God is a spirit: and those that worship him must worship him in spirit and in truth."
.... John 4:24

GOD CREATED THE BODIES OF ADAM AND EVE – Genesis 2: 7, 21- 24

In Genesis 2:7 **God created** Adams **Body** so he would have an earthly vessel to house Adams spirit and soul.

"And the Lord formed man of the dust of the ground, and breathed into his nostrils the breath of life; and man became a living soul."
.... Genesis 2:7

In Genesis 2: 21-24 God created Eves body.

"And the Lord God caused a deep sleep to fall upon Adam and he slept: and he [God] took one of his ribs, and closed up the flesh instead thereof; and the rib which the Lord God had taken from man, made he a woman, and brought her unto the man. And Adam said. This is now bone of my bones, and flesh of my flesh: she shall be called woman [man with a womb] because she was taken out of man. Therefore shall a man leave his father and his mother, and shall cleave unto his wife: and they shall be one flesh."
… Genesis 2: 21-24

If you have any Catholic or Jewish friends you might show them this about the separate creation of the 'Spirit and Body', some think there is a redundancy or contradiction within the scriptures.

25.

"Thus saith God the Lord, He that created the heavens, and stretched them out: He that spread forth the earth, and that which cometh out of it; he that giveth **breath unto the people** upon it, and **spirit to them that walk therein:**"
… Isaiah 42: 5

When men die the body, spirit and soul separate;

"Then shall the dust (body of man) return to the earth as it was: and the spirit (of man) shall return unto God who gave it."
… Ecclesiastes 12: 7

What does your Spirit, the real you look like?

You look very much the same in your spirit form as you do in the physical, earthly, bodily form. There were two men that lived and died on the earth and the Bible records in the book of Luke that they recognized each other after their deaths:

"And there was a certain beggar named Lazarus, which was laid at his [the rich mans] gate, full of sores, and desiring to be fed with the crumbs which fell from the rich mans table: Moreover the dogs came and licked his sores. And it came to pass that the beggar died, and was carried away by the angels into Abraham's bosom: The rich man also died, and was buried; And in hell he lift up his eyes, being in torments, and seeth Abraham afar off, and Lazarus in his bosom. And he cried and said, Father Abraham, have mercy on me, and send Lazarus, that he may dip the tip of his finger in water, and cool my tongue: for I am tormented in this flame."
… Luke 16: 20-24

Both men died, one was confirmed buried. Both left their bodies on the earth and their spirits were conscious and communicating with each other. The rich man recognized both Abraham and Lazarus. Since he recognized Abraham, it is possible that when we get to heaven we may know everyone we encounter. As recorded in the above verse, when we die, we, our spirits and souls, leave our bodies and go to one of two places: either heaven or hell.

"For the body without the spirit is dead, so faith without works is dead also."
... James 2: 26

"Therefore we are always confident, knowing that, whilst we are at home in the body, we are absent from the Lord: (For we walk by faith, not by sight:) We are confident, I say, and willing rather to be absent from the body [physically dead], and to be present with the Lord [life eternal]."
.... 2 Corinthians 5: 6-8

Men are responsible for what is happening on the earth. When Jesus left the earth he left us in control: He left us with the Comforter or the Holy Spirit to help Christians throughout their lives. God the Father (Jehovah) is sitting on a throne in heaven (a planet or structure) and Jesus is sitting on a throne right next to him.

"For there are three that bear record in heaven, the Father, the Word [Jesus], and the Holy Ghost: and these three are one."
... 1 John 5: 7

Jesus said, "Hereafter shall the son of man [Jesus] sit on the right hand of the power of God."
... Luke 22: 69

"For the eyes of the Lord run to and fro throughout the whole earth, to shew himself strong in the behalf of them whose heart is perfect toward him."
... 2 Chronicles 16: 9

27.

The day a Christian dies the 'spirit and soul' leave for heaven and the body, the carnal, sinful part of man through Satan's corruption stays on the earth unredeemed and it returns to dust.

The soul of a man contains his mind, will and emotions and his soul is central to all he thinks, does and feels and is the beginning point for everything you do. What you think, speak and hear are recorded in your soul. All of your memories are stored in your soul and everything you learned here on the earth is recorded in your soul. The day your body dies and you leave; your soul goes with your spirit. Your mind is not your brain, the brain is physical, the mind is spiritual, the electrical component, and leaves the physical brain behind. Science claims that men only use a small portion of their brains, maybe 10 or 20%, perhaps the other 80 or 90% are reserved for spiritual use.

There was a researcher that did a series of experiments to see if a persons soul could be confirmed by weight. He found a group of willing test subjects at a home for Tuberculosis patients in Dorchester Massachusetts in 1901.
His name was Dr. Duncan McDougle. His hypothesis was that a soul would be a material object and if material, it would have mass and weight. He theorized that the soul leaves the body when the spirit leaves the body, so, upon the death of a person, there should be a measurable difference, before and after, in body weight. Dr. McDougle engineered a measure–arm scale that can measure very small precise weight variances and built it into a hospital bed. He then performed these experiments on 4 patients over time depending upon their 'End of Life' prognosis.

Patient #1 recorded a ¾ ounce loss of weight upon death.
Patient #2 recorded a 2 ounce loss of weight upon death.
Patient #3 recorded a 1 ½ ounce loss of weight upon death.
Patient #4 recorded a 3/8 ounce loss of weight upon death.

Dr. McDougle closely monitored each patient and was present at the point of death for each person. The loss of weight could not be attributed to body fluid release at death since it would still be present and weigh-able on the bed.

The Bible says that men can renew their minds by replacing old thoughts with new thoughts. Every word you say or hear and every thought you think is recorded in your soul. Perhaps some people have larger souls because they were more mentally active; thinking and saying more during their lifetimes and as a means of storage our souls grow as we think.

Dr. McDougle wondered if only men had souls. He performed the same experiment on several dogs; there was no change in weight upon death. Animals are apparently only two part beings, spirit and body, which would make sense as the soul is a recorder of thoughts through language and animals are not held accountable for their actions on earth. The soul stores a life long record of every event in every mans life and then goes to heaven or hell with him.

OFFENSE, A MANS HEART AND SOUL WILL PHASE IT OUT

What happens in our souls when we get hurt deeply by someone we know, respect or love? There is a built-in process that takes place within your soul that brings about the settlement of offenses, whether they were purposeful or unpurposeful, that occur to your heart or soul.

If, for example, you are married and your spouse offends you; you start out with a **wounded heart**. You feel betrayed or wronged and if there is not a mending of the offense very soon you develop a **cold heart** and you begin to become embittered because you are feeling less loved and you feel your feelings just don't matter to your spouse yet you still have strong emotions for your spouse. If there is not a reconciliation soon that cold heart will turn into a **hard heart**, you feel embittered, unloved and unwanted and the offense escalates to fighting; physically or verbally, there is still a chance to reconcile your marriage because an emotional bond is still present. If there is no resolution and apologies are not made and a reconciliation is not sought you will develop an **apathetic heart**. The emotional bond is broken, with an apathetic heart you will care little for the person from which the offense came. Indifference and a lack of emotion towards your spouse may lead to a separation; only God can repair a relationship at this point. The task is not to let an offense linger until it gets to that point. This process takes months or even years. Marriages don't end in a day as they did not begin in a day. The common thread throughout each phase is the lack of reconciliation. Apologize immediately and if you don't believe your spouse knows they offended you, let them know about it so you can work towards a resolution. This is part of the emotional healing process that's embedded into the souls of men and women. Offense is usually born from anger through angry words spoken to a person. As you will see in later chapters, offense is an area that Satan uses in personal relationships to destroy them.

"Be ye angry, and sin not: let not the sun go down upon your wrath [anger]: Neither give place to the devil."
.... Ephesians 4: 26-27

"But now ye also put off all these; anger, wrath, malice, blasphemy, filthy communication out of your mouth."
.... Colossians 3: 8

"Wherefore, my beloved brethren, let every man be swift to hear, slow to speak, slow to wrath: for the wrath of man worketh not the righteousness of God."
... James 1: 19- 20

"Put away from thee a froward [deceitful] mouth, and perverse lips put far from thee."
... Proverbs 4: 24

"A wrathful [hot-tempered] man [or woman] stirreth up strife: but he that is slow to anger appeaseth strife."
.... Proverbs 15: 18

GODS TWO DEFINITIONS OF DEATH

Gods defines death as:
1. When a flesh and blood body dies [bodily death]
2. Separation from God [your spirit does not die but you are spiritually dead to God]

Men that live on the earth can experience one or both of these deaths.
The only way to escape the 2nd form of death is to surrender to God through Jesus.
The 2nd death culminates in being sentenced to a prison inside the earth called Hell and eventually the person enters the Lake of Fire that is also inside the earth.

There are no two Christians alike, we all come from different backgrounds and have unique qualities and we all have to renew our minds into Gods way of thinking by reading his thoughts sent to us in the form of the Bible: 'Gods thoughts written by him through men – through dictation or inspiration of God'. The Bible is God and reading it will cause an intimate knowledge of our 'Creator' and you will know exactly what he desires of you and for you.

"In the beginning was the Word [Jesus], and the Word was with God, and the Word was God. The same was in the beginning with God. All things were made by him; and without him was not anything made that was made. In him was life; and the life was the light of men. And the light shineth in darkness; and the darkness comprehended it not... And the Word was made flesh [Jesus, Emmanuel* – Hebrew word meaning: God with us], and dwelt among us, (and we beheld his glory, the glory as of the only begotten of the father,) full of grace and **truth**."   *[or Immanuel]

... John 1: 1-5, 14

Jesus was at the beginning of creation - **creating** with God the Father.

There are some Christians who rarely read the Bible to attain Gods thoughts (Carnal Christians) and unfortunately non–Christians look at their lives and their conduct and they don't look any different from the rest of the world because they don't know God through his Word. Many non–Christians look at carnal Christians and they judge God and Jesus by what they observe in the carnal Christians lives. You can only truly judge Christianity through your own personal relationship with God , Jesus and the Holy Spirit. Your not joining a Christian believer, your joining God in heaven.

There are no perfect men on the earth today, Gods plan was that all men would seek perfection but none have attained it, save one, he lived almost 2000 years ago, and through Jesus's sinless perfection he could legally die for the redemption or purchase back of all of mankind's sins. Satan has no choice but to relinquish his ruler-ship over the earth to men as they receive Jesus's atonement one by one. Satan's plan was to work through the Jews, Pharisees and the Romans to kill Jesus but he did not realize that by killing Jesus he was ending his own ruler-ship over the earth. The Bible says that by "Sin" death entered into the world, (men were separated from God and Satan took over) Jesus had never sinned (Jesus was not part of the "Fallen state of Man" through mans disobedience- He had the DNA of Father God which allowed him to circumvent the "Sin Nature" of Adam) and therefor should have never died, (A sinless man cannot legally die, there was no death prior to Adams fall- men were created immortal) Jesus had to 'give up' his **Spirit** on the cross to allow himself to die. (Restoring mans immortality) – More on mans sinless nature through Christ in a later chapter.

32.

"But with the precious blood of Christ, as of a lamb without blemish [sin] and without spot: Who verily was foreordained before the foundation of the world, but was manifest in these last times for you."
... 1 Peter 1: 19- 20

"For all have sinned and come short of the Glory of God; being justified freely by his grace through the redemption [purchase back] that is in Christ Jesus."
.... Romans 3: 23-24

"Jesus saith unto him, I am the way, the truth, and the life: no man cometh unto the father but by me."
... John 14: 6

God (Jehovah, Jesus, and the Holy Spirit) created heaven, God is the legal owner of the planet or structure called "Heaven" and both of the other heavens 1 and 2. God lives in heaven, God makes the decision of who is allowed in and who is excluded from heaven and God says there is only one way to himself in heaven...

"No man cometh unto the Father [who is in heaven] but by me [Jesus]"
... John 14: 6.

The God of the Christian Bible wrote the above verse. His name is 'Jesus' and 'Jehovah' and the 'Holy Spirit'; they are a 3 in 1 or a three-part, triune God.

Buddha is not included in that verse!
Mohammed and Allah are not included in that verse!
The Saptarshi's or the Rishis of Hinduism are not included in that verse!
No other religions or prophets or gods on the earth are included in that verse!

33.
No one else is included in the ownership of heaven **EXCEPT** born again Christians, when we become part of the body of Jesus we become 'Heirs of the Heavens'.

The term "Heaven" is not a generic "catch phrase" that includes everything outside of the earth. The heavens are specific places created by a specific God for a specific purpose and have been hijacked or perverted into a universal catchall for any and all to falsely claim as their own and for their own use. The God that created the universe owns all the heavens and he alone decides what happens in them. Some believe that a loving merciful God would not allow the pain and suffering that's happening on the earth to exist so they don't allow God to exist in their thoughts and lives. God gave the earth to men to rule over and manage, Satan is working against men and God, the pain and suffering on the earth is because men have not maintained God in their minds and they don't know how to manage Satan in the world—its through Gods word by faith and obedience that anything associated with peace, prosperity, compassion, selflessness and love could manifest on the earth and when that's in place pain and suffering will diminish. It's possible that you can believe in Jesus but have absolutely no faith in Jesus.

There was a poll taken in the U.S. about God and Heaven;

Do you believe there is a God?
……………………………………………..Majority answer-Yes
Do you believe in the God of the Bible?
……………………………………………..Majority answer-Yes
Do you believe Jesus is God?
……………………………………………..Majority answer-Yes
Do you believe there is a Heaven?
……………………………………………..Majority answer-Yes
Do you believe you are going to Heaven?
……………………………………………..Majority answer-Yes

34.

Are you heaven bound by asking Jesus into your heart?
....Majority answer-No
Do you plan on asking Jesus into your heart?
....Majority answer-No

Q: Why not? A: If Jesus was a merciful God, he would not allow all this pain and suffering in the world.
My questions are;
How do you plan on getting to heaven since God says Jesus is the only way to get there?
Jesus says that men have got to verbally ask him to be their God and to repent of their sinful past!
Which God are you relying on to stop the pain and suffering?
Does pain and suffering automatically prove there is not a merciful, loving God?
Do you know how to stop the pain and suffering?
Do you know that Satan is the God of this present world and hates the existence of men?
Do you know that Satan causes the pain and suffering of this world?
Do you know that Satan desires to destroy all men?
Do you know God left man in charge of the earth and men are responsible for destroying Satans works?Do you know that God gave us the key to destroying Satan's plans of "Pain and Suffering"?
Have you researched Gods word to see what may be required of you?
Is the 'Pain and Suffering' answer the only factor?
Did you know that on judgment day there will be no excuses?

Men have failed...not God

There is only one way to heaven and its exclusive to any other claim in the world, ask Jesus in sincerity, he would be happy to let you in.

35.

"Death and life are in the power of the tongue: and they that love it shall eat the fruit thereof."
… Proverbs 18: 21

"And you shall know the truth and the truth shall make you free."
… John 8: 32

GOD TREATS OUR REBORN SPIRITS DIFFERENTLY THAN OUR FLESH BODIES

The only two parts of man that are responsible for sinning are our bodies and souls. Your soul is constantly learning and, if a devout Christian, constantly being perfected into the image of God or the likeness of Jesus, it takes time to replace your old carnal thoughts with new spiritual thoughts. Your spirit was instantly renewed or regenerated the day you received Jesus's ministry and became saved or born again. At the point of salvation, your spirit was sealed by God to receive "Eternal Life". Furthermore, it is no longer your spirit that is capable of sinning but rather your body controlled by an un-renewed soul (mind, will, emotions) that transgresses Gods moral laws. The Bible records that the body (or flesh) wars against the spirit and sometimes the body wins and that action is called sin, transgression or lawlessness-the act is a "Sin" but you are no longer a "Sinner". Your body does not go to heaven when you die, anything that goes to heaven has to be redeemed by the blood of Jesus and the blood was applied only to mans spirit and soul. Your reborn spirit and soul are required to control the carnal flesh appetites of the body since the body is, in no way, being renewed or cleansed to go to heaven yet you still are in need of your body even though it still has the fallen nature from Satan. If your spirit and soul fail to keep your body from transgressing Gods word or law, then God will step in and correct you for allowing your soul to allow the body to act lawlessly. Even though our spirits and souls are sealed by God as "sinless" they still have to endure corrections from God for allowing the body to dominate the spirit and soul. When a Christian allows his body to rule over his life this is called living 'carnally' or 'after the flesh' and ruled by selfish lusts and desires which remains in the domain of Satan.

"Whosoever is born of God doth not commit sin; for his seed remaineth in him: and he cannot sin, because he is born of God."
..... 1 John 3: 9

"There is therefore now no condemnation to them which are in Christ Jesus, who walk **not after the flesh, but after the Spirit**. For the law of the Spirit of life in Christ Jesus hath made me free from the law of sin and death."
... and if Christ be in you, the body is dead because of sin; but the spirit is life because of righteousness.
... for as many as are led by the Spirit of God, they are the sons of God."
... Romans 8: 1-2,10,14

"For whom the Lord loveth he corrects; even as a father the son in whom he delighteth. happy is the man that finds wisdom, and the man that gets understanding."
... Proverbs 3:12-13

"In whom [Jesus] you also trusted, after that you heard the word of truth, the gospel [good news] of your salvation: In whom also after that you believed, you were sealed with that Holy Spirit of promise."
... Ephesians 1: 13

"And grieve not the Holy Spirit of God, whereby you are sealed unto the day of redemption."
... Ephesians 4: 30

Jesus speaking:

"Father, the hour is come: glorify thy son, that thy son also may glorify thee: As thou hast given him power over all flesh, that he

should give eternal life to as many as thou hast given him. And this is life eternal, that they might know thee, the only true God, and Jesus Christ, whom thou has sent."
.... John 17: 1-3

"That whosoever believeth in him should not perish, but have eternal life. For God so loved the world, that he gave his only begotten son, that whosoever believes in him should not perish but have everlasting life."
.... John 3: 15-16

MANS INTERNAL STRUGGLE

The following is an account of the struggle within mankind, between body and spirit, as illustrated by the Apostle Paul in the book of Romans; it's as if our spirit has one mind within us and our carnal flesh body has a separate mind within us and our soul is struggling over which of the two to obey and there is a constant argument between these two opposing minds. The Apostle Paul writes:

"For we know that the law is spiritual: but I am carnal, sold under sin, for that which I do I allow not: for what I would, that do I not; but what I hate that I do. If then, I do that which I would not, I consent unto the Law that it is good. Now then it is no more I [my own reborn spirit] that do it, but sin [in my imperfected soul and unredeemed body] that dwelleth [lives] in me. For I know that in me (that is, in my flesh), dwelleth no good thing; for to will is present with me; but how to perform that which is good I find not. For the good that I would I do not: But the evil which I would not, that I do. Now if I do that I would not, it is no more I [my reborn Spirit] that do it, but sin that dwells in me [carnal flesh]. I find then a law, that, when I would do good, evil is present with me, for I delight in the law of God after their inward man: But I see another law in my members [fleshly body], warring against the law of my mind [in my soul], and bringing me into captivity to the law of sin which is in my member [body]. O wretched man that I am! Who shall deliver me from the body of

this death? I thank God through Jesus Christ our Lord. So then with the mind [in your soul] I myself serve the law of God; but with the flesh [body] the law of sin [unwillingly]."
… Romans 7: 14-25

The spirit and soul, when reborn, are attached to God the Father, Jesus and the Holy Spirit.
The body is still attached to Satan through Adams fall and needs to be kept in control by mans spirit and soul. The soul needs to have new information (the Bible) so it will know Gods thoughts and, thus, know who to obey: Spirit (Gods) or body (Satans).
As you can see from the war that is waging between the Apostle Paul's flesh and spirit he is doing things that he really does not like to do and he is not doing things he knows he should be doing. Every man alive has experienced this internal argument in their lives. The fallen nature of the world that each man was born into -" verses "- the righteous nature of God that, hopefully, all men will be reborn into and perfected in. The internal war between 'law and lawlessness' or 'morality and immorality' may be lost when man allows his flesh to take control and he ignores the prompting and correction of the Holy Spirit either through the scriptures that we have read and are recorded in our souls or by mans 'internal moral law' as written on our hearts.
That is what happened to Hitler, Stalin and others as they set out to **"falsely" purify** the world by murdering their own people and the Jewish people that they deemed inferior races of men.

"For we wrestle not against flesh and blood [men], but against principalities, against powers, against the rulers of the darkness of this world, against spiritual wickedness in high places…..Above all, taking the shield of faith [the Word of God, Bible] whereby ye shall be able to quench all the fiery darts [thoughts, ideas, and suggestions] of the wicked [Satan]"
… Ephesians 6: 12,16

Satan launched 'Fiery Darts' at Darwin, Hitler and **Stalin. These** darts are; "thoughts, ideas and suggestions" and they were spoken into the minds of these three men in hopes that Satan could use them for his **destructive** purposes. They did not know enough of Gods word or have faith in Gods word, the Bible, to realize what was happening to them and they fell for Satan's plan to start a new false religion and use that religion to destroy millions. They were all ignorant of Satan's presence and plans and when they were given these **destructive** thoughts by Satan they **thought** they were thinking their own thoughts but they were not. They then would dwell on the thoughts, the thoughts grew within and Satan added more and more ideas or suggestions until these thoughts took on lives of there own and they each thought that they were superior to other human beings because they were more evolved; physically, socially, intellectually and morally and it was acceptable as a more advanced member of a more advanced race to destroy lesser advanced races of men as do animals in the animal **kingdo**m destroy to survive.

"The fool has said in his heart,There is no God. They are corrupt, they have done abominable works, there is none that doeth good."
… Psalms 14: 1

"Either make the tree [man] good, and his fruit [works] good; or else make the tree corrupt, and his fruit corrupt: for the tree is known by his fruit."
… Mathew 12: 33

The fruit or works done by Darwin, Hitler and Stalin were definitely corrupt and its clear to see which God they served. These men acted upon the thoughts that Satan spoke into their thoughts and the whole world suffered. Thousands upon thousands of other men have also listened to Satan and today our prisons are overflowing, cemeteries house the corpses of men and women who have been victimized by men who allowed Satan's thoughts to guide them. **Drug** users, pornographers, organized crime members and others have all listened to Satan's fiery darts and allowed Satan to use them for his purposes- to destroy the lives of men and women.

GOD'S CAPABILITIES

The definition of God is "The Supreme Being"

God created all things for his pleasure according to the Bible and his greatest creation is man. We were created like him in spirit form and we are here on the earth, in bodily form, to learn and watch God fulfill the Bible and through its fulfillment he reveals Jesus Christ to the world- the King of Kings.

In other words, the entirety of the Bible was written to reveal Jesus the Messiah to all men. There have been over 600 prophecies in the Bible that have been fulfilled and, as of this writing, we are just steps away from the rapture and the return of the Lord. To show Gods capabilities I have included a few descriptors and scriptures that will leave you with a better understanding of how God could write a book of future events (prophesy) and have them all come to pass over the ensuing centuries, God is:

OMNISCIENT..........OMNIPOTENT..........OMNIPRESENT

Complete ....Infinite and....................Encompassing.....		
Awareness ....Absolute Power............. the Universe........		

Unlimited.....................Unlimited................ Present Everywhere
Knowledge .... Capability .... Simultaneously......

Unlimited ....Unlimited........................Complete ....
Understanding ....Authority.......................Perception........
 ....Almighty

Jesus was speaking to a group of Jews who were asking him questions:

"Jesus said unto them, Verily, verily, I say unto you, Before Abraham was, **I am**."[present tense]

… John 8:58

Abraham walked the earth centuries prior to Jesus walking the earth. Jesus did not say "I was" he said "I am" speaking directly to his 'Omnipresence', Jesus pre-existed Abraham even though Abraham had long since died and Jesus was a descendant of Abraham in bodily form. Jesus [God] is in the present tense all throughout earth history. At year zero during the creation, during Abrahams lifetime and during your lifetime Jesus would answer "I am". Before creation he is "I am", before and after Abraham he is "I am", before and after Ronald Reagan he is "I am" or at any point along earths time-line.

Jesus is the great "I AM". Our eternal omnipresent creator God that exists in the past, present and future simultaneously. When you have complete perception, knowledge, understanding and unlimited authority combined with omnipresence it is easy to write a book when you can see everything that happens throughout earths history right in front of you at the same instance.

SPIRIT SOUL AND BODY AND OTHERS WITHIN

Along with our own spirit and soul we can have other spirits join us within our bodies. When you are born again the Holy Spirit moves in and becomes a resident alongside your spirit in the same body. He sees, hears, feels everything you do and he assists you when needed- especially when you specifically ask him for assistance. There are others that also may indwell your body with you and these are not welcomed as the Holy Spirit would be welcomed. The following is an account that's recorded in the Bible where Jesus encounters the Madman of the Gadarenes;

42.

"And they came over unto the other side of the sea, into the country of the Gadarenes, and when he [Jesus] was come out of the ship, immediately there met him out of the tombs a man with an unclean spirit, who had his dwelling among the tombs; and no man could bind him, no, not with chains because he had been often bound with fetters [shackles] and chains, and the chains had been torn apart by him, and the fetters broken in pieces: neither could any man tame him. And always, night and day, he was in the mountains, and in the tombs, crying, and cutting himself with stones. But when he saw Jesus afar off, he ran and worshiped him, and cried with a loud voice, and said, "WHAT HAVE I TO DO WITH THEE, JESUS, THOU SON OF THE MOST HIGH GOD? I ADJURE THEE BY GOD, THAT THOU TORMENT ME NOT." For he [Jesus] asked him, "What is thy name?" And he answered, saying, my name is Legion: for we are many. And he besought him much that he would not send them away out of the country. Now there was there nigh [close] unto the mountains a great herd of swine feeding. And all the devils [dwelling inside the man] besought him, saying, "Send us into the swine that we may enter into them." And forthwith Jesus gave them leave, and the unclean spirits went out, and entered into the swine; and the herd ran violently down a steep place into the sea, (they were about 2000 swine) and were chocked in the sea...
...and they came to Jesus, and seeing him that was possessed with the devil and had the Legion [of devils], sitting, and clothed, and in his right mind; and they were afraid."
.... Mark 5: 1-13,15

Like the Holy Spirit, demonic spirits can see through a mans eyes, hear through his ears, speak through his vocal cords and can carry on an intelligent conversation. Do not negotiate or converse with demonic spirits, cast them out or find a believing Christian to cast them out.

A legion is 6000, even when the demons left the man and went into the 2000 pigs there were maybe 3 demons per pig. Prior to

Jesus this mans life was absolutely ruined. Jesus commanded the demons to leave the man, likewise a believing Christian can command demons to leave a man in the name of Jesus. Men have power over demonic spirits as recorded in the book of Mark, Jesus speaking;

"And these signs shall follow them that believe; **In my name [Jesus] they shall cast out devils**; they shall speak with new tongues; they shall take up serpents; and if they drink any deadly thing it shall not harm them; they shall lay hands on the sick and they shall recover."
… Mark 16: 17-18

As illustrated in the above scripture about the madman of the Gadarenes, Satan **does not** have the authority to kill a man outright. Satan has to set traps, place thoughts, ideas and suggestions into unwary men. He lies in wait for opportunities to attack- Satan arranges situations where a person gets offended and he is at his weakest. He pits men against men. About 30 seconds to a minute after these demonic spirits left the man and entered the swine all the swine were dead. Satan does not have the same restrictions on animals as he does men. Satan has to trick men into harming each other. If you don't realize or recognize what is happening to you through demonic manipulation you can't fight against it. Its imperative to know the word of God so you can recognize Satan's attacks and what you can do and can't do to resist. Satan uses men against men and we do not fight against flesh and blood [men], we fight against "Spiritual Wickedness". As I stated earlier, our prisons are full of men that were manipulated by Satan's demonic spirits and these men yielded their bodies [for Satan's use] to commit crimes that landed them in jail or the cemetery. Mans spiritual combat against Satan is through the name of Jesus combined with verses in the Bible.

"THE HOLY SPIRIT"; PRESENCE, MANIFESTATION AND INDWELLING

******VERSES******

"SATANIC OR DEMONIC"; INFESTATION, OPPRESSION AND POSSESSION

There are 3 characteristic levels of Holy Spirit activity on the earth, his presence, his manifestation and his indwelling of Christians.

There are 3 characteristic levels of demonic spirit activity on the earth, his infestation, his oppression of men and when he enters and possesses the body of a man.

A Holy Spirit Presence occurs in an area or building, characterized by overt positive Spirit activity; may see light flashes, light colored shapes or clouds, unexplainable noises, voices or music- temperature fluctuations, pleasant odors. Perceptible sense of peace and love and attraction.

A Demonic Infestation occurs in an area or building, characterized by overt negative spirit activity; may see articles move; may see dark clouds or images, shapes and shadows, unexplainable noises, voices or music- temperature fluctuations, foul odors. Perceptible sense of dread and danger and repulsion.

A Holy Spirit Manifestation occurs when the Holy Spirit ministers to individuals by manifesting his presence to them personally through a myriad of different mechanisms to allow his presence to be known. He manifests a loving presence both inwardly and outwardly in the personal affairs of men. He is gentle, kind and loving.

Demonic Oppression occurs when a demonic spirit targets a person or family; oppression is an outward manifestation of a demonic spirit. May see fully manifested demonic spirits or dark shapes, clouds or moving shadows accompanied by foul odors and temperature fluctuations. These spirits force themselves on their victims, are rude and they thrive on fear. They may cause electronic interference designed to create fear or annoyance, items move or are thrown. They may cause physical harm.

Holy Spirit Indwelling occurs when invited into a believer's life the Holy Spirit enters the human body, wellness usually occurs. A positive shift in personality occurs. Values change to holiness and an unselfish pattern emerges. The Holy Spirit gives gifts to men. In Galatians chapter 5 the Bible records the fruit of the Holy Spirit; Love, Joy, Peace, Long Suffering, Gentleness, Goodness, Faith, Meekness and Temperance [Moderation or Abstinence].

Demonic Possession occurs when a demonic spirit enters a human body by means of purposeful , unpurposeful or unwitting invitation; Example, Ouija boards, spirit dowsing, conversation, direct invitation, etc. A negative shift in personality occurs, illness may occur, values shift to carnality, fearfulness, selfishness and a destructive pattern emerges. Physical harm usually occurs, self mutilization or mutilization (cutting) by the demonic spirit may occur, destruction of property may occur.
Galatians chapter 5, the Bible records the manifestations of carnality:
"**Adultery, fornication, uncleanness,** lasciviousness [sensuality], idolatry, witchcraft, hatred, discord, emulations, wrath, strife, seditions, heresies [speaking against Gods word], envyings, murders, **drunkenness** and revelings [wild parties]."... Galatians 5

s stated earlier, a demonic spirit cannot kill a man outright, he has to plant the thoughts of murder, death or suicide into a mans mind and try to cause the man to act on his suggestions. The only way a man can expel or cast out a demonic spirit is **through** a **Christian with the Holy Spirit** using the name of Jesus Christ against the demonic spirit.

"And the seventy returned again with joy, saying, Lord even the devils [demonic spirits] are subject unto us through thy name, and he [Jesus] said unto **them, I** beheld Satan as lightning fall from **heaven**. Behold, I give unto you power to tread on serpents [devils] and scorpions, and over all the power of the enemy: and nothing shall by any means hurt you."
… Luke10: 17-19

Again, Jesus speaking: …."**In my name [Jesus] they shall cast out devils**; they shall speak with new tongues;..."
… Mark 16: 17

Back in the 1970's, a movie came out called 'The Exorcist', it was based on a true event that happened in Missouri back in the 1940's. A 14 year old boy and his **aunt** were playing with a **Ouija** board and they unwittingly invited a demonic spirit to indwell them. The 14 year old boy started to experience demonic oppression as described earlier. The demonic activity escalated more and more until the demon possessed the boy and his parents decided to call a Catholic **priest** to see if he could help their son. The **priest** asked for and received permission (from the Catholic Church leaders) to perform an exorcism on the boy. They began the **exorcism** in **the boy's home**…weeks went by and the **priest** decided to move the boy to a hospital where they would spend hours and hours each night praying Latin prayers over the boy. The Catholic priests had specific prayers and protocols they had to follow in an exorcism; It's made up of very strict guidelines and pre-written prayers and they are **read** straight from the exorcism handbook. The **priests** prayed for this boy night after

night for hours on end for over a month. Towards the end, the demonic spirit in the boy began to mock the priests and said through the boys vocal chords **"I am not going anywhere. You didn't say the Word"**. The priests inquired of the demonic spirit about the "Word" that he was referring to but the demon spirit would not elaborate further. The priests finally got the boy delivered through an Arch-Angel that came and entered the boy along-side the demonic spirit. The Arch-Angel, as did the demonic spirit, spoke through the boys vocal chords; ---- **'The Lord Dominus commands you to go, Go Now- Go Now- Go Now!'**
The demonic spirit immediately left the boy.

The **"Word"** was Jesus which is God in word form; Dominus is a Latin derivative of 'Christ' which is who Jesus is! "The Lord" is also who Jesus is. The demonic spirit himself was mocking the priests by telling them what they were missing that would make him leave.

"In the beginning was the **Word** and the **Word** was with God and the **Word** was God....and the **Word was made flesh [Jesus]**, and dwelt among us, (and we beheld his glory, the glory as of the only begotten of the father), full of grace and truth."
   ... John 1: 1,14

I believe that all the Catholic priests had to do was pray in the name of Jesus and they would have saved 100's of hours. In the Catholic Exorcisms, there is a conspicuous absence of the name 'Jesus' from their prayers, they pray to Saints. The Arch-Angel only said about a dozen words and the demonic spirit left. A Christian has to combine the name of Jesus and faith to his prayers and he will get the same result.
Jesus speaking; "He that is not with me is against me: and he that gathereth not with me scattereth. When an unclean spirit is gone out of a man, he walks through dry places, seeking rest; and finding none, he saith, I [the demonic spirit] will return unto my

house [the man he was cast out of] whence I came out. And when he comes, he finds it swept and garnished. Then goes he [the demonic spirit], and takes to him seven other spirits more wicked than himself; and they enter in, and dwell there: and the last state of that man is worse than the first." (instead of only 1 demon, he now has 8 demons)
... Luke 11: 23-26

As you can see from the above scripture you are not alone in this life. You have intelligent, invisible beings all around you 24 hours a day, 7 days a week since the day you were born and until the day you die and beyond. Some work for the Lord Jesus and some work as demons for Satan. They hear everything you say, they are privy to every conversation you ever had or will have. Some may dwell inside your body with you. As mentioned before, Satan uses his demonic spirits to inject thoughts into your mind to upset you or to get you offended by others or to offend others, mankind is their career in a sense, working on mankind is all they do.

"Put on the whole armor of God that you may be able to stand against the wiles [trickery, deceit, schemes, lies and fiery darts: thoughts, ideas and suggestions] of the devil."
... Ephesians 6: 11

"Lo, he [God] goeth by me, and I see him not: he passeth on also, but I perceive him not."
... Job 9: 11

Angels and Demons are especially tuned into what you actually speak or say to other people. God is a speaking Spirit and men are speaking spirits, whether it's known and agreed with or not. The following verse from the book of Mark emphasizes the importance of speaking as it pertains to a man. If you believe in what you are saying then you shall have whatsoever you speak. The Angels or Demons will bring it to pass. If you are speaking of something righteous and good the heavenly Angels will work on your behalf, if you are speaking of something destructive or bad then the demons will hear you and they will work to bring that to pass.

"For nothing is secret, that shall not be made manifest [known]; neither anything hid, that shall not be known and come abroad."
.... Luke 8 : 17

"For verily [truthfully] I say unto you, that whosoever shall say unto this mountain, be thou removed, and be cast into the sea; and shall not doubt in his heart, but shall believe that those things which he saith shall come to pass; he shall have whatsoever he saith. Therefore I say unto you, What things soever ye desire, when ye pray, believe that ye receive them, and ye shall have them."
.... Mark 11: 23-24

The 'saying and receiving' work both in the positive and the negative. They are both activated by 'faith' and believing. What you believe in your heart is recorded in your soul and needs to be protected from the attacks launched by Satan and his demons.

"Keep thy heart with all diligence; for out of it are the issues of life."
.... Proverbs 4: 23

Darwin, Hitler and Stalin, if they truly had a relationship with God in their youths, did not keep a guard over what they knew of Gods word. They chose to believe and act upon a Satanic lie.

GOD GIVES GIFTS UNTO MEN

God has, for all of those who seek him, exclusive gifts, 'free downloads' of knowledge, faith, healing power, miracle working power, etc., As recorded in the book of Corinthians:

"Now concerning Spiritual gifts, brethren, I would not have you ignorant. Now there are diversities of gifts, but the same Spirit [the Holy Spirit]. And there are differences of administrations, but the same Lord [Jesus], And there are diversities of operation, but it is the same God which worketh all in all. But the manifestation of the Spirit is given to every man to profit by. For to one is given by the Spirit the word of wisdom; to another the word of knowledge by the same Spirit; To another faith by the same Spirit; to another the gifts of healing by the same Spirit; To another the working of miracles; to another prophecy; to another discerning of Spirits; to another various kinds of tongues [speaking a language that's unknown to you]; to another the interpretation of tongues, But all these worketh that one and self same Spirit [the Holy Spirit], dividing to every man individually as he will."
... 1 Corinthians 12: 4-11
... **Plus** the Spirit of Truth.......... John 14: 17
... **Plus** the Spirit of Meekness... Galatians 6: 1

Every Christian may have one or more spiritual gifts from God as required to complete their work on the earth. Wisdom is one spiritual gift that can be had by anyone simply by asking God for it.
Unfortunately, Satan also has spirits that he can send to men to oppress their lives on the earth, some examples of what Satan uses to inflict men with are recorded below;

SATANIC SPIRITS SENT TO INDWELL MEN

The spirit of uncleanness .... Mathew 5: 8
The spirit of jealousy .... Numbers 5:14
The spirit of sorrow................... 1 Samuel 1: 15
A lying spirit .... 1 Kings 22: 22
A perverse spirit .... Isaiah 19:14
A familiar spirit .... Isaiah 29: 4
A dumb and deaf spirit .... Mark 9: 25

An evil spirit .... Acts 19: 15
The spirit of fear....................... 2 Timothy 1: 7

"Ye are of your father the Devil [Satan], and the lusts of your **father** you will do, he was a murderer from the beginning, and abode not in the truth, because there is no truth in him. When he **speaketh** a lie, he **speaketh** of his own: For he is a liar and the father of it."
... John 8: 44

By looking at the above list of Satanic **spirits, it's** easy to tell who is either oppressed by or serving Satan by the nature of the spirit that leads or oppresses them.

"How art thou **fallen** from heaven, O Lucifer [Satan], son of the morning! How art thou cut down to the ground, **which didst weaken the nations** [through Satan's attacks with deceit, death, disease, wars, evolution and other false religions]!"
... Isaiah 14: 12

"**and** the **great** dragon **was** cast **out, that** old serpent, called the Devil, and Satan, which **deceiveth** the whole world; he was cast out into the **earth**; and his angels [demonic spirits] **were** cast out with him."
... Revelation 12: 9

Satan used men that yielded themselves to him, they voluntarily or unknowingly gave their 'free will to choose' to **accept** Satan's plan of destruction and then Satan sent demonic **spirits** to indwell them. Satan sent spirits that were liars, evil, perverse, jealous, unclean, murderers, etc. Those men gave up their connection to God to create a plan, unknown at the time, to lead people away from God and his Word and into something that would cause the deaths of millions during Hitler and Stalin's time and is still in effect today and it's still causing the destruction of souls. The evolution religion is still in operation as it was with Hitler and there is another religion that's just as dangerous and potentially devastating as the 3rd Reich was- Islam; another immoral and violent religion with a Satanic agenda to destroy mens lives. (More on Islam later)

Jesus speaking "The thief [Satan] cometh not, but for to steal, and to kill, and to destroy: I am come that they might have life and have it more abundantly. I am the good shepherd; the good shepherd giveth his life for the sheep [men]"
… John 10: 10

All of the Spirit world is a living, thinking, intelligent group of beings on both sides that influence your thoughts, they know each and every one of your thoughts and the intentions of your heart so lying to someone does not go undetected by any indwelling spirit, they know when you are being deceitful and what your motives are for lying. Keep in mind that Jesus himself is the "Word of God" as you read the following:

The Lord puts it this way;
"For the word of God is quick and powerful, and sharper than any two edged sword, piercing even to the dividing asunder of soul and spirit, and of the joints and marrow, **and is a discerner of the thoughts and intents of the heart.**"
… Hebrews 4: 12

"Evolution is unproven and unprovable, we believe it because the only alternative is special creation, and that is unthinkable."
..... Sir Arthur Keith

Why is special creation unthinkable to humanists or evolutionists? Because they would be required to relinquish the command of their own souls to the Lord. They can't be the captains of their own souls if the Lord Jesus is the Captain of their souls. It could be that they would have to give up all of their favorite pass times like **drunkenness**, fornicating, lying, stealing, cheating, etc, including their own thoughts of how they, through their education and intellect, have attained to Homo **Sapien Sapien (Wise** Wise Men) status. Again, If you truly want to become a wise wise man- **wisdom** is freely given to all men through believing in Jesus and by asking God for his gift of wisdom.

"If any of you lack wisdom, let him ask of **God, that giveth** to all men liberally, and **upbraideth** not; and it shall be given him. But let him ask in faith, nothing wavering... "
... James 1: 5-6

"Wisdom is the principal thing; therefor get wisdom. And with all thy getting, get understanding."
... Proverbs 4: 7

As stated earlier, what Sir Keith was saying in the above quote was that if the evolution religion were to ever fail the default position would **fall** back to Christianity and 'Gods Creation Model'. Gods Creation **Model** is the only model that has never been dis-proven or shown to be false or in error and where all the geology of the earth; artifacts and fossils within may be explained without deceitful **manipulation** and **cover-up** as evolution does. (More on manipulation and cover-ups later)
Darwin's **evolution** hypothesis and the 'Evolution Religion' **have** both failed the test of time- they have had over 150 years with zero results to confirm it. Gods word has never gone against the formation of the geologic record or the existence of fossilized bones. To the contrary, evidence for the flood exists all around the world in every nation. In this debate- **the** last man standing is Jesus who created all things in heaven and earth. Evolutionists are still undermining Christianity and Jesus and our freedoms of speech and worship in America. They have taken God out of our government offices and schools including crosses, prayer and the 10 commandments. Some university professors push or force evolution as a fact under the threat of a "bad grade" and at the same time bash Christianity as a **dead** religion for the inferior,

uneducated types that cannot think intelligently for themselves. The way they tell it not one man of intellect has ever been a Christian but I challenge that claim with a list of quotes that I have compiled to show the world that there are Christian men who do love Jesus (Who is God) and have contributed to the advancement of the 'Human Condition'.

QUOTES FROM GODLY INTELLECTUAL MEN WHO HAVE MADE GREAT CONTRIBUTIONS TO HUMANITY
Contrary to what Evolutionist Professors tell our children

"Without the assistance of the Divine being, I cannot succeed, with that assistance, I can not fail..."
"We trust Sir, That God is on our side, it is more important to know that we are on Gods side."....
"I am profitably engaged in reading the Bible. Take all of this book that you can by reason and the balance by faith, and you will live and die a better man. It is the best book which God has given to man."
….. Abraham Lincoln

"Within the covers of the Bible are the answers for all of the problems men face."
"Gods miracles are to be found in nature itself, the wind and waves, the wood that becomes a tree – all of these are explained biologically, but behind them is the hand of God."
….. Ronald Reagan

"I am sure that never was a people, who had more reason to acknowledge a Divine interposition in their affairs, than those of the United States: And I should be pained to believe that they have forgotten that agency, which was so often manifested during our Revolution, or that they failed to consider the Omnipotence of that God who is alone able to protect them.".........
"It is impossible to rightly govern the world without God and the Bible."
….. George Washington

"As a child I received instruction both in the Bible and in the Talmud. I am a Jew, but I am enthralled by the luminous figure of the Nazarene.... No one can read the Gospels without feeling the actual presence of Jesus. His personality pulsates in every word. No myth is filled with such life"…..
"Few are those who see with their own eyes and feel with their own hearts..."
"I want to know how God created this world, I am not interested in this or that phenomenon in the spectrum of this or that element. I want to know Gods **thoughts, the** rest are details."
….. Albert Einstein

"**The** gift of mental power comes from **God,** Divine Being, and if we concentrate our minds on that **truth, we** become in tune with this great power."
….. Nicola Tesla

"There are more sure marks of authenticity of the Bible than in any profane **history.**"
….. Sir Isaac Newton

"Oh Lord, thou **givest** us everything, at the price of an effort....I obey thee Lord, first for the **love I ought,** in all reason to bear thee; secondly for that thou canst shorten or prolong the lives of men. Our body is dependent on heaven and heaven on the Spirit...."
"....His [mans] external form, appears to thee marvelously constructed, **remember** that it is nothing as compared with the soul that dwells in that structure [body]; For that indeed, be it what it may, is a thing divine."
.... Leonardo Da Vinci

"The Bible is no mere book, but a living creature, with the power that conquers all that oppose it."
"I know men and I tell you that Jesus Christ is no mere man.

56.

Between him and every other person in the world, there is no possible term of comparison. Alexander, Caesar, Charlemagne and I have founded empires. But on what did we rest the creation of our genius? Upon force, Jesus Christ founded his empire upon love; and at this hour millions of men would die for him."
..... Napoleon Bonaparte

"As Gods only son, Jesus came to earth and gave his life so that we may live, his actions and his words remind us that service to others is central to our lives and that sacrifice and unconditional love must guide us and inspire us to lead lives of compassion, mercy, and justice."
.....George W. Bush, 43

"(My) great joy and glory that, in occupying an exalted position in the nation, I am enabled to preach the practical moralities of the Bible to my fellow countrymen and to hold up Christ as the hope and savior of the world.
..... Theodore Roosevelt

"It is a very good thing that you read the Bible... The Bible is Christ, for the Old Testament leads up to this culminating point... Christ alone... has affirmed as a principle certainty, eternal life, the infinity of time, the nothingness of death, the necessity and the 'raison d'etre' of serenity and devotion. He lived serenely, as a greater artist than all other artists, despising marble and clay as well as color, working in living flesh, that is to say, this matchless artist... made neither statues nor picture nor books; He loudly proclaimed that he made... living men, Immortals."
..... Vincent Van Gogh

57.

"So great is my veneration for the Bible that the earlier my children begin to read it the more confident will be my hope that they will prove useful citizens of their country and respectable members of society. I have for many years made it a practice to read through the Bible once every year."
..... John Quincy Adams

"The New Testament is the very best book that ever was or ever will be known in the world."
..... Charles Dickens

"Nothing higher exists than to approach God more than other people, and from that to extend His Glory among humanity."
..... Ludwig Van Beethoven

"It is of great consolation for me to remember that the Lord, to whom I had drawn near in humble and childlike faith, has suffered and died for me, and that he will look on me in love and compassion."
..... Wolfgang Amadeus Mozart

"It cannot be emphasized to clearly and to often that this nation was founded, not by religionists, but by Christians, not on religion, but on the Gospel of Jesus Christ, for this very reason, peoples of other faiths have been afforded asylum, prosperity, and freedom of worship here."
..... Patrick Henry

The next time you come across one of these anti-Christian educators that thinks like Sir Arthur Keith, Lyell, Darwin or Hitler- that he is a 'Man of Supreme Talent' who is capable of thinking for himself and is not blinded by the authority of Gods Word, show him this list of quotes and ask him; "Shouldn't I be afforded the right to believe whom I choose to believe?" The Bible records that all men have the knowledge that God exists either through observation of the creation or the internal moral law revealed through our consciences (the inner thoughts of our mind).

"Science without religion is lame, religion without science is blind...a legitimate conflict between science and religion cannot exist."
… Albert Einstein

Chapter 3

GODS BIG BANG or BIG STRETCH

God pre-existed our known physical universe and is not bound by the physical laws that we, as men, are limited by. Mans dimensional space was created by "Gods Big Bang", God set "Time, Space and Matter" into existence through his 'Big Bang'. In Gods version of the Big Bang or Big Stretch no laws of physics were violated, "the conservation of energy and matter" did not exist to be violated. He created the heavens from nothing since prior to its creation there was no place for it to exist and no need for the laws of physics. Matter had no place to exist without space to exist in. Space and matter could not exist without a time to exist in. These three: time, space and matter cannot exist independently of each other. Our three-dimensional universe has boundaries and limitations but God is extra-dimensional, he's timeless, boundless and limitless. God's realm includes our dimension and he and his messengers [Angels] can come and go at will in and out of our three-dimensional space (the physical realm) undetected. God is a Spirit, He and his angels do not have physical bodies made from the elements of this universe but he can transform himself and take on an earthly form, he is not limited by the laws of physics as men are. Men have to experience time linearly but God observes time at any point past, present and future as he desires. God sees prior to the Holy Spirit hovering over the waters in Genesis and he can see Jesus on the throne in his millennial reign and every point in between simultaneously as described earlier when "Omnipresence" was defined.

"The extraordinary thing is that scientists accept the Big Bang and in the same breath deride [ridicule] the creationists."
... Wallace Thornhill, Physicist, Co-author of Electric Universe, 2007, Thunderbolts of the Gods, 2005

The scientific community has, in part, caught up with the Bible concerning the creation of the heavens and the earth. Early on, scientists hypothesized that something the size of a small moon exploded; and over time they kept shrinking the explosive down further and further until today; they say that nothing exploded. The explosion that is referred to as the Big Bang happened in Gods extra-dimensional realm and that created our dimension of time-space-matter. **It may not have been an explosion at all, God says he "stretched forth the heavens" implying that everything has a place and God placed everything where he desired it to be - God says he hung the earth on nothing.** Our own solar system was built with the precision of a Swiss clock. Prior to the formation of our universe [**uni**-single, **verse**-spoken sentence], the only place that anything could exist was outside of what we are familiar with today – Gods domain was and still is a place where time, space and matter **as we know it** does not exist. God created the universe to house his highest creation- men. God created the earth for the habitation of men. The "Goldilocks Zone" describes a location for a planet that is conducive for life to exist in any solar system. A life sustaining planet is located at the perfect distance from the sun in its corresponding solar system and the temperature extremes are not to hot and not to cold. The earth didn't accidentally hit upon the right ingredients to sustain life, God hung the earth in the Goldilocks Zone and he added everything that men needed to survive.

"For thus saith the LORD that created the heavens; God himself that formed the earth and made it; he hath established it, he created it not in vain, **he formed it [the earth] to be inhabited [by men]**: I am the LORD; and there is none else."
… Isaiah 45: 18

"He stretcheth out the north over the empty place, **and hangeth the earth upon nothing**."
… Job 26: 7

61.

There are trillions and trillions of stars that exist today and not only did God create each and every one of them but he also named each and every one.

"He [God] telleth the number of the stars; He calleth them all by their names."
.... Psalms 147: 4

"By the word of the Lord were the heavens made; and all the Host [Heavenly bodies and Angelic beings] of them by the breath of his mouth, he gathereth the waters of the sea together as an heap: He layeth up the depth in storehouses. Let all the earth fear the Lord: Let all the inhabitants of the world stand in awe of him.. For he spake, and it was done; He commanded, and it stood fast. The Lord bringeth the counsel of the heathen to nought [nothing]: he maketh the devices of the people of none effect."
...... Psalms 33: 6-10

"For the invisible things of him from the creation of the world are clearly seen, being understood by the things that are made, even his [Gods] eternal power and Godhead; so that they are without excuse. Because that, when they knew God, they glorified him not as God, neither were thankful; but became vain in there imagination [thinking the earth and the creatures in it evolved without him], and there foolish heart was darkened, professing themselves to be wise they became fools, and changed the glory of the incorruptible God into an image made like corruptible man, and the birds, and four footed beasts, and creeping things."
… Romans 1: 20-23

Thus saith the Lord thy redeemer, and he that formed thee from the womb, I am the Lord that maketh all things; that stretcheth forth the heavens alone; that spreadeth abroad the earth by myself."
… Isaiah 44: 24

"For by him were all things created, that are in heaven, and that are in earth, **visible and invisible**, whether they be thrones, or dominions, or principalities, or powers, all things were created by him and for him."
..... Colossians 1: 16

"In the beginning, God created the heaven and the earth."
.... Genesis 1: 1

THE BIBLICAL AGE OF THE EARTH

The Epistle of Barnabas from approximately 200 A.D. is the starting point scholars use when piecing together earths Biblical history to arrive at the age of the earth. The 7000 year plan of God was derived by Barnabas from two verses in the Bible;

"For a thousand years in thy sight are but as yesterday when it is past, and as a watch in the night."
.... Psalms 90: 4

"But, beloved, be not ignorant of this one thing, that one day is with the Lord as a thousand years, and a thousand years as one day."
... 2 Peter 3: 8

From Gods 7 day 'Creation and Rest' plan Barnabas, and others, have been given a revelation by God through Psalms 90 and 2nd Peter 3 that each day of 'creation and rest' means God will allow 1000 years per day for mans eventual redemption equaling **6000 years of pre-millennial earth history**. At the end of 6000 years Christ returns for his church and sets up his "Millennial Kingdom" to reign on the earth with Christians for the final 1000 years.
The four Gospels; Mathew, Mark, Luke and John, were written at approximately the same time as the Epistle of Barnabas. As with

the authors of the books of the Bible, Barnabas claims to have been inspired by God through the divine revelation of the Holy Spirit.

This 7000 year plan will be divided up into 4 time spans;

0 ------ 2000 leads up to Abraham
2000 – 4000 leads up to the Messiah Jesus's birth and sacrifice
4000 – 6000 leads up to the return of the Messiah for his Church
6000 – 7000 are the millennial reign of Christ Jesus the Messiah with his Church

THE EPISTLE OF BARNABUS

"...Of the Sabbath he **speaketh** in the beginning of creation; 'And God made the works of his hands in 6 days and he ended on the 7th day, and rested on it, and he hallowed it, give heed, children, what this **meaneth**.' 'He ended in 6 days' He **meaneth** this, that in 6000 years the Lord shall bring all things to an end, for the day with him **signifieth** a thousand years; and this he himself **beareth** me witness, saying, 'behold, the day of the Lord shall be as a thousand years.' Therefore, children, in 6 days, that is in 6 thousand years, everything shall come to an end'. And he rested on the 7th day'. This he **meaneth**; when his son [Jesus] shall come, and shall abolish the time of the **lawless** one [Satan], and shall judge the ungodly [non-Christians], and shall change the sun and the moon and the stars, then shall he truly **rest** on the 7th day."
….. Epistle of Barnabas, Chapter 13: 3-6

Look at what this Epistle does not say; it does not say that God created the heavens and the earth in 6000 years or billions of years; it says **"in 6000 years the Lord shall bring all things to an end "**[as it pertains to Satan's ruler-ship over the earth]. Jesus the Messiah and his body of believers; the Church, are taking over the earth.

In Creation ------------------------------ 1 day = 1 day
In Gods chronology of earth ----------- 1 day = 1000 years each; as patterned after the 7 day creation.

The Bible records each patriarch from Day 5 of creation starting with Adam and records an unbroken line of succession of one patriarch's wife giving birth to the next (future) patriarch; Abraham was 52 years old in the 2000th year anniversary of the earths creation.

Patriarch ....Verse...Age at sons birth.....**Years from creation**

(Earths creation)... Genesis 1: 1 .... 0 0
Adam.................... Genesis 5:1 .... 130 130
Seth .... Genesis 5:3 .... 105 235
Enos .... Genesis 5:6 .... 90 325
Cainan .... Genesis 5:9 .... 70 395
Mahalaleel .... Genesis 5:12 .... 65 460
Jared .... Genesis 5:15 .... 162 622
Enoch .... Genesis 5:18 .... 65 687
Methuselah .... Genesis 5:21 .... 187 874
Lamech .... Genesis 5:25 .... 182 1056
Noah .... Genesis 5:28-29 .... 502 1558
*******World Wide Flood********** 1656
Shem .... Genesis 5:32 .... 100 1658
Arphaxad .... Genesis 11:10 .... 35 1693
Salah .... Genesis 11:12 .... 30 1723
Eber .... Genesis 11:14 .... 34 1757
Peleg .... Genesis 11:16 .... 30 1787
Reu .... Genesis 11:18 .... 32 1819
Serug .... Genesis 11:20 .... 30 1849
Nahor .... Genesis 11:22 .... 29 1878
Terah .... Genesis 11:24 70 (at Abraham's birth).... 1948
Abraham ...(from earths creation)......... 52 years old 2000

*An interesting side-note about names in the Bible, they all have meaning. The meaning of the first 10 Patriarchs in the above list are recorded below;

Adam .... Man
Seth ....Appointed
Enos ....Mortal
Cainan ....Sorrow
Mahalaleel ...The Blessed God
Jarod ....Shall come down
Enoch .... Preaching
Methuselah .... His death shall bring
Lamech ....The despairing
Noah .... Rest

By taking the meanings of each name in succession there is a message for us;

Man appointed mortal sorrow, The blessed God shall come down preaching. His [Jesus's] death shall bring the despairing rest.

Jesus took upon himself a mortal body on the earth to preach the Kingdom of Heaven and then died, as planned, on a tree, [Galatians 3: 13] 'the Cross', for the redemption of all mankind who have been oppressed by Satan's ruler-ship.
In between Abraham and Jesus the Bible records that there are 42 generations and they are broken down in Mathew chapter 1 verse 17;

"So all the generations from Abraham to David and 14 generations; and David until the carrying away into Babylon are 14 generations; and from the carrying away into Babylon unto Christ are 14 generations."
… Mathew 1: 17

There have been Biblical scholars over the centuries that have attempted to date these 42 generations in order to find the exact age of the earth from the creation week to Christ. The list below names a few of these men with the corresponding results that they obtained;

Researcher .... Year of Calculation .... Derived date B.C. [Before Christ]

Martin Anstey 1913 4042
W. Lange .... N/A 4041
E. Reinholt .... N/A 4021
J. Cappelus 1600 4005
James Usher 1656 4004
E. Greswell 1830 4004
Floyd Jones 1993 4004
E. Faulstich 1986 4001
D. Petavius 1627 3983
..... AnswersinGenesis.org/articles/2007

The discrepancies between the dates derived by these scholars were due to several causes. Any time a book printer rewrites the Bible or other text in the public domain they are required to change it by at least 10% in order to have a version that they may copyright as their own work and then sell under copyright protection laws. Some translations have Methuselah living past the flood. Some translations were from differing manuscripts and are missing hundreds of verses. Not all of the historical data agree with each other or is available. It's not clear as to which Babylonian captivity should be used in the calculation; Daniel said that Nebuchadnezzar had taken captives before he was King of Babylon. The Jewish Historian Josephus had written an account similar to Daniels account of Nebuchadnezzar. Prior to his becoming King, he went to war and defeated the Egyptian army at Carchemish in Syria in the Spring of 605 B.C. where he sent Jewish, Phoenician, Syrian and Egyptian captives to Babylon

19 years prior to their "National" captivity in 586 B.C. These reasons and many more make it very difficult to calculate an exact date with a high level of confidence in the results.

For illustration purposes only, we are going to use what has been historically the most popular calculation of the age of the earth. a...James **Ushers** 4004 B.C., and b...**The Epistle of Barnabus:**

Adam to Abraham..................................a. 1948 ….............b. 2000
Abraham to Christs first appearance …
…............................... (**4004** – 1948) ... 2056 2000
Christs 1st to Christs 2nd Coming .... 2000* 2000*
…...6004 …............6000
*any day

Abraham died when he was 175 years old! We have his birth date as part of our calculation in (a) above, the year 1948 since creation. What part of a mans life should a person use in the calculation? That's another area that's unclear when trying to calculate an accurate result. There are those that have tried to track down the **birth day** and death **day** records of each person in the generations listed in Mathew **chapter** 1. As any genealogist knows, record keeping on each person may not have been as trustworthy as you would need it to be for this purpose. Personally, I think everyone is wasting their time trying to nail down an exact date because if you could find the exact date then you would know the exact date of the return of the Lord and God records that we cannot know the day and hour of his return. Add that to the re-working of the Gregorian calender at least 3 times that I am aware of and early dates become altered nearly beyond reconciliation. Julius Caesar and Caesar Augustus both wanted their own months named after them so the months of July and August were added to the calender. In another instance two weeks were removed from the calendar, the calender jumped two weeks in one day.

... "but of that day and hour [of Jesus's return] knoweth no man, no, not the angels of heaven, but my father only"
..... Mathew 24: 36

Just by using Barnabas's revelation of 2000, 2000 and 2000 we can derive a starting point for the length of a generation. Abraham to Christ is 2000 years. 2000 divided by 42 is 47.6 years.
As you can see by the numbers in the above illustration the return of the Lord is imminent no matter which one of the researchers were the closest to the actual date.

THE JEWISH TALMUD, FROM ABOUT 70 A.D., ALSO SPEAKS ABOUT THE AGE OF THE EARTH

"The Tanna debe Eliyyahu teaches: The world is to exist 6000 years. In the first 2000 there was desolation; [i.e. no Torah, it is a tradition that Abraham was 52 years old when he began to convert men to the worship of the true God; from Adam until then, 2000 years elapsed] 2000 years the Torah flourished; and the next 2000 years is the Messianic era, [i.e. Messiah will come within that period] but through our many iniquities all these years have been lost [He should have come at the beginning of the last 2000 years, the delay is due to our sins.]"
..... Sanhedrin 97

Good news Israel --- The delay never happened --- Jesus the Messiah did come and he fulfilled all prophecy concerning his first coming, he 'gave up' his life on a cross in Jerusalem, he is about to come again. The supposed 'Delay' that's spoken of in the Talmud was in order that the fullness of the Gentiles or 'non Jewish peoples' may come in [ushered into the Kingdom of Heaven]. For the past 2000 years, Jesus has been gathering the men and women that make up his 'Gentile and Jewish' Church. Israel has been, figuratively speaking, kept in the dark concerning the Gentiles coming into the Messiahs Kingdom.

69.

"For the days shall come upon thee [Israel], that thine enemies shall cast a trench about thee, and compass thee round, and keep thee in on every side. And shall lay thee even with the ground, and thy children within thee: And they shall not leave in thee one stone upon another [The destruction of the Jewish Temple in 70 A.D.] ; because thou **knowest** not the time of thy visitation [Jesus, at the appointed time walked and preached the kingdom on the streets then died and was resurrected in Jerusalem]."
…. Luke 19: 43-44

"Which none of the princes [Satan's demonic forces] of this world knew; for had they known it, they would not have crucified the Lord of Glory [Jesus]."
…. 1 Corinthians 2: 8

"I [Jesus] am the vine, you are the branches [new Gentile converts]: He that **abideth** in me, and I in him, the same **bringeth** forth much fruit: for without me you can do nothing. If a man **abideth** not in me, he is cast forth as a branch, and is withered, and men gather them, and cast them into the fire, and they are burned."
… John 15: 5 – 6

"And if some of the branches be broken off, [the Jewish people], and thou, being a wild olive tree [a Gentile made spiritually Jewish], wert grafted in among them, and with them **partakest** of the Root and Fatness [the spiritual gifts from the Messiah] of the olive tree; boast not against the branches. But if thou boast, thou **bearest** not the root [Jesus], but the root thee. Thou wilt say then, the branches were broken off, that I might be grafted in. Well; because of unbelief they [the Jews] were broken off, and thou **standest** by faith. Be not high minded [Gentiles:non-Jews], but fear: For if God spared not the natural branches [the Jewish people], take heed also lest he spare not thee. Behold therefor the goodness and severity of God: on them which fell, severity; but toward thee, goodness, if thou continue in his goodness:

otherwise thou also shalt be cut off. And they also, if they abide not still in unbelief, shall be grafted in: for God is able to graft them [Israel] in again. For if thou wert cut out of the Olive tree which is wild by nature, and wert grafted contrary to nature into a good Olive tree: how much more shall these, which be the natural branches [the Jewish people], be graffed into their own Olive tree? For I would not, brethren, that you should be ignorant of this mystery, lest you should be wise in your conceits; **that blindness in part has happened to Israel, until the fulness of the Gentiles be come in. And so all Israel shall be saved**: as it is written, there shall come out of Sion the Deliverer, and shall turn away ungodliness from Jacob [Israel]: For this is my covenant unto them, when I shall take away their sins.
.... Romans 11: 17-27

The Messiah speaking "**And I say also unto thee, that thou are Peter, and upon this rock I will build by Church [Gentile and Jewish believers in Christ]**; and the gates of Hell shall not prevail against it. And I will give unto thee the keys of the Kingdom of Heaven; and whatsoever thou shalt bind on earth shall be bound in heaven: and whatsoever thou shall loose on earth shall be loosed in heaven."
..... Mathew 16: 18-19

"I say then, have they [Israel] stumbled that they should fall: God forbid; but rather through their fall salvation is come unto the Gentiles [non-Jewish peoples], for to provoke them [Israel: Jews] to jealousy."
..... Romans 11: 11

THE LAUNCH OF THE MESSIAHS MINISTRY IN ISRAEL

In about 100 B.C., a Jewish prophet, Isaiah, foretells the coming of the Jewish Messiah:

"The Spirit of the Lord GOD is upon me; because the LORD hath anointed me to preach good tidings unto the meek; he hath sent me to bind up the broken hearted , to proclaim liberty to the captives, and the opening of prison to them that are bound; To proclaim the acceptable year of the LORD,..."
… Isaiah 61: 1- 2

A century after Isaiah records his prophecy [the foretelling of a future event] about the Messiah- Jesus stands before a synagogue in Nazareth to announce his arrival:

"The Spirit of the LORD is upon me, because he has anointed me to preach the gospel to the poor; he has sent me to heal the broken hearted, to preach deliverance to the captives, and recovery of sight to the blind, to set at liberty them that are bruised. To preach the acceptable year of the Lord. ..... **This day is this scripture fulfilled in your ears."**
….Luke 4: 18- 19, 21

Jesus was immediately rejected by the Jewish community in his day:

"And they in the synagogue, when they heard these things, were filled with wrath, and rose up and thrust him out of the city, and led him unto the brow of the hill whereon their city was built, that they might cast him down headlong."
… Luke 4: 28- 29

"And He [Jesus] taught daily in the temple. But the chief priests and the scribes and the chief of the people sought to destroy Him."
… Luke 19: 47

Since the Jewish community rejected Jesus as their Messiah, this paved the way for the Gentiles to be included in Gods plan of salvation and the Gentile entrance into the Kingdom of Heaven:

"Then Paul and Barnabas waxed bold, and said, it was necessary that the word of God [Jesus and his gift of eternal life] should first be spoken unto you [the Jewish people]: but seeing you put it [Gods Word – Jesus] from you, and judge yourselves unworthy of everlasting life, lo, **we turn to the Gentiles**."
… Acts 13: 46

"For by one Spirit are we all baptized into one body, whether we be Jews or Gentiles, whether we be bond or free; and have been all made to drink into one Spirit."

… 1 Corinthians 12: 13

When Paul, Barnabas and the other early church leaders **turned to the Gentiles** to deliver them into Gods kingdom they were not speaking of only the Gentiles in the immediate area around Judea, they were speaking of the entire world.

"And this gospel [the restoration of eternal life by God] of the kingdom **shall be preached in all the world for a witness unto all nations** [both Jewish and Gentile nations]; and then shall the end come." … Mathew 24: 14

The Jewish nation is Israel.

The Gentile nations around the world include the following:

Afghanistan… Akrotiri… Albania… Algeria… American Samoa… Andorra… Angola… Anguilla… Antarctica… Antigua and Barbuda… Argentina… Armenia… Aruba… Ashmoreland Cartier Islands   Australia… Austria… Azerbaijan… The Bahamas… Bahrain… Bangladesh… Barbados… Basses da India Belarus… Belgium… Belize… Benin… Bermuda… Bhutan… Bolivia… Bosnia and Herzegovina…   Botswana… Bouvet Island… Brazil… British Indian Ocean Territory… British Virgin Islands… Brunei… Bulgaria… Burkino Faso… Burma… Burundi… Cambodia… Cameroon… Canada… Caper Verde… Cayman Islands… Central African Republic… Chad… Chili… China… Christmas Island… Clipperton Island… Cocos (Keeling) Islands… Colombia… Comoros… Congo, Democratic Republic… Congo, Republic… Cook Islands… Coral Sea Islands… Costa Rica… Cote d"Ivoire (Ivory Coast)... Croatia... Cuba... Cyprus... Czech Republic... Denmark... Dhekelia... Djibouti... Dominica... Dominican Republic. Ecuador... Egypt... El Salvador... Equatorial Guinea... Eritrea... Estonia... Ethiopia... Europa Island... Falkland Islands (Islas Malvinas)... Faroe Islands... Fiji... Finland... France... French Guiana... French Polynesia... French Southern and Antarctic Lands... Gabon... Gambia, The... Gaza Strip... Georgia... Germany... Ghana (Gold Coast)... Gibraltar... Glorioso Islands... Greece... Greenland... Grenada... Guadeloupe... Guam... Guatemala... Guernsey.... Guinea.... Guinea–Bissau... Guayna... Haiti... Heard Island and Mcdonald Islands... Holy See (Vatican City)... Honduras... Hong Kong... Hungary... Iceland. India... Indonesia (Netherlands East Indies, Dutch East Indies)... Iran (Persia)... Iraq... Ireland... Isle of Man... Italy... Jamaica... Jan Mayen... Japan... Jersey... Jordan... Juan de Nova Island... Kazakhstan or Kazakstan... Kenya... Kiribiti... North Korea... South Korea... Kosovo... Kuwait... Kyrgystan... Laos... Latvia... Lebanon... Lesotho... Liberia... Libya... Liechtenstein... Lithuania... Luxembourg... Macau... Macedonia... Madagascar... Malawi... Malaysia... Maldives... Mali... Malta... Marshall Islands... Martinique... Mauritania... Mauritius... Mayotte... Mexico... Micronesia, Federated States of... Moldova... Monaco... Mongolia... Montserrat... Morocco... Mozambique... Myanmar... Namibia... Nauru (Pleasant Island)... Nauassa Island... Nepal... Netherlands... Netherlands Antilles... New Caledonia... New Zealand... Nicaragua... Niger... Nigeria... Niue (Savage Island)... Norfolk Island... Northern Mariana Islands... Norway... Oman... Pakistan... Palau... Panama... Papua New Guinea... Paracel Islands... Paraguay... Peru... Philippines... Pitcairn Islands... Poland... Portugal... Puerto Rico... Qatar... Reunion... Romania... Russia... Rwanda... Saint Helena... Saint Kitts and Nevis... Saint Lucia... Saint Pierre and Miquelon... Saint Vincent and the Grenadines... Samoa... San Marino... Sao Tome and Principe... Saudi Arabia... Senegal... Serbia and Montenegro... Seychelles... Sierre Leone... Singapore... Slovakia... Slovenia... Solomon Islands... Somalia... South Africa... South Georgia and the South Sandwich Islands... Spain... Spratly Islands... Sri Lanka

(Ceylon)... Sudan... Suriname... Svalbard... Swaziland... Sweden... Switzerland... Syria... Taiwan... Tajikistan... Tanzania... Thailand... Timor-Lcstc. Togo... Tokclau... Tonga (Friendly Islands)... Trinidad and Tobago... Tromelin Island... Tunisia... Turkey... Turkmenistan... Turks and Caicos Islands... Tuvala... Uganda... Ukraine... United Arab Emirites... United Kingdom (Great Britain)... United States... Uruguay... Uzbekistan... Vanuatu... Venezuela... Vietnam... Virgin Islands (Danish West Indies)... Wake Island... Wallis and Futuna... West Bank... Western Sahara (Spanish Sahara)... Yemen... Yugoslavia... Zaire (Belgian Congo)... Zambia... Zimbabwe.

Today we have instant communication through satellites and cell phones and video feeds and its fairly common to preach in one nation and have the sermon broadcast to other nations very quickly. Today we have automobiles and aircraft to cut down on travel time. We have printing presses so we don't have to write each book laboriously by hand one by one as the early church had to . Today we have electronic books or ebooks that can be uploaded onto the internet and they are almost instantly made available around the world for someone to download; usually within hours. The biggest reason Jesus has not returned yet is because every nation needed to hear the gospel as recorded in Mathew 24: 14 above. The early church walked everywhere they went or rode a donkey or possibly boarded a ship. What took them months to do back in Jesus's time only takes hours today and the nations around the world are wired for satellite communications so they are hearing the gospel right now.

There were prophets in the Old Testament that spoke about the coming messiah of Israel, 4 of them: Micah, Isaiah, Hosea, Jeremiah talked about Jesus's beginnings:

Born in Bethlehem..............Micah 5: 2
fulfilled............................Mathew 2: 1

Born of a virin...................Isaiah 7: 14
fulfilled............................Mathew 1: 20- 23

Anointed by God................Isaiah 11: 2

fulfilled...............................Mathew 3: 16– 4: 1
Mary was foretold of him....Isaiah 7: 14
fulfilled...............................Mathew 1: 20- 23
Fled to Egypt.......................Hosea 11: 1
fufilled...............................Mathew 2: 13- 15
Slaughter of the innocents...Jeremiah 31: 15
fulfilled...............................Mathew 2: 16 – 4: 1

OLD TESTAMENT PROPHESIES ABOUT THE MESSIAH [JESUS] AND THE CORRESTPONDING NEW TESTAMENT FULFILLMENT OF THOSE PROPHESIES

There are over 300 prophecies concerning Jesus; the Jewish Messiah or Gentile Savior recorded in the Bible, over 90% have been fulfilled to date. A partial list follows:

"Your throne, O God, is forever and ever; a scepter of righteousness is the scepter of your kingdom, You love righteousness and hate wickedness; therefore God, your God, has anointed you with the oil of gladness more than your companions.....Of old you laid the foundation of the earth, and the heavens are the work of your hands. They will perish, but you will endure; yes, all of them will grow old like a garment; like a cloak you will change them, and they will be change. But you are the same, and your years shall have no end."
….. **Old Testament,** Psalms 45: 7,102:25-27

"But to the son he says: "Your throne, O God, is forever and ever; a scepter of righteousness is the scepter of your Kingdom, You have loved righteousness and hated lawlessness; therefore God, Your God, has appointed you with the oil of gladness more than your companions, And : You, Lord, in the beginning laid the foundation of the earth,, and the heavens are the work of your

hands; they will perish, but you remain; and they will all grow old like a garment; like a cloak you will fold them up, and they will be changed, but you are the same, and your years will not fail."
..... **New Testament**, Hebrews 1: 8-12

"Of the increase of His [Jesus's] government and peace there will be no end, upon the throne of David and over his kingdom, to order it and establish it with judgment and justice from that time forward, even forever, the zeal of the Lord of Hosts will perform this."
...... **Old Testament**, Isaiah 9: 7

"He will be great, and will be called the son of the Highest; and the Lord God will give him the throne of his father David. And he will reign over the house of Jacob [Israel] forever, and of his kingdom there will be no end."
...... **New Testament**, Luke 1: 32-33

"When Israel was a child, I loved him, and out of Egypt I called my Son."
.... **Old Testament**, Hosea 11: 1

"When he arose, he took the young child and his mother by night and departed for Egypt, and was there until the death of Herod, that it might be fulfilled which was spoken by the Lord through the prophet, saying "Out of Egypt I called my Son"."
.... **New Testament**, Mathew 2: 14-15

"Therefore the Lord himself will give you a sign: Behold, the virgin shall conceive and bear a son, and shall call his name Immanuel [God with us]."
.... **Old Testament**, Isaiah 7: 14

"Now in the 6th month the angel Gabriel was sent by God to a city of Galilee named Nazareth, to a virgin betrothed to a man

whose name was Joseph, of the House of David. The virgins name was Mary... Then the angel said unto her, 'Do not be afraid, Mary, for you have found favor with God. And behold, you will conceive in your womb and bring forth a son, and shall call his name Jesus'." [Immanuel-God with us]
…….. **New Testament**, Luke 1: 26-27,30-31

"I will declare the decree: The Lord has said to me, "You are my Son, today I have begotten you."
….. **Old Testament**, Psalms 2: 7

"And suddenly a voice came from heaven, saying, "This is my beloved son, in whom I am well pleased."
…... **New Testament**, Mathew 3: 17

"The Lord your God will raise up for you a prophet like me [Moses] from your midst, from your brethren, him you shall hear."
…... **Old Testament**, Deuteronomy 18: 15

"And that he may send Jesus Christ, who was preached to you before,…For Moses truly said to the father. "The Lord your God will raise up for you a prophet like me from your brethren. Him you shall hear in all things, whatever he says to you."
…... **New Testament**, Acts 3: 20,22

"Rejoice greatly, O Daughter of Zion! Shout, O Daughter of Jerusalem! Behold, Your King is coming to you; He is just and having salvation, lowly and riding on a donkey, a colt, the foal of a donkey."
…... **Old Testament**, Zechariah 9: 9

"Then they brought the colt to Jesus and threw their garments on it, and He sat on it.... Then those who went before and those who followed cried out, saying: "Hosanna! Blessed is he who comes in the name of the Lord!"....And Jesus went into Jerusalem and into the Temple. So when he had looked around at all things, as the hour was already late, he went out to Bethany with the 12."
...... **New Testament**, Mark 11: 7,9,11

These next scriptures deal with the disciple Judas, the betrayer of the Messiah;

"Then I said unto them, 'If it is agreeable to you, give me my wages; and if not, refrain.' So they weighed out for my wages 30 pieces of silver."
...... **Old Testament**, Zechariah 11: 12

"Then one of the twelve, called Judas Iscariot, went to the chief priests and said, 'What are you willing to give me if I deliver him to you?' And they counted out to him 30 pieces of silver."
.... **New Testament**, Mathew 26: 14-15

"The Lord has sworn and will not relent. 'You are a Priest forever according to the order of Melchizedek'."
...... **Old Testament**, Psalms 110: 4

"...So also Christ did not Glorify himself to become High Priest. But it was he who said to him: 'You are my son, today I have begotten you! As he also says in another place. 'You are a Priest forever according to the order of Melchizedek."
.... **New Testament**, Hebrews 5: 5-6

"You have ascended on high, you have led captivity captive; You have received gifts among men; even among the rebellious, that the Lord God might dwell there."
......**Old Testament**, Psalms 68:18

"So then after the Lord had spoken to them, he was received up into heaven, and sat down at the right hand of God."…..**New Testament**, Mark 16:19

"Therefore he says: 'When he ascended on high, **He** led captivity captive, and gave gifts to men."
…...**New Testament**, Ephesians 4:8

EVOLUTIONS AGE OF THE EARTH AND THE REASON HOMOSEXUALITY EXISTS

Currently, but subject to change, evolutionists say that the earth is 4.8 billion years old. Evolution says that life on the earth is 3.8 billion years old and the universe is 20 plus billion years old. Evolutionists claim that all living things came from wet rocks by evolving slowly starting 3.8 billion years ago and morphing into more advanced organisms until today where men are at the pinnacle of the evolutionary tree [even though there is no evidence for this ever happening].
Would it be reasonable to say that today's evolutionists respect, admire, revere and are devoted to the evolution religion? I would say so.
Would it also be reasonable to say that evolutionists guard evolution because it affords them social status (doctors, professors) and a career? Possibly.
Could the beliefs born from their careers have lead to their mutual respect and admiration they have for each other due to their belief that they have a greater understanding (intellectually, not spiritually) of how the creation came to be which excluded Gods creation claim? Probably.
Could it be that today's evolutionists who think like Darwin, Lyell and others, just do not think it is intellectually acceptable and would be embarrassing to admit that there could be something in our universe that exists that they cannot explain using their intellect so they deny it altogether, namely God? Definitely.

Homosexuality and lesbianism are both direct results of the nations turning away from God and worshiping Gods creation, through evolution, more than God himself.

"For the invisible things of him <u>from the creation of the world are clearly seen</u>, being understood by the things that are made, even his eternal power and Godhead; so that they are without excuse: Because that, when they knew [by the law written on our hearts] God, they glorified him not as God, neither were thankful, **but became vain in their imagination and their foolish heart was darkened. Professing themselves [evolutionists] to be wise [homo sapien sapien: wise wise man], they became fools**, and changed the Glory [deserved credit] of the incorruptible God into an image made like to a corruptible man, and to birds, and four-footed beasts, and creeping things."
….. Romans 1: 20-23

God says that men should recognize that he created the earth by observing the entire creation (the things that God made in the beginning; the universe, planets, man, animals, fish, insects, etc.) and that he should be getting the credit for creating the earth and everything in it, not men for imagining that the earth created itself from an evolutionary standpoint and creating their own stories of the way the universe, earth and life formed. As with idol worship, by teaching evolution, men have intellectually brought God down to the level of the natural world alongside corrupted men and creatures. The above scriptures are speaking of man made idols of animals, men and mans evolutionary replacement of Gods creation. Including, what men have done with the fossils of animals that were dug from the ground and how they relate to today's animals. Evolutionists piece bones together and create stories through their imaginations of how they came to exist through a slow evolutionary process supposedly, but never proven, from one creature to another creature disregarding God altogether. If God hates the idolatry of men worshiping a golden bull or a Buddha statue how much more would God be grieved if men worshiped his entire creation and excluded him and his Word in the process. Men claim that God had nothing to do with the formation of the universe or the planets and stars, they created themselves. Men claim that God did not create the life that exists on the earth, it created itself. Men have excluded God from the schools where they teach others how everything known to man just happened by chance over billions of years without a divine creator. To God an idol is anything that is worshiped instead of Him.

Continuing;
"Wherefore God also gave them up to uncleanness through the lusts of their own hearts, to dishonor their own bodies between themselves: Who changed the truth of God [creation] into a lie [evolution], **and worshiped and served the creature** [creatures evolving] more than the Creator [**who created the creatures**], who is blessed forever. Amen."
…... Romans 1: 24-25

Evolutionism, both the religion and the supposed science, are disregarding God concerning his 6 day creation and they created their own religion to worship what they suppose is a self generating, multi-billion year old random event that came straight out of their imaginations with absolutely zero proof for their claims and they are forcing their beliefs on everyone in the public schools.

Continuing;
"**For this cause God gave them up unto vile affections [homosexuality]**: for even their women did change the natural use into that which is against nature. And likewise also the men, leaving the natural use of the woman, burned in their lust one toward another; men with men working that which is unseemly, and receiving in themselves that recompense [payment] of the error which was meet."
….. Romans 1: 26-27

By worshiping the "creation" through both the evolution religion or 'supposed' science -the judgment on the earth was homosexuality for both men and women.

Merriam-Webster defines "Worship" in part as; respect, admiration or devotion to an object of esteem. Honor and reverence.

Evolution has been in the school systems in earnest since President Eisenhower [in the U.S.] allocated a billion dollars to include it in the science text books in the early 1960's. Of course, at the time, no one really knew the damage it would cause but today the damage has become evident just by observing the moral decline of America. When we take a hard look at the decades since its inception then its destructive effects become very clear. [More on the statistics of evolution later]. Evolution is so entrenched today we see its evidence everywhere, kids books, commercials on television, any nature documentary usually has multiple references concerning evolution. Its been taught as a 'Fact' for so long that most people believe it because they, like myself, thought the educational system should have been teaching only something that had it's foundations in truth. Unfortunately, in this instance they are unwittingly teaching an agenda launched by Satan through ungodly men from the middle of the 1800's. We all 'fell for it' at first but the truth will always prevail. Evolution has failed to meet the criteria of any and all scientific methodology and as you will see later, many university professors know that it has failed and they openly admit it.

Personally, I have returned to believing Gods creation claim, there is nothing that can refute it and there are volumes that refute the evolution hypothesis. One last word on homosexuality and lesbianism, God hates those sins as he does all sins but he loves the people that have been trapped [by Satan's agenda] in them. He can and will forgive you and receive you into his kingdom just as he can and will receive anyone else. The door is open! God doesn't look upon one sin as being greater or lesser that any other sin. -- Sin is sin and all sin has to be recognized, confessed and resisted.

"Submit yourselves therefore to God. Resist the devil, and he will flee from you."
.... James 4: 7

"For all have sinned, and come short of the Glory of God; Being justified freely by his grace through the redemption that is in Christ Jesus:".... Romans 3: 24-25

Don't blame God for homosexuality in the world;
Suppose I wrote you a letter that said you would have an automobile accident if you drove with a blindfold over your eyes. Would it be my fault if you drove with a blindfold and crashed your car? No; what I said was designed to warn you and keep you from having a wreck not to cause it. We fell right into Satan's hands when America adopted evolution and kicked God out of our school systems. As mentioned earlier, men are responsible for what happens on the earth, God left man in charge and disregarding God cost us dearly. The book of Romans along with Gods warning has been in the Bible for centuries, long before Darwin launched Satan's plan to draw men from God. Homosexuality was part of the price the world paid for turning away from God and worshiping Gods creation through the teaching of evolution rather than teaching our children the truth that God created the heavens and the earth.

QUOTES ABOUT THE SHORTCOMINGS OF EVOLUTION AS A SCIENCE

There are some evolutionists that have been honest about the shortcomings of the evolution religion and science. Not all of the following quotes are from evolutionists but most are. Keep in mind it's been over 150 years since the hypothesis was launched and there still has not been one shred of evidence save a few exposed hoaxes. If we haven't found any evidence in over 150 years maybe it's time to call it what it is, a false hypothesis, and form another hypothesis.

"Both the origin of life and the origin of major groups of animals remains unknown."
.... Alfred Fisher, Grolier Encyclopedia, 1998

"The evolutionary trees that adorn our textbooks have data only at the tips and nodes of their branches; the rest is inference [guesswork], however reasonable, not the evidence of fossils."
.... Stephen Gould, Harvard University, Evolutions Erratic Pace, Natural History, vol.5

"One of the ironies of the evolution-creation debate is that the **creationists have accepted the mistaken notion** that the fossil record shows a detailed and orderly progression and they have gone to great lengths to accommodate this "Fact" in their flood genealogy."
..... David Raup, Evolution and the Fossil Record, science, vol. 213

"In the years after Darwin, his advocates hoped to find predictable progressions [missing links, proof for evolution]. In general, these have not been found – yet the optimism has died hard, **and some pure fantasy has crept into** the textbooks."
..... David Raup, University of Chicago, Science, vol.213

"I fully agree with your comments on the lack of evolutionary transitions [missing links] in my book. If I knew of any, fossil or living, I would certainly have included them. I will lay it on the line – there is not one such fossil..."
..... Dr. Colin Patterson, Darwins Inigma, 1988

85.

"The absence of fossil evidence for intermediary stages...has been a persistent and nagging problem for...**evolution.**"
..... Dr. Stephen Gould, Harvard University, **Theorized Punctuated** Equilibrium

"Paleontologists have tried to turn Archeopteryx into an earth bound feathered dinosaur. But it's not, it's a bird, a perching bird. And no amount of "**paleobabble**" is going to change **that**."
.... Alan Feduccia, University of North Carolina, Chapel Hill, One of the Worlds foremost authorities on birds

"Evolution is a fairy tale for grownups. The theory has helped nothing in the progress of science. It is useless."
..... Professor Louis Bounoure, Director of the Strasbourg Zoological Museum

"The origin of bird is largely a matter of deduction, there is no fossil evidence of the stages through which the remarkable change from reptile to bird was achieved."
......W.E. Swinton, British Museum of Natural History

"Evolution is promoted by its practitioners as more than mere science. Evolution is promulgated as an ideology, a secular religion – A full fledged alternative to Christianity, with meaning and morality. I am an ardent evolutionist and an Ex-Christian, but I must admit that in this one complaint – And Mr. Gish is but one of many to make it – the **literalists** are absolutely right. Evolution is a **religion**. This was true of evolution in the beginning, and it is true of evolution still today."
..... Dr. Michael Ruse, Professor of Philosophy and Zoology, University of Guelph

"**I myself am convinced that the theory of evolution**, especially the extent to which it has been applied, **will be one of the greatest jokes in the history books of the future.** Posterity will marvel that so flimsy and dubious **an hypothesis** could be

accepted with the incredible credulity [with slight evidence] that it has."
….. Malcolm Muggeridge, [His book: "Something beautiful from God" about Mother Teresa of India.] **Philosopher, Lecturer, Journalist,** Pascal Letters, University of Waterloo, ….. Canada

"Apart from very "modern" [non-fossilized] examples, which are really **archeology**. I can think of no cases of radioactive decay being used to date fossils."
….. Derek Ager, Fossil **Frustrations**, New Scientist, Vol. 100

"It is as if though they [all animal fossils] were just planted here, without any evolutionary history."
…... Richard Dawkins, Biologist

The Christian Creation response to the lack of evolutionary history as mentioned above:
There are no missing links to be found, God created everything in it's completed form during the 6 days of creation. They did not need to evolve because they were made perfectly the first time. As you will see later, they can't evolve because the DNA of all species prohibits evolution from happening.
An animal or plant has to be buried before it can fossilize and there **are** over a thousand flood legends pointing towards a worldwide flood about 4400 years ago. Fossils seem to be planted because within one year all animals died and settled out in the sediment or mud as undersea earthquakes caused **tsunamic** activity worldwide. In the mixing of rock, pebbles, sand and mud laden water during the flood **the layers** were sorted by hydrologic action and settled out **trapping the** carcasses of everything that died. The mud sediments hardened into rock over the last 4400 years.
This also explains the petrified trees, **polystrate** fossils, that are found worldwide in fossil forests, intruding through dozens of layers of geologic or, more accurately described, hydrologic strata that are supposedly each millions of years old, some of these trees

are found upside down, and they certainly did not live millions of years to allow sediments to bury them.

"Evolution is not a fact, evolution doesn't even qualify as a theory or as a hypothesis, it is a Metaphysical Research Program, and it is not really **testable** science."
.... Dr. Karl Popper, Philosopher of Science

"99% of all fossils found in a species that lived and went extinct were always found in the same state of development throughout their entire existence. From the first to the last in the fossil record, 1% variation. The 1% remaining could be explained by disease, age, lack of nutrition, injury or a variant in its genetic makeup."
.... Dr. Kent Hovind Seminar, 2005

"I was a young man with unformed ideas. I threw out queries, suggestions, wondering all the time over everything; and to my astonishment the ideas took like wildfire. People made a religion out of them!"
.... Charles Darwin on his own theory of evolution

Darwin himself had serious doubts and legitimate concerns about his own theory of evolution.

"...I am quite conscious that my speculations run beyond the bounds of true science... It is a mere rag of **an** hypothesis with as many **flaw**[s] & holes as sound parts."
.... Charles Darwin to Asa Gray, Darwin,New York: W.W. Norton and Company, 1991,pg.456,475

"...Why, if species have descended from other species by insensibly fine graduations, do we not see everywhere innumerable transitional forms? Why is not all nature in confusion, instead of the species being, as we see them, well defined?"
... Charles Darwin

"The number of intermediate varieties which have formerly existed on earth must be truly enormous. Why then is not every geological formation and every stratum full of such intermediate links? Geology assuredly does not reveal any such finely graduated organic chain; and this, perhaps, is the most obvious and gravest objection which can be urged against my theory."
…. Charles Darwin, 1902, ……..The Origin of Species………..

"Darwin admitted that millions of 'missing links', transitional life forms, would have to be discovered in the fossil record to prove the accuracy of his theory that all species had gradually evolved by chance mutation into new species. Unfortunately for his theory, despite hundreds of millions spent on searching for fossils worldwide for more than a century, the scientists have failed to locate a single missing link out of the millions that exist if their theory of evolution is to be vindicated."
….. Grant Jeffery, The Signature of God, [Mr. Jeffery is obviously a creationist]

"To suppose that the eye…could have been formed by natural selection seems, I freely confess, absurd in the highest degree."
….. Charles Darwin, The Origin of Species by Means of Natural Selection or the Preservation of Favored Races in the Struggle for Life. 1859, pg. 217

"If it could be demonstrated that if any complex organ [the eye] existed, **which could not possibly have been formed by numerous, successive, slight modifications**, my theory would absolutely break down. But I can find out no such case."
… Charles Darwin

God had a "case" waiting for Charles-
"The hearing ear, and the seeing eye, the LORD hath made even both of them."
… Proverbs 20: 12

"I can indeed hardly see how anyone ought to wish Christianity to be true."
..... Charles Darwin from his autobiography by M. Grano, The Faith of Darwinism

"Why do geologists and archeologists still spend their scarce money on costly radiocarbon determinations? They do so because occasional dates appear to be useful. While the method cannot be counted on to give good, unequivocal results, the number[s] do impress people, and save them the trouble of thinking excessively. Expressed in what look like precise calendar years, figures seem somehow better... 'Absolute' dates determined by a laboratory carry a lot of weight, and are extremely helpful in bolstering weak arguments.
No matter how 'useful' it is, though, the radiocarbon method is still not capable of yielding accurate and reliable results. There are gross discrepancies, the chronology is uneven and relative, and the accepted dates are actually selected dates. This whole bless thing is nothing but 13th Century Alchemy, and it all depends upon which funny paper you read."
..... Robert E. Lee," Radiocarbon: Ages in error", Anthropological Journal of Canada, vol. 19, 1981

"Contrary to what most scientists write, the fossil record does not support the Darwinian theory of evolution because it is this theory (there are several) which we use to interpret the fossil record. By doing so we are guilty of circular reasoning if we then say the fossil record supports this theory."
..... Ronald R. West, PhD (paleoecology and geology), Assistant Professor of Paleobiology at Kansas State University, "Paleoecology and uniformitarianism". Compass, vol. 45, May 1968, pg. 216

"The likelihood of the formation of life from inanimate matter is one out of 10 to the power of 40,000... It is big enough to bury Darwin and the whole theory of evolution. There was no primeval

soup, neither on this planet nor on any other, and if the beginnings of life were not random, they must therefore have been the product of purposeful intelligence."
.... Sir Fredrick Hoyle, Professor of Astronomy, Cambridge University

"Scientists who go about teaching that evolution is a fact of life are great con-men, and the story they are telling may be the greatest hoax ever. **In explaining evolution, we do not have one iota of fact.**"
.... Dr. T. Tahmisian (Atomic Energy Commission, USA), The Fresno Bee, 8/1959

"The theory suffers from grave defects, which are becoming more and more apparent as time advances. It can no longer square with practical scientific knowledge, nor does it suffice for our theoretical grasp of the facts....No one can demonstrate that the limits of a species have ever been passed. These are the Rubicons which evolutionists cannot cross... Darwin ransacked other spheres of practical research work for ideas... But his whole resulting scheme remains, to this day, foreign to scientifically established zoology, since actual changes of species by such means are still unknown."
... Albert Fleischmann, "The Doctrine of Organic Evolution in the Light of Modern Research," Journal of the Transactions of the Victoria Institute 65 (1933)

"Evolution requires plenty of faith; a faith in L-proteins that defy chance formation; a faith in the formation of DNA codes which, if generated spontaneously, would spell only pandemonium; a faith in a primitive environment that, in reality, would fiendishly devour any chemical precursors to life; a faith in experiments that prove nothing but the need for intelligence in the beginning; a faith in a primitive ocean that would not thicken, but would only hopelessly dilute chemicals; a faith in natural laws of thermodynamics and biogenesis that actually deny the possibility

for the spontaneous generation of life; a faith in future scientific revelations that, when realized, always seem to present more dilemmas to the evolutionists; faith in improbabilities that treasonously tell two stories—one denying evolution, the other confirming the Creator; faith in transformations that remain fixed; faith in mutations and natural selection that add to a double negative for evolution; faith in fossils that embarrassingly show fixity through time, regular absence of transitional forms and striking testimony to a worldwide water deluge; a faith in time which proves to only promote degradation in the absence of mind; and faith in reductionism that ends up reducing the materialist's arguments to zero and forcing the need to invoke a supernatural Creator."
.... R.L. Wysong, The Creation-Evolution Controversy, 1981, pg.455

"The facts must mold the theories, not the theories the facts.... I am most critical of my biologist friends in this matter. Try telling a biologist that, impartially judged among other accepted theories of science, such as the theory of relativity, it seems to you that the theory of natural selection has a very uncertain, hypothetical status, and **watch** his reaction. I'll bet you that he gets red in the face. This is 'religion', not 'science', with him."
..... Burton, "The Human Side of the Physiologist: Prejudice and Poetry", Physiologist 2, 1957

"No one can think of **ways to test it [the evolutionary hypothesis]**. Ideas **with** [or] without basis or **based on a few laboratory experiments** carried out in extremely simplified systems, **have attained currency far beyond their validity**. They have become part of an evolutionary dogma accepted by most of us as part of our training."
.... L.C. Birch and P. Ehrlich, Nature, April 22, 1967

"I find it as difficult to understand a scientist who does not acknowledge the presence of a superior rationality behind the existence of the universe as it is to comprehend a theologian who would deny the advances of science."
....Wernher von Braun, Tornado in a junkyard by James Perloff, Refuge books, 1999, pg.253

"In fact [subsequent to the publication of Darwin's book, Origin of Species], evolution became, in a sense, a scientific religion; almost all scientists have accepted it and **many are prepared to 'bend' their observations to fit with it.** To my mind, the theory does not stand up at all...If living matter is not, then, caused by the interplay of atoms, natural forces, and radiation, how has it come into being?... I think, however, that we must go further than this and admit that the only acceptable explanation is creation. I know that this is anathema to physicists, as indeed it is to me, but we must not reject a theory that we do not like if the experimental evidence supports it."
..... H.S. Lipson, "A Physicist Looks at Evolution", Physics Bulletin, Vol. 31, pg. 138 1980

Chapter 4

GOD USES MEN TO DO HIS WILL ON THE EARTH

In this chapter we begin with Gods specific assignments for certain men on the earth. As Johannes Brahms points out later - some of these men know they are being used by God and some of them do not. I have selected a group of three well-known men that God has worked specifically through during their careers to advance mankind through science, music and mathematics.

NIKOLA TESLA ------------------- SCIENCE

First up is Nicola Tesla; The inventor of A/C electricity, the electric motor, the fluorescent light bulb, the Tesla coil. Nikola was the first to wire a city block for electricity. The first hydro-electric power plant was built by Tesla at Niagara Falls, New York using his designs including electrical conversion and distribution systems. Nicola was working on a system of electrical generation and wireless distribution that would provide free electricity to the entire world but lost his financial backing. Tesla writes:

"We could irrigate arid deserts, create lakes and rivers, and provide motive power in unlimited amounts. This would be the most efficient way in harnessing the sun to the uses of man. The consummation depended on our ability to develop electric forces of the order of those in nature. It seemed a hopeless undertaking, but I made up my mind to try it and immediately on my return to the United States in the summer of 1892, after a short visit to my friends in Watford, England: Work was begun which was to me all the more attractive, because a means of the same kind was <u>necessary for the successful transmission of energy without wires.</u> At this time I made a further careful study of the Bible, and discovered the key in Revelation. The first gratifying result was obtained in the spring of the succeeding year, when I reached a

tension of about 100,000,000 volts – one hundred million volts – with my conical coil [Tesla Coil], which I figured was the voltage of a flash of lightning. "
….. Nicola Tesla, Autobiography

In 1939 when Tesla was in his 80's, he wrote a letter to a friend, Miss Pola Fotitch, which shows that God planted the seed of electricity in Tesla's mind as a young man living at home with his parents. By Tesla's admission, God was the catalyst that led him to study and work on all manner of electrical devices in his career. A portion of Tesla's letter to Miss Fotitch;

"Now, I must tell you of a strange experience which bore fruit in my later life... We had a cold [snap] drier that ever observed before. People walking in the snow left a luminous trail behind them and a snowball thrown against an obstacle gave a flare of light like a loaf of sugar hit with a knife. [As I stroked the cat] MaA'aks back, [it became] a sheet of light and my hand produced a shower of sparks. ...My father... remarked, this is nothing but electricity, the same thing you see on the trees in a storm. My mother seemed alarmed. Stop playing with the cat, she said, he might start a fire. I was thinking abstractly. Is nature a cat? If so, who strokes its back? **It can only be God, I concluded.** … I cannot exaggerate the effect of this marvelous sight on my childish imagination. Day after day I asked myself what is electricity and found no answer. Eighty years have gone by since and I still ask the same question, unable to answer it."
…….Nikola Tesla, Letter to Miss Pola Fotitch, Cited in Marc Seifers Book,"Wizard: The Life and Times of Nikola Tesla", 1998

In my personal life, I have never seen static electricity the way Nikola describes it in his letter. I believe God caused that to happen to Nikola at his boyhood home to plant an unending curiosity for electricity inside of a young Nikola's mind which led him to study and research and to build all of the electrical devices and systems that he built.

Nikola claimed that if he sat in a quiet place and concentrated on the issues that he was working on eventually he would be given the solution in his mind. He could visualize the inner workings of electrical components in operation before he ever attempted to make a prototype of the electrical device he was working on. He could model all of his inventions in his mind to see if certain components worked or not in the finished product.

"Peace can only come as a natural consequence of universal enlightenment and merging of races, and we are still far from this blissful realization, because few indeed, will admit the reality that God made man in His image in which case all earth men are alike. There is in fact but one race, of many colours. Christ is but one **person, yet** he is of all people, so why do some people think themselves better that some other people?"
… Nikola Tesla in his Autobiography

DR. JOHANNES BRAHMS ------------- MUSIC

Secondly we have Dr. Johannes Brahms- music composer, Dr. Brahms was asked questions about what inspired him to compose his music. Below are excerpts from Arthur Abells book; "Talks with Great Composers";

"I will now tell you and our young friend here about my method of communication with the infinite, for all truly inspired ideas come from God. Beethoven, who was my ideal, was well aware of this."
….. Dr. Johannes Brahms, page 3

"To realize that we are one with the **Creator, as** Beethoven did, is a wonderful and awe-inspiring experience. Very few human beings ever come to that realization and that is why there are so few great composers or creative geniuses in any line of human endeavor. I always contemplate all this before commencing to compose. This is the first step. When I feel the urge I appeal directly to my maker and I first ask him the three most important questions pertaining to our life here in this world, - whence, wherefore, whither?"

Brahms continued, "I immediately feel vibrations that thrill my whole being. These are the Spirit illuminating the soul-power within, and in this exalted state, I see clearly what is obscure in my ordinary moods; then I feel capable of drawing inspiration from above, as Beethoven did. Above all, I realize at such moments the tremendous significance of Jesus' supreme revelation, 'I and my Father are one'. Those vibrations assume the forms of distinct mental images, after I have formulated my desire and resolve in regard to what I want – namely, to be inspired so that I can compose something that will uplift and benefit humanity- something of permanent value. Straightway the ideas flow upon me, directly from God, and not only do I see distinct themes in my minds eye, but they are clothed in right forms, harmonies and orchestration. Measure by measure, the finished product is revealed to me when I am in those rare, inspired moods...I have to be in a semi-trance condition to get such results – A condition when the conscious mind is in temporary obeyance and the subconscious is in control, for it is through the subconscious mind, which is part of omnipotence, that the inspiration comes. I have to be careful, however, not to lose consciousness, otherwise the ideas fade away."
.... Dr. Johannes Brahms, pages 5- 6

"Spirit is the light of the soul". Brahms continued. "Spirit is universal. Spirit is the creative energy of the cosmos. The soul of man is not conscious of its powers until it is enlightened by spirit. Therefore, to evolve and grow, man must learn how to use and develop his own soul forces [cooperating with the Holy Spirit]. All great creative geniuses do this, although some of them do not seem to be as conscious of the process as others."
... Dr. Johannes Brahms, pages 6- 7

Brahms goes on;
"As I said before, when I enter that dreamlike state, I am in a trance-like condition- hovering between being asleep and awake; I am still conscious but right on the border of losing consciousness, and it is at such moments that inspired ideas come. All true inspiration emanates from God, and he can reveal himself to us only through that spark of Divinity within- through what modern psychologists call the subconscious mind."
….. Dr. Johannes Brahms, page 9

As is clearly evident by Dr. Brahms descriptions as to where his inspiration comes from - he knows God is providing and inspiring everything he needs and desires as it pertains to composing. One last thought for the up and coming composer from Dr. Brahms;

"The Muse [thought] is a very jealous entity, like Jehovah in the commandments, and she flies away on the slightest provocation."
…. Page 60
Find a place where you can work uninterrupted!

The Bible records something similar to what Dr. Brahms describes;

"In a dream, in a vision of the night, when deep sleep falleth upon men, in slumbering upon their bed; then he openeth the ears of men, and sealeth their instruction."
……. Job 33:15-16

Our final example is of a man used by God that propelled mathematics well beyond the 20th century.

SRINIVAS RAMANUJAN ------ MATHEMATICS

Ramanujan was the most mathematically enlightened man that ever lived on earth that I am aware of. There are a couple of different stories associated with his inspiration of how he came up with his mathematical formulas:

The first account; an angel would visit him in the night and show him different formulas in a dream. After he awoke the next morning he would write them all down and then prove them mathematically.

The second account; he would see a red wall in a dream and a disembodied hand would write formula after formula on the wall and when he awoke in the morning, as previously, he would prove them all mathematically.

The Bible records something similar to this in the books of Daniel and Ezekiel;

"In the same hour came forth fingers [disembodied] of a mans hand, and wrote over against the candlestick upon the plaster of the wall of the Kings Palace; and the King saw the part of the hand that wrote."
…. Daniel 5: 5

"But thou, son of man, hear what I [God] say unto thee: Be not thou rebellious like that rebellious house: open thy mouth, and eat that I give thee. And when I looked, behold, a hand was sent unto me; and, Lo, a roll of a book was therein."
…... Ezekiel 2: 8-9

The following is an excerpt from "Ramanujan, Greatest Indian Mathematician" from Mayyam.com.

99.

"Today's mathematicians-- armed with supercomputers – are still star-struck, and unable to solve many theorems the young man from India proved quickly by pencil and paper....In his day, these equations were mainly pure mathematics, abstract computations that math sages often felt describe God's precise design for the cosmos. While much of Ramanujan's work remains abstract, many of his theorems are now the mathematical power behind several 1990's disciplines in astrophysics, artificial intelligence and gas physics. According to his wife – Janaki, who still lives outside Madras – her husband predicted "his mathematics would be useful to mathematicians for more than a century." Yet, before sailing to England, Ramanujan was largely ignorant of the prevailing highest-level math. He flunked out of college in India. Like Albert Einstein, who toiled as a clerk in a Swiss patent office while evolving his Special Theory of Relativity at odd hours, Ramanujan worked as a clerk at a port authority in Madras, spending every spare moment contemplating the mathematical face of God. It was here in these sea-smelling, paper-pushing offices that he was gently pushed into destiny – a plan that has all the earmarks of divine design."
..... Mayyam.com

G.W. Hardy at Cambridge University was considered to be the brightest mathematician in England. He received a letter or resume from Ramanujan asking for a job at Cambridge. Here is what Hardy had to say about Ramanujan;

"Ramanujan's letter and equations fell to them like a broadcast from alien worlds. At first they dismissed it as a curiosity. Then, they suddenly became intrigued by the Indian's musings."
Hardy later wrote;
"A single look at them is enough to show that they could only be written down by a mathematician of the highest class. They must be true, for if they were not true, no one would have the imagination to invent them."
... G.W. Hardy, Cambridge University

Side note * The apostle Paul also received 'letters' or 'epistles' from heaven and he wrote them down to share them with mankind as did all of the writers of the Bible, Paul wrote 2/3 of the new testament as conveyed through Divine inspiration from God:

"But I [Paul] **assure you, brethren**, that the gospel which was preached of me is not after man. For I neither received it of man, neither was I taught it, but by the revelation of Jesus Christ."
...Galatians 1 : 11 – 12

I believe Mr. Hardy was correct when he said; "A broadcast from alien worlds"
The most common definition for an extraterrestrial is, according to the 'New American Webster Dictionary': **"Beyond the limits of the earth".**

GOD IS AN ALIEN OR 'EXTRATERRESTRIAL' ... by mans definition!

I believe that, according to the definition, any life form that is from outside of the earth's atmosphere would qualify as an 'Alien or Extraterrestrial Life form" even if that life form does not have a physical, flesh and blood body. Remember in "Gods Big Bang" God, who is a Spirit, set our 3 dimensional universe into existence and the fact that he pre-existed the earth's formation and created everything we know today from an invisible realm. Heaven #1 is the surface of the earth and its atmosphere. Heaven #2 is all of the cosmos excluding heavens #'s 1 and 3. Heaven #3 is a planet or a constructed city, by God, where God lives, it's very earth-like, complete with mountains, rivers, trees, animals, men, angels,etc.
Gods plan is to eventually get planet earth (H1) the same as planet heaven (H3), populate it with believers that are faithful to him, then move here and live with us on earth. That's why I believe

that unbelievers will be imprisoned within the earth, away from God and his faithful sons and daughters.

"After this manner therefore pray ye: Our Father which art in heaven, hallowed be thy name. Thy kingdom come, thy will be done in earth, as it is in heaven."
.... Mathew 6: 9-10

"I knew a man in Christ above 14 years ago, (whether in the body, I cannot tell; or whether out of the body, I cannot tell: God knoweth;) **such an one caught up to the 3rd heaven**....How that he was caught up into paradise, and heard unspeakable words, which is not lawful for a man to utter [speak]."
… 2 Corinthians 12: 2, 4

EVERY MAN, WOMAN AND CHILD ON THE PLANET ARE , IN PART, EXTRATERRESTRIAL

The spirits of men are sent to the earth to be placed in a human body while in the mother's womb. These spirits came from heaven #3 and they are eternal spirits and will exist somewhere after the death of the body. The body is the only part that was originally from the earth or made from the dust [elements] of the ground. Since Adam and Eve's time, our spirits are made outside of the earth and will return to heaven where they were made if and only if we receive Jesus Christ as our Lord. As stated earlier, if a person fails to receive Jesus then their spirits will dwell in the Lake of Fire inside the earth and separated from the God of heaven but with the God of this world – Satan. Since our spirits are from the planet or super-structure called heaven #3 then by definition, we are at least 1/3 alien. The Bible records that God breathes the breath of life into men and they become a living soul, I believe or souls come into existence the instant God breathes his life into us on earth but the soul stays with the spirit in either heaven or hell depending upon which God we serve. The following verse confirms that prior to the formation of our physical bodies God has in intimate knowledge of each one of us, our spirit, before we ever come to the earth.

"Before I formed thee in the belly I knew thee; and before thou camest forth out of the womb I sanctified thee, and I ordained thee a prophet unto the nations."
... Jeremiah 1 : 5

BIBLICAL UFO'S

The following is an account given by an elderly John, the last surviving disciple from Jesus's earthly ministry while he was exiled on the Isle of Patmos. An angel (messenger from God) showed him in a vision- the "Holy Jerusalem" that God is going to dwell in on the earth. If God brought this to the earth today, people would be terror-struck by its enormous size. They would be thinking 'alien invasion' but not the type of invasion they would imagine. Here is what John was shown in his vision:

"And he [the angel] carried me away in the spirit [the angel took Johns spirit from his body temporarily to show him this] to a great and high mountain, and showed me that great city, the Holy Jerusalem, descending out of heaven from God [this would happen centuries in the future close to our time today], having the Glory of God: and her light was unto a stone most precious, even like a Jasper stone, clear as crystal; and had a wall great and high, and had 12 gates, and at the gates 12 angels, and names written thereon, which are the names of the twelve tribes of the children of Israel: On the east three gates; on the north three gates; on the south three gates; and on the west three gates. And the wall of the city had 12 foundations, and in them the names of the 12 apostles of the Lamb [Jesus]. And he that talked with me had a golden reed to measure the city, and the gates thereof, and the wall thereof. And the city lieth foursquare, and the length is as large as the breadth: and he measured the city with the reed, 12,000 furlongs [1500 miles]. The length and the breadth and the height of it were equal. And he measured the wall thereof, an hundred and forty and four cubits, according to the measure of a man, that is, of the angel. And the building of the wall of it was of Jasper: and the city was pure gold, like unto clear glass. And the foundations of the wall of the city were garnished with all manner of precious stones. The first foundation was jasper; the second, sapphire; the third, a chalcedony; the fourth, an emerald; the fifth, sardonyx; the sixth, sardius; the seventh, chrysolite; the eighth, beryl; the ninth, a topaz; the tenth, a chrysoprasus; the eleventh, a jacinth; the twelfth, an amethyst. And the 12 gates were 12 pearls; every several gate was one pearl: and the street of the city was pure gold, as it were transparent glass. And I saw no temple therein: for the Lord God Almighty and the Lamb[Jesus] are the temple of it. **And the city had no need of the sun, neither of the moon, to shine in it; for the Glory of God did lighten it, and the Lamb is the light thereof.** And the nations of them which are saved [became followers of Jesus] shall walk in the light of it; and the kings of the earth do bring their glory and honor into it. And the gates of it shall not be shut at all by day: for there shall be no night there."....

…....."And he showed me a pure river of water of life, clear as crystal, proceeding out of the throne of God and of the Lamb. In the midst of the street of it, and on either side of the river, was there the tree of life, which bare 12 manner of fruits, and yielded her fruit every month: and the leaves of the tree were for the healing of the nations.... And there shall be no night there; and they need no candle, neither light of the sun; for the Lord God giveth them light; and they shall reign forever and ever. And he said unto me, these sayings are faithful and true: and the Lord God of the Holy Prophets sent His Angel to show unto his servants the things which must shortly be done."

…... Revelation 21: 10-25------- + --------Revelation 22: 1-2,5-6

The Holy Jerusalem will be the largest airborne city or craft the world will probably ever see unless God has something larger in the works that he hasn't told us about yet. This "city" will be coming to the earth in the very near future. There has been debate over what form the 1500 mile equidistant sided city will take. It

could be in the form of a cube or it could be in the form of a pyramid. If it's cubic in shape then it will have approximately 3,375,000,000 cubic miles of interior space. If it's pyramidal in shape then it will have approximately 1,125,000,000 cubic miles of interior space. For comparison, today on the earth there is 57.5 million square miles of surface area of land which is about 29% of the earths surface. The other 71% of earths surface area is what remains of the pre-flood seas and the flood water that was released when the underground fountains of the deep (aquifers) broke open. Either version of the above Holy Jerusalem would be enormous floating cities descending from the sky; plenty of room to stretch out in, that also includes the aforementioned mountains and rivers and trees, etc. that are inside of the city.
This could be heaven #3 or the city was built in heaven #3, either way it's headed towards the earth.

"Him that overcometh will I make a pillar in the Temple of my God, and he shall go no more out; and I will write upon him the name of my God, and the name of the city of my God, which is New Jerusalem, which cometh down out of heaven from my God; and I will write upon him my new name."
…. Revelation 3 :12

In the book of 2 Kings there is an account of ' unearthly craft' called a 'Chariots of Fire'. There was a large gathering of these 'Chariots' in the spirit dimension and Elisha, Gods prophet, asked God to let his frightened servant "See" into the spirit dimension to show his servant that God had sent help for them.

"And one of his [the King of Syria's] servants said, None, my lord, O king: but Elisha, the prophet that is in Israel, telleth the king of Israel the words that thou speakest in thy bedchamber. [God, through his omnipresence is hearing the King of Syria who thinks he is speaking in private, God tells his prophet Elisha and Elisha tells the King of Israel what the King of Syria is planning]. And he [the King] said, Go and spy where he is, that I may send

and fetch him. And it was told him, saying, behold, he is in Dothan. Therefore sent he thither horses, and chariots, and a great host: and they came by night, and compassed the city about. And when the servant of the man of God was risen early, and gone forth, behold, **an** host compassed the city both with horses and chariots. And his [Elisha's] servant said unto **him**, Alas, my master! How shall we do? And he **answered**, Fear not: for they that be with us are more than they that be with them. And Elisha prayed, and **said**, Lord, I pray thee, open his eyes, that he may see. And the Lord opened the eyes of the young man; and he saw: **and, behold**, the mountain was full of horses and **chariots of fire** round about Elisha. And when they came down to him, Elisha prayed unto the Lord, and said, Smite this people, I pray thee, with blindness. And He [God] smote them with blindness according to the word of Elisha."
..... 2 Kings 6: 11-18

These chariots of fire, as theorized by myself and other researchers, may actually be referring to nuts and bolts craft which were clearly from another dimension outside of our 3 dimensions. They were there for a specific purpose: To protect the prophet of God and the prophet's servant from the **King** of Syria's army.
Entering into and out of another dimension, at least for men, possibly may only be a product of our minds which, as mentioned, are part of our souls. In this account where Elisha asked God to 'Open his servants eyes' - **this** tells us how men may operate in another spiritual dimension at least in part. God 'switched on' the servants **ability** to see what was already there and possibly already visible to Elisha. This same thing happened to me when God allowed me to see in the spirit dimension. (more on this later). **The spirit** world does not suddenly come upon us or visit us from time to time, it's always there, however, men are not continually 'switched on' and able to see in that dimension.

In the book of Ezekiel Chapters 1 and 2 Ezekiel describes a flying craft that God used to pay Ezekiel a visit in; this craft flew towards him and then around him. After his description of the craft, he went on to say that God spoke to him and Gods Spirit entered into him and gave him instructions to follow concerning Israel. From the book of Ezekiel:

"Now it came to pass in the thirtieth year, in the fourth month, in the fifth day of the month, as I was among the captives by the river of Chebar, that the heavens were opened, and I saw visions of God. In the fifth day of the month, which was the fifth year of king Jehoiachin's captivity, The word of the Lord came expressly unto Ezekiel the priest, the son of Buzi, in the land of the Chaldeans by the river Chebar; and the hand of the Lord was there upon him. And I looked , and, behold, a whirlwind came out of the north, a great cloud, and a fire infolding itself, and a brightness was about it, and out of the midst thereof as the colour of amber, out of the midst of the fire. Also out of the midst thereof came the likeness of four living creatures. And this was their appearance; they had the likeness of a man. And every one had four faces, and every one had four wings. And their feet were straight feet; and the sole of their feet was like the sole of a calf's foot: and they sparkled like the colour of burnished brass. And they had the hands of a man under their wings on their four sides; and they four had their faces and their wings. Their wings were joined one to another; they turned not when they went; they went every one straight forward. As for the likeness of their faces, they four had the face of a man, and the face of a lion, on the right side: and they four had the face of an ox on the left side; they four also had the face of an eagle. Thus were their faces: and their wings were stretched upward; two wings of every one were joined one to another, and two covered their bodies. And they went every one straight forward: whither the Spirit was to go, they went; and they turned not when they went. As for the likeness of the living creatures, their appearance was like burning coals of fire, and like the appearance of lamps: it went up and down among the living creatures; and the fire was bright, and out of the fire went forth lightning. And the living creatures ran and returned as the appearance of a flash of lightning. Now as I beheld the living creatures, behold one wheel upon the earth by the living creatures, with his four faces. The appearance of the wheels and their work was like unto the colour of a beryl: and they four had one likeness: and their appearance and their work was as it **were** a wheel in the middle of a wheel. When they went, they went upon their four sides: and they turned not when they went. As for their rings, they were so high that they were dreadful; and their rings were full of eyes round about them four. And when the living creatures went, the wheels went by them: and when the living creatures were lifted up from the earth, the wheels were lifted up. Whithersoever the Spirit was to **go , they** went, thither was their Spirit to go; and the wheels were lifted up over against them: for the Spirit of the living creature was in the wheels. When those went, these went; and when those stood, these stood; and when those were lifted up from the earth, the wheels were lifted up over against them: for the Spirit of the living creature was in the wheels. And the likeness of the firmament upon the heads of the living creature was as the colour of the terrible crystal, stretched forth over their heads above. And under the firmament were their wings straight, the one toward the other; **every one** had two, which covered on this side, and every one had two, which covered on that side, their bodies. And when they went, I heard the noise of their wings, like the noise of great waters, as the voice of the Almighty, the voice of speech, as the noise of an host: when they stood, they let down their wings. And there was a voice from the firmament that was over their heads, when they stood, and had let down their wings. And above the firmament that was over their heads was the likeness of a throne, as the appearance of a sapphire stone: and upon the likeness of the throne was the likeness as the appearance of a man above upon it. And I saw as the colour of amber, as the appearance of fire round about within it, from the appearance of his loins even upward, and from the appearance of his loins downward, I saw as it were the appearance of fire, and it had brightness round about. As the appearance of the bow that is in the cloud in the day of rain, so was the appearance of the brightness round about. This was the appearance of the likeness of the glory of the Lord. And when I saw it, I fell upon my face, and I heard a voice of one that spake.

And He said unto me, Son of man, stand upon thy feet, and I will speak unto thee. **And the Spirit entered into me when he spake unto me**, and set me upon my feet, that I heard him that spake unto me. And He said unto me, Son of man, I send thee to the children of Israel, to a rebellious nation that hath rebelled against me: they and their fathers have transgressed against me, even unto this very day. For they are impudent children and stiffhearted. I do send thee unto them; and thou shalt say unto them, This saith the Lord GOD. And they, whether they will forbear, (for they are a rebellious house,) yet shall know that there hath been a prophet among them. And thou, son of man, be not afraid of them, neither be afraid of their words, though briers and thorns be with thee, and thou dost dwell among scorpions: be not afraid of their words, nor be dismayed at their looks, though they be a rebellious house. And thou shalt speak my words unto them, whether they will hear, or whether they will forbear: for they are most rebellious. But thou, son of man, hear what I say unto thee; Be not thou rebellious like that rebellious house: open thy mouth, and eat that I give thee. And when **I looked, behold, an hand was sent unto me**; and, lo, a roll of a book was therein; And he spread it before me; and it was written within and without: and there was written therein lamentations, and mourning, and woe.........
.........Then the Spirit took me up, and I heard behind me a voice of a great rushing, saying, Blessed be the Glory of the Lord from his place. I heard also the noise of the wings of the living creatures that touched one another, and the noise of the wheels over against them, and a noise of a great rushing. "
.........1st and 2nd Chapters of Ezekiel and 3:12-13

If God existed prior to the creation of the universe and a select group of mens eternal spirits also were created prior to the formation of the earth would it be reasonable to say that not only is God an extraterrestrial but so are we; men!

I am talking about the part of you that lives forever; your body is made from the elements of this earth and it's going to dissolve back into the earth but your spirit and possibly your soul are made by God in heaven. If your spirit was made in heaven with a predetermined purpose then God had a plan for your life on the earth.

"According as he has chosen us in him **before the foundation of the world**, that we should be Holy and without blame before him in love: Having predestinated us unto the adoption of children of Jesus Christ to himself, according to the good pleasure of his will,..."
…… Ephesians 1: 4-5

"Moreover whom he did predestinate, them he also called: and whom he called, them he also justified: and whom he justified, them he also glorified. What shall we then say to these things? If God be for us who can be against us."
…. Romans 8 : 30-31

"Before I formed thee in the belly I knew thee: and before thou camest forth out of the womb I sanctified thee, and I ordained thee a prophet unto the nations."
…… Jeremiah 1: 5

"God standeth in the congregation of the mighty; **he judgeth among the gods**."
…… Psalms 82: 1

"I have said, **ye are gods**; and all of you are children of the most high."
…… Psalms 82:6

Apparently not only are men aliens but we are alien gods. We aren't going to be ruling the universe; God with a capital G would have something to say about that but we will be ruling over the earth with Jesus in his Millennial reign and beyond.

"Jesus answered them, is it not written in your law, I said, you are gods? If he called them gods, unto whom the word of God came, and the scripture cannot be broken; say you of him, whom the Father hath sanctified, and sent into the world, thou blasphemest; because I said, I am the son of God? If I did not the works of my Father, believe me not. But if I do, though you believe not me, believe the works: that you may know, and believe, that the Father is in me, and I in him."
…... John 10: 34-38

"But as it is written, eye hath not seen, nor ear heard, neither have entered into the heart of man, the things which God has prepared for them that love him. But God has revealed them unto us by his Spirit: for the Spirit searches all things, yea. The deep things of God.. ..But the natural man (non- Christian) receiveth not the things of the Spirit of God: For they are foolishness unto him [the intellectual man]; neither can he know them, because they are Spiritually discerned [understood]."
…. 1 Corinthians 2 : 9-10, 14

The only way a man on this earth will ever see heaven and enjoy all of the things that God has for us throughout eternity is to receive Jesus as the Lord and Savior of their life. Don't let Satan win and deceive you and cause you wind up in a place that was never meant for men to be locked up in. God created this planet for men to enjoy and rule over, Satan took that away partly but we are soon to have it back completely.

TODAYS CHARIOTS OF FIRE, AKA; UFO's

Mufon, the '**M**utual **U**nidentified **F**lying **O**bject Network', has been busy for years recording different accounts of sighting of UFO's by citizens in all walks of life. Mufon has been working mostly in the United States but the phenomenon is not limited to the United States by any means. The U.S. Air Force had a reporting agency called "Project Blue Book" that operated from 1952 to 1969 and received over 16,000 reports of which not one was deemed a threat to national security. Today Mufon has trained investigators that go out into the 'field' (your house if you call them) and ask a series of questions about the encounter and try to collect any evidence available to prove the existence of UFO's. Mufon is not the only reporting agency available if a person had a sighting and desired to report it. Since the Air Force closed down their research office concerning UFO's there have been several private organizations that took their place and are actively collecting data for research purposes and they all have opinions as to why they are here and what they want with the earth.
From an evolutionists stand-point the earth and the cosmos just happened billions of years ago and life sprang up everywhere and some of that life became intelligent and now aliens are out cruising the cosmos looking for resources and some could be hostiles searching for worlds to conquer, sound familiar, the survival of the fittest. Some even fear that all of our television and radio broadcasts are giving these supposedly hostile aliens a homing beacon and those older broadcasts are leading them right to us! **"They" are already here**.
From a Christian perspective God created everything and knows everyone that exists in the universe even the ones flying around the heavens. I believe these craft belong to both sides; God and his Angels and Satan and his lieutenants or princes (Spiritual wickedness in high places). They war in the heavens; God against Satan, they war on the earth; God and man against Satan. Today Christian men have an advantage over Satan since Jesus conquered Satan and stripped him of his power within three

days of Jesus's atonement on the cross.

"For by him [Jesus] were all things created, that are in heaven, and that are in earth, visible and invisible, whether they be thrones, or dominions, or principalities, or powers; all things were created by him and for him: And he is before all things, and by him all things consist. And he is the head of the body, the Church, who is the beginning, the firstborn from the dead; that in all things he might have preeminence [first place]."
….. Colossians 1: 16-18

God knows everyone and everything in the entire universe by name, he designed it. God would know if there were any hostiles coming toward earth- he would have had to create them. The only hostiles that men need to be concerned with are recorded in the Bible. When Satan and 1/3 of the angels, now demonic, were cast out of heaven #3 they became hostile towards God and everything God holds dear. Satan desires to destroy men and that's why Satan deceived Eve in the garden of Eden and that's why he deceived Darwin and that's why he deceived Mohammed and Hitler and Stalin and Manson and (fill in the blank)_____. Every false religion in the world was started through men that either unknowingly or knowingly allowed Satan to use them for his purposes, to keep men from Christianity [God]. Satan knows what Gods Church looks like so he made other religions that are patterned after what God ordained for men. Complete with Gods, angels, demonic spirits, worship, offerings, meeting places; Satan hijacked what God created for men as a means to worship and fellowship with him. When Satan deceived Eve he took the control of the earth from man; that was the fall of man. Satan has been plotting and scheming for our destruction ever since. Satan uses men in his efforts to destroy but God says that we don't fight against men because they are unwitting pawns being used by Satan to bring mans destruction on the earth. That's one of the best reasons I know to read the Bible so you can recognize what Satan has attacked men with. Men are required to use the Word of God and our faith in that Word to destroy Satan's plans on the earth.

"For we wrestle not against flesh and blood [men], but against principalities [demonic spirits], against powers, against the rulers of the darkness of this world, against spiritual wickedness in high places."
..... Ephesians 6: 12

"I am he [Jesus] that liveth, and was dead; and behold, I am alive forevermore, Amen; and have the keys of Hell and Death."
.... Revelation 1: 18

"Let every soul be subject unto the higher powers. For there is no power but of God: the powers that be are ordained of God."
..... Romans 13:1

"Which He [God] wrought [made] in Christ [Jesus], when He raised him from the dead, and set Him at His own right hand in heavenly places. Far above all principality, and power, and might, and dominion, and every name that is named, not only in this world, but also in that which is to come: And hath put all things under His [Jesus's] feet, and gave Him to be the head over all things to the Church. **Which is His body** [Christians themselves have taken the place of Jesus on the earth], the fulness of Him that filleth all in all."
.... Ephesians 1: 20-23

If men are predestined by God to be rulers with God, the Creator of the universe, I don't believe being taken out by a chance encounter with an intergalactic sniper would fit into Gods plan for us. Throughout earth history, there have been hundreds of thousands of sightings of unidentified aerial craft in earth's atmosphere, two accounts, as mentioned earlier, were straight from the Bible. There are other possibilities from the Bible:

THE CLOUDS OF GOD

Dr. Bill Birnes, a U.F.O. investigator, hypothesizes that UFO's can cloak themselves to look like a cloud in the sky. I am not aware of the full extent of Dr. Birnes hypothesis, but I also believe that to be the case. I myself witnessed a spirit being that vanished before my eyes. He looked exactly like a man and then turned into a thick white cloud and the cloud slowly diminished until he was gone from sight. I also believe UFO's may operate the same way since they are from a spiritual or an extra dimensional realm; they can start out looking like a nuts and bolts craft and just vanish at will. They operate under a different physics than men do, I believe they have physical bodies from a greater dimensional realm and their capabilities are far greater than ours. As stated earlier some of mans limitations are limits within our souls (our minds) and God has to switch on those capabilities temporarily to allow us to experience other dimensions.

God is a Spirit, there are many instances in the Bible that talk about the Lord being inside of a cloud or on a cloud or speaking out of a cloud. I have compiled a number of these accounts below;

"**And the Lord went before them [Israel] by day in a pillar of a cloud, to lead them the way**; and by night in a pillar of fire, to give them light; to go by day and night; He took not away the pillar of the cloud by day, nor the pillar of fire by night, from before the people."
….. Exodus 13: 21-22

The Lord was in this cloud leading Israel for over 40 years

"And the Angel of God, which went before the camp of Israel, removed and went behind them; **and the pillar of the cloud went from before their face**, and stood behind them: And it came to

pass between the camp of the Egyptians and the camp of Israel; and it gave light by night to these; so that the one came not near the other all the night."
….. Exodus 14: 19-20

"And it came to pass, that in the morning watch **the Lord looked unto the host of the Egyptians through the pillar of fire and of the cloud**, and troubled the host of the Egyptians."
…. Exodus 14: 24

In the above account; the Egyptians were frightened because they could see the Lord observing them from inside the cloud.

"**And all the people saw the cloudy pillar stand at the tabernacle door**; and all the people rose up and worshiped, every man in his tent door. And the Lord spake unto Moses face to face, as a man speaketh unto his friend…"
…... Exodus 33: 10-11

"**And the Lord descended in the cloud**, and stood with him there, and proclaimed the name of the Lord. And the Lord passed by before him, and proclaimed, 'The Lord, The Lord God, Merciful and gracious, long-suffering, and abundant in goodness and truth'."
….. Exodus 34: 5-6

"**And the Lord came down in a cloud**, and spake unto him, and took of the Spirit that was upon him, and gave it unto the seventy elders: and it came to pass, that when the Spirit rested upon them, they prophesied, and did not cease."
…... Numbers 11: 25

"**And the Lord came down in a pillar of the cloud**, and stood in the door of the tabernacle, and called Aaron and Miriam: and they both came forth. And he said, hear my words: If there be a

prophet among you, **I the Lord will make myself known unto him in a vision, and will speak unto him in a dream."**
…… Numbers 12: 5-6

"And the Lord appeared in the tabernacle in a pillar of a cloud: and the pillar of the cloud stood over the door of the tabernacle."
……. Deuteronomy 31: 15

"And it came to pass, when the Priests were come out of the Holy Place, **that the cloud filled the house of the Lord**, so that the Priests could not stand to minister because of the cloud: for the Glory of the Lord had filled the house of the Lord."
….. 1 Kings 8: 10-11

"It came even to pass, as the trumpeters and singers were as one, to make one sound to be heard in praising and thanking the Lord: and when they lift up their voice with the trumpets and symbols and instruments of musick, and praised the Lord, saying, for he is good: for his mercy endureth forever: that then **the house was filled with a cloud**, even the house of the Lord. So that the priests could not stand to minister by reason of the cloud: for the Glory of the Lord had filled the House of God."
…… 2nd Chronicles 5: 13-14

"Who layeth the beams of his chambers in the waters: **who maketh the clouds his chariot**: who walketh upon the wings of the wind:
….. Psalms 104: 3

"Now the Cherubims [Angels] stood on the right side of the house, when the man went in; and the cloud filled the inner court. Then the Glory of the Lord went up from the Cherub, and stood over the threshold of the house, **and the house was filled with the cloud,** and the court was full of the brightness of the Lords Glory."
…… Ezekiel 10: 3-4

"While he yet spake, behold, **a bright cloud overshadowed them: and behold a voice out of the cloud**, which said, 'This in my beloved son [Jesus], In whom I am well pleased. Hear ye him'."
….. Mathew 17: 5

"And after six days Jesus taketh with him Peter, and James, and John and leadeth them up into a high mountain apart by themselves; and he [Jesus] was transfigured before them. And his raiment [clothing] became shining, exceeding white as snow; so as no fuller on earth can white them.... **And there was a cloud that overshadowed them; and a voice came out of the cloud, saying. 'This is my beloved Son, hear Him'.** "
….. Mark 9: 2-3, 7

Jesus speaking: "And there shall be signs in the sun, and in the moon, and in the stars; and upon the earth distress of nations, with perplexity; the sea and the waves roaring; mens hearts failing them for fear, and for looking after those things which are coming on the earth: for the powers of heaven shall be shaken. And then shall they **see the son of man [Jesus] coming in a cloud with power and great glory**. And when these things begin to come to pass, then look up, and lift up your heads; for your redemption draweth nigh [near]."
…... Luke 21: 25-28

"And then he [Jesus] said unto them, 'It is not for you to know the times or the seasons, which the Father hath put in his own power. But you shall receive power, after that the Holy Ghost is come upon you: and you shall be witnesses unto me both in Jerusalem, and in all Judea, and in Sumeria, and unto the uttermost part of the earth.' And when he had spoken these things, while they beheld (looked), **he was taken up; and a cloud received him out of their sight.**"
…... Acts 1: 7-9

"And they heard a great voice from heaven saying unto them, come up hither. **And they ascended up to heaven in a cloud; and their enemies beheld them.**"
…..... Revelation 11: 12

BINARY CODE FROM A CHARIOT OF FIRE

There is a modern day UFO account that happened on two successive nights that is worth exploring further; sightings at Rendlesham Forest on December 26th and 27th, 1980. These accounts were witnessed by dozens of serious minded, professional military personnel tasked with guarding and operating a nuclear capable U.S. Air Force base. The highest ranking officer to witness the craft was Deputy Base Commander Lt. Col. Charles Holt who followed the craft through the forest and onto a neighboring farm on the 2nd night. The first night, December 26th, the craft was first noticed on radar by RAF radar-men in Norfolk, England. The craft was over the North Sea moving towards Bentwaters Air Force Base which was next door to a Royal Air Force base in Suffolk, England. It was about 3:00 am.. The lights of the craft were seen by the security police on the back side of the base as it descended into the trees of the neighboring forest; the entire forest was lit up by the lights of the craft. As is so often the case in 'close proximity' encounters - electronics fail to work properly, radios, lights or anything electrical are effected by these craft and both nights electronic interference effected their equipment. Two men from **base security**, Pinniston and Burroughs, went into the forest with a search team thinking that there could have been a crash of some sort. They witnessed the craft as it was lowering and eventually landing on the ground. The craft sat on 3 legs equidistant to each other, the craft was approximately nine feet on each side, triangular in shape, and six feet thick. Castings of the landing pads and measurements taken in the following days confirmed the size approximations. Sgt. **Pinniston** approached the craft and touched it with his hand. He recorded that it was warm to the touch... **then** he noticed hieroglyphs on the sides of the craft. As he touched the largest of the **hieroglyphs**, there was an impartation of information from the craft to Sgt. **Pinniston**. He immediately began to record the information that he had been given through the **craft** but he did not record **the entirety of the message at the time**. Burroughs has no recollection that Sgt. **Pinniston** approached and touched the **craft. They** each had their own unique encounter with the craft. Sgt. **Pinniston**, later that night, says that when he closed his eyes he could see nothing but binary code (1's and 0's) flashing through his mind and it kept repeating over and over again. Since these codes kept repeating in his minds eye over and over he eventually wrote the entire sequence of code in his **notebook** from start to finish and at the point in time when he finished recording them, they stopped repeating . At the time, in 1980, Sgt. **Pinniston** had no idea what binary code was and he did not report the code to his superiors. Flash forward to 2010, Pinniston and Burroughs met again and they were talking about the incident that night in Rendlesham Forest and the conversation turned to the sequence of 1's and 0's that Pinniston had written down 30 years earlier; he showed Burroughs the original note book that he used. Burroughs recognized the sequence as binary code and thought maybe there could be information in Pinnistons note **book** from whoever was in the craft. Binary code is what computer programmers use to encode information. **Pinniston** took the 1st 6 of the 16 pages of binary to a computer **programmer** named Nick Ciske to analyze it and see if he could decipher what it meant. As it turned out there was meaningful information encoded in the binary, some of the information is recorded below:

"Exploration of Humanity
52" 09' 42.532 N
13" 13' 12.69 W
Conti[nuous] Planetary Advance"

These are longitudinal and latitudinal coordinates that are off the coast of Ireland in the Atlantic Ocean. A place called Hy Brasil. There were other coordinates recorded in the code within the following state and countries;

"Sedona Arizona
Central America
South America
Greece
Egypt
China"

Mr. Pinniston put forth his own hypothesis as to what he experienced and who he thought they were. He thought the markings or hieroglyphs on the craft looked a great deal like Air Force markings only not our current Air Force. He thought the vehicle may have been an Air Force craft from the future that came back in time to deliver the above message.

My beliefs are, the earth belongs to Jesus and the Bible says that all things were created by Him and he continues to inspire our designs through men on the earth and perhaps through angels in the heavens, not only mathematics, music and the sciences but also the lay-out of cities on the earth and the way government structures look. He may influence or inspire the designs of the way the military command is structured down to the smallest detail; the insignias on uniforms and symbols of our armed forces.

As God gave science, mathematics and music to Tesla, Ramanujan and Brahms, perhaps God gave Sgt. Pinniston a message. What is at each of those coordinates remains to be seen, I would hope that it's something that points right to our creator. God has an intimate knowledge of the world because he made it and probably inspired the latitudinal and longitudinal coordinate system. He has advanced craft, he can give men messages directly into our souls, cause us to record it and save it then wait 30 years to divulge the information, he is technologically superior, he can work inside a mans mind or soul showing us things at his will. They are with us... they have always been with us because they made us and never left us.

Man has been led on this planet since creation either through heavenly forces or Satanic forces, God desires that men discover him for themselves with the aid of other men. Knowing God takes faith, if he just came back and exclaimed to the world that he's back then faith would not be required. Gods plan as recorded in the Bible is that men preach to other men and each man discovers God through the faith developed through the preaching of Gods letter to us – the Bible. The Bible says 'faith comes by hearing', and through hearing we believe and when we believe we may receive. Why can't God just send his angels to preach to men? After all, so many men have made inaccurate assumptions about the Bible which caused all of the different denominations.
The short answer is "It's not the job of angels to preach until after the rapture". Men have the job of bringing other men to the Lord.

"Wherefore he [Jesus] saith, when he ascended up on high, he led captivity captive, and gave gifts unto men... And he gave some apostles; and some, prophets; and some, evangelists; and some, pastors and teachers. For the perfecting of the saints, for the work of the ministry, for the edifying of the body of Christ."
.... Ephesians 4: 8, 11 - 12

Notice in the above verse; He 'gave gifts unto men', not angels, men preach and teach until this current dispensation of grace is ended.

That is the reason why Jesus [God himself] had to physically indwell [place his own eternal Spirit inside] the flesh and blood body of a man so he could have the authority on the earth to preach and teach and; through Satan's illegal destruction of him, die and deliver us from our fallen nature of sin.

"For the Son of Man [Jesus] is as a man taking a far journey [back to heaven], who left his house [the earth], **and gave authority to his servants [Christians]**, and to every man his work, and commanded the porter to watch."
… Mark 13: 34

"Wherefore, **as by one man [Adam] sin entered into the world, and death by sin**; and so death passed upon all men, for that all have sinned:"
…. Romans 5: 12

Romans 5: 12 above says 'by one man [Adam] sin entered into the world, and death by sin' -
This verse alone proves there was no pre-Adamite civilization prior to Adam and Eve. When Adam and Eve sinned in the garden that brought death into the world, that was the introduction of death. Their body's went from incorruptible to corruptible, from immortality to mortality. If there were civilizations prior to Adam and Eve then men would have been dying prior to the introduction of death. Prior to the disobedience of Adam and Eve all men were immortal- death did not exist. The Bible says Adam was "The First Man" and he lost mans immortality. Jesus who is the Second Adam restored our immortality through his sacrifice – if we would but receive our immortality by receiving the one who supplies it.

The original creation was eternal; death did not exist until Satan came along and deceived Eve. Jesus circumvented that death that 'passed upon all men' in the above verse. When Father God himself overshadowed Mary; Jesus, the son of God who is also "God" - placed himself in the 'man class' by allowing himself to be born through Mary. The DNA that was from God excluded Jesus from the nature of the 'death of Adams fall' and anyone that receives Jesus receives that regeneration by Father Gods blood placed in Jesus. The blood comes from the father; hence, 'paternity test'- The nature of sin is in the blood, the nature of sinlessness is also in the blood. God placed His sinless blood in Jesus through Mary and Jesus was born without the 'sin nature' that natural men are born with. That is the reason it was illegal for Satan to destroy Jesus- he was a man with no blood connection to Adam and Eve or the "Fall of Man". A man in the fallen state; as Adam and Eve caused, may die of sin, but Jesus never sinned because he didn't have the nature of sin from Satan and it was illegal for him to die. Sin is not an act, it's a nature or "state of existence"- **men are not sinners because they sin- they are sinners because they are born into Adam's fallen nature passed through his blood.** Disobedience changed the nature of man from God's perfection to Satan's imperfection. Adam and Eve took all mankind from Gods incorruption into Satan's corruption. Men who are Christians [with the new sinless nature] can act out and sin against God but remain sinless because of the 'New Nature' that they received from Jesus's gift of salvation. Men can 'sin' by walking after their fleshly, carnal lusts and disregarding the Holy Spirits guidance. Even when men sin they are still sinless and they can be restored from their lawless actions by repenting [turning away].

"If we say that we have no sin, we deceive ourselves, and the truth is not in us. If we confess our sins, he is faithful and just to forgive us our sins, and to cleanse us from all unrighteousness."
… 1 John 1: 8- 9

Think of this analogy, Gods nature is like a software system that is perfect, powerful, creative and down-loadable. Gods software is designed to be used in men to give them authority, power and victory on the earth. Satan's nature is also like a software system but his is corrupted with viruses having self destructive elements built into it. Gods all-powerful software is called "Sinless Nature" and Satan's destructive software is called "Sinful Nature"- both operate in the human soul but Gods all-powerful software has much greater capabilities and the results are far superior to Satan's self destruct software. Gods software is incorruptible, creative and has built-in anti virus elements – Satan's software is temporary, corrupted with built-in viruses and self-destructs the man that it's downloaded into. Men are born with the "Sinful Nature" but God desires that every man upgrades to his "Sinless Nature" by receiving Jesus- the one who paid for and provides the new "Sinless Nature" software as a gift to men. Men's hard drives are our souls and God's software "Sinless Nature" operates at maximum proficiency when God's Word, the Bible, is loaded onto our hard drives to work hand in hand with the software.

"For what the law could not do, in that it was weak through the flesh, God sending his own son [Jesus] in the likeness of sinful flesh, and for sin, condemned sin in the flesh; that the righteousness of the law might be fulfilled in us, who walk not after the flesh, but after the Spirit. For they that are after the flesh do mind the things of the flesh; but they that are after the Spirit the things of the Spirit."
….... Romans 8: 3-5

"And without controversy great is the mystery of Godliness: God [Jesus] was manifest in the flesh, justified in the Spirit, seen of angels, preached unto the gentiles, believed on in the world, received up into Glory."
… 1 Timothy 3: 16

"But [Jesus] made himself of no reputation and took upon him the form of a servant [a flesh body], and was made in the likeness of men...and that every tongue should confess that Jesus Christ is Lord."
..... Philippians 2: 7,11

Men also get rewarded for preaching the Gospel of Christ: "Feed the flock of God which is among you, taking the oversight thereof, not by constraint, but willingly, not for filthy lucre [wealth], but of a ready mind;...and when the Chief Shepard [Jesus] shall appear, ye shall receive a crown of glory that fadeth not away."
..... 1 Peter 5: 2,4

The Holy Spirits role is to assist and to guide men into truth partly through helping them as apostles, prophets, evangelists, pastors and teachers as recorded in Ephesians 4: 11 for our perfection.

"And I will pray the Father, and he shall give you another Comforter [the Holy Spirit], that he may abide with you forever. Even the Spirit of truth; whom the world cannot receive [outside of salvation], because it seeth him not, neither knoweth him: But you know him; for he dwelleth with you and shall be in you."
.... John 14: 16-17

Faith is a Spiritual Law set forth by God. Every one of Gods elect has got to live by faith;

The following verses in Hebrews are affectionately known as **The Hall of Fame of Faith**:
"By faith Abel offered unto God a more excellent sacrifice than Cain, by which he obtained witness that he was righteous, God testifying of his gifts: and by it he being dead yet speaketh. By faith Enoch was translated that he should not see death; and was

not found, because God had translated him: for before his translation he had this testimony, that he pleased God. But without faith it is impossible to please him [God]: For he that cometh to God must believe that he is, and that he is a rewarder of them that diligently seek him. By faith Noah, being warned of God of things not seen as yet, moved with fear, prepared an Ark to the saving of his house; by the which he condemned the world, and became heir of the righteousness which is by faith. By faith Abraham, when he was called to go out into a place which he should after receive for an inheritance, obeyed: and he went out, not knowing whither he went. By faith he sojourned in a land of promise, as in a strange country, dwelling in tabernacles with Isaac and Jacob, the heirs with him of the same promise."
....Hebrews 11: 4-9

"Through faith also Sara herself received strength to conceive seed, and was delivered of a child when she was past age, because she judged him faithful who had promised."
... Hebrews 11: 11

... Hebrews 11: 20...By faith Isaac...
... Hebrews 11: 21...By faith Jacob...
... Hebrews 11: 22...By faith Joseph...
... Hebrews 11: 23...By faith Moses...
.... Hebrews 11: 31...By faith the harlot Rahab perished not with them that believed not,..."

"Now faith is the substance of things hoped for, the evidence of things not seen."
...... Hebrews 11: 1

"Through faith we understand that the worlds were framed by the word of God, so that things which are seen were not made of things which do appear [Everything was made from the Spirit realm]."
...... Hebrews 11: 3

"Now the just shall live by faith: but if any man draw back, my [Gods] soul shall have no pleasure in him."
….. Hebrews 10: 38

"For we walk by faith, not by sight. We are confident, I say, and willing rather to be absent from the body [physically dead], and to be present with the Lord [Spiritually alive]."
…… 2 Corinthians 5: 7-8

"Where is boasting then? It is excluded. By what law? Of works? Nay: but by the law of faith."
…... Romans 3: 27

"So then faith cometh by hearing, and hearing by the word of God."
…….. Romans 10: 17

"And the scripture, foreseeing that God would justify the heathen through faith, preached before the Gospel unto Abraham, saying. In thee shall all nations be blessed."
…... Galatians 3: 8

"But no man is justified by the law in the sight of God, it is evident: for, the just shall live by faith."
…... **Galatians** 3: 11

As you can clearly see in the scriptures, faith is a large determinant in the way God deals with men. God is pleased when you have faith in him, just believe that he is. Your faith in his word activates the power behind his word. When you pray Gods own words in the scriptures back to him in faith his power is activated. God is in a sense concealed from mankind to allow all of those who believe in him through the preaching of his word to realize that he exists and respond to him by the faith that grows from that preaching. However, the gathering of the church is almost over, the 6th day has drawn to a close and preaching by men will cease, today is the acceptable day of salvation, don't delay.

THE EXTRA-DIMENSIONAL SPIRIT WORLD

The spirit world is an extra-dimensional world, spirits can indwell people, influence people, speak into men's minds as a thought, appear and disappear, they are not limited by natural mans physical laws.
In similar fashion, UFO craft are operating like they are not limited by earths physical laws. Crypt-ids (crypto-zoologicals) could also be extra-dimensional spirit beings that are not limited by our natural or physical laws. Big Foot or Sasquatch are largely unstudied by science yet multiple thousands of sightings have happened worldwide. The same goes for other crypt-ids such as the Lock Ness monster, Thunderbird's, the Jersey Devil, the Moth Man; these and others may all be spirit beings that appear and disappear at will. Some of the characteristics of the UFO phenomenon are;

Materialize [appear]
Dematerialize [disappear]
Fly so fast through our atmosphere that they should melt from friction
Turn 90 degrees at speed with no apparent G load issue
Start or stop at speed or from speed with no apparent G load issue
Fly out of the earths atmosphere in the blink of an eye
Jump from one point to another in an instant

These craft, like God himself, can operate outside of the known laws of physics, God created those laws and he is capable of circumventing them or moving into one dimension from another. Unfortunately- men are temporarily trapped here in our limited bodies in this limited dimension. The day we are released from our bodies I believe we will be able to see the fullness of the spirit world, the different beings, the craft, other technologies,etc. The Bible claims that God created and therefor owns all the heavens and as men on earth use man made craft such as planes, automobiles, boats etc. maybe we should consider that Gods angels or Satan's demons use their own craft also. In Ezekiel chapter 1, recorded earlier, God visited Ezekiel from within such a craft. God who is omnipresent can also use a physical craft to move from place to place, and personally visit individuals face to face.

"And they heard the voice of the LORD God walking in the garden in the cool of the day: and Adam and his wife hid themselves from the presence of the LORD God amongst the trees of the garden."
… Genesis 3: 8

"And when Abram [Abraham] was ninety years old and nine, the LORD appeared to Abram, and said unto him, I am the Almighty God; walk before me, and be thou perfect."
… Genesis 17: 1

GOD KNOWS YOUR DNA SEQUENCE

There have been claims made over the years that some of these craft from outside of the earth have crashed here; Roswell NM, Aurora TX, etc, and left bodies behind. If a government or governments were hiding them, it could be that, while studying them, they discovered they have DNA similar to DNA on the earth. If they do have earth-like DNA that would be the final nail in the coffin of Darwin's evolution theory. That would mean life did not spontaneously evolve on earth from wet rocks as the evolutionists claim. Life is scattered throughout the heavens and I believe that there may be physical bodied life in the cosmos that has DNA which could have similarities to earth-like DNA that is sequenced to meet their particular needs. All life on earth has DNA that is sequenced for a specific purpose, both plant and animal. It's just the sequencing of the DNA string or the order each amino acid is attached in sequence that determines the overall attributes to each life form. God knows the name of every planet in the universe, he knows the names of every man that ever lived, he knows how many hairs are on the heads of every man that ever lived. God knows the exact sequencing of your DNA code that made your body. He knows yours, he knows mine, he knows Princess Dianna's DNA code, a T-Rex's DNA code, a roses DNA code,etc. If you took a strand of DNA and rearranged the sequencing to match Princess Diana's exact sequence you could grow a body that looks exactly like Princess Dianna. Her spirit and soul are a separate matter, they have left the earth and if she was a Christian, you would have to talk to God about reuniting them in her new body to rejoin her mind, will, emotions, memories, knowledge and personality with her body. You don't need a mosquito trapped in amber to grow a T-Rex. If you knew the code of any T-Rex and re-sequenced any DNA strand you could grow your own less it's spirit. However, as you will see later, it's not a good idea to rework DNA or mix different species for any reason. Maybe that's how God can reassemble a person's body if, for instance, they were cremated. God can create your glorified body in heaven based upon the same DNA code that you had here on the earth. Your new body will look like the same body you spent your life in here on the earth. Perhaps, at Adams fall, the "Sin nature" of man corrupted our DNA and we went from living eternally to having abbreviated life spans. Our glorified bodies will be restored to their former state of immortality by restoring our DNA back to its previous state. God is going to give us an incorruptible body, more powerful, beautiful or handsome and physically fit than what we enjoyed on the earth. You will look similar to your earthly body, then your spirit and soul will be placed inside and you become at least a three part being again; spirit, soul and body. God promised the Holy Spirit would abide with us forever so maybe we will become four part beings since 'forever' would be a permanent condition.

"For the truth's sake, which dwelleth in us, and shall be with us forever."
….. 2 John 1: 2

IF WE WERE "CREATED" WOULD WE BE ROBOTS OR MACHINES- OR SOMETHING ALTOGETHER DIFFERENT

Scientists have spent years and millions if not billions of dollars working on robotics that perform like the human body. At the same time, computer scientists have been working towards "Artificial Intelligence" (AI) technology trying to get a computer to think like a man, feel (emotions) like a man, act like a man. It's already been done, in a sense, you are a self replicating biological robot (or machine) with a computer for a brain to match. Your wired similar to a computer only with a spirit... your soul (mind-will-emotions) would be the equivalent to the computer and your body would be the equivalent to the robot. Your soul has something a computer will never have; emotion, an 'AI' system will never have a spirit and soul unless God gives it one, emotion resides in the soul and souls are the sole domain of God. The best you will ever see is a mimic, an emotional response programmed into the 'AI' computer software based upon what the programmer believes the response should look like after a specific stimulus. There will be no actual 'feelings or emotions' present, but they will act like they have emotions through their programming.

The Bible records;

"I [King David] will praise thee [God]; for I am fearfully and wonderfully made: Marvelous are thy works; and that my soul knoweth right well."
….. Psalms 139: 14

"The Spirit of God hath made me, and the breath of the Almighty has given me life."
….. Job 33: 4

"For by Him were all things created, that are in heaven, and that are in earth, visible and invisible..."
…… Colossians 1: 16

"For we are His [Jesus's] workmanship, created in Christ Jesus unto good works, which God has before ordained that we should walk in them."
…… Ephesians 2: 10

DNA RESEARCHERS HAVE DISCOVERED THAT DNA ITSELF EXCLUDES THE POSIBILITY THAT EVOLUTION COULD HAPPEN – Gods fail-safe

"Dr. Barney Maddox, a leading genetic genome researcher said, concerning the genetic differences between chimpanzees and man,

"Now the genetic difference between human and his nearest relative, the chimpanzee, is at least 1.6%. That doesn't sound like much, but calculated out, that is a gap of at least 48,000,000 nucleotides, and a change of only 3 nucleotides is fatal to an animal; there is no possibility of change."
….. Human Genome Project; Quantitative A disproof of evolution. CEM Facts Sheet, cited in Doubts ….. about Evolution

Newer research in 'Nature', May 27, 2004 pg, 382-388 says there is an even greater difference than what was originally calculated. It jumped from a 1.6% difference to 7.7%. "In fact, we share less that 95% of our genetic material, a 3 fold increase in the variation between us and chimps."
…….. Cited in Dr. Hovinds Creation Seminar 2005

133.

The possibility or chance of **life forms** spontaneously changing or 'evolving' as suggested by the theory of Darwinian evolution is zero. The **evolutionary** process would have to take place here on a DNA level by re-sequencing amino acids along the chain. The best you could get in a **variation** from the original parent organism would be 1 or 2 / **48,000,000 change** in nucleotides and if the organism survives it would be a mutation and there has never been a proven beneficial mutation.

Chapter 5

IS THE SPIRIT WORLD POWERED BY ELECTICITY AND ELECTROMAGNETISM?

Einstein said that if we could hyper accelerate ourselves to 35 trillion miles per second we would turn into energy. $E = MC$ squared or Energy = Mass x (186,000 mps x 186,000 mps)! Thanks to Einsteins equation men now understand that energy and mass are interchangeable, they are not exclusively separate constructs but one in the same. **In Physics** there are only two ways for anything to exist in our universe- mass and energy. We can convert mass to energy and energy to mass.
Part of the different energy forms created from the matter of mass using Einsteins equation are :

Nuclear Energy ......Gamma Rays...... Radio Waves ......Visible Light ..... X-Rays .... Electricity

If the spirit world is based on any of the above energy forms then the dimension they exist in could be manipulated. If men can theoretically accelerate and turn into energy then the reverse could be said- energy can be decelerated and turned into mass. Many UFO sightings include the accounts of craft moving extremely fast or just disappearing or appearing suddenly. Many are described as glowing like a light in the sky during the day or night. Could they be nuts and bolts craft that are hyper-accelerating or decelerating or can they suspend themselves in a less energetic state indefinitely making themselves visible to us in our 3 dimensions. The spirit world could easily be based on energetic matter (plasma) and the physical world is based on physical matter(mass) and energy (electricity or plasma). Today men transmit energy for many reasons: radio waves, television signals, x-rays, lasers, lights, gps, radar, Tesla's theorized electricity transmissions. The entire earth is a giant dynamo that creates electricity that envelopes the earth. Our bodies are powered by electrical impulses: our nervous system, our thoughts, our muscles contract from electrical energy that was sent either voluntarily or involuntarily from our minds through our brains and into our nervous systems. Our eyes see light energy and through electrical manipulation in our brains we image, in the form of a thought, what we see inside of our minds. The entire physical world is turned into images and stored as thoughts, electronically, in our souls. Our thoughts are nothing more than electric impulses that are used to reason in our minds, store in our souls, or use in our nervous systems to provide locomotion with our bodies which are electrically wired for us as spirit beings. Telepathic thought transfer may be an ability, if switched on, to send electric signals outside of the mind itself or the ability to receive thought signals. If the spirit world is all electric then that would not be an issue. The Bible records that both Gods Spirit and Satanic spirits speak thoughts into the minds of men. A portion of the thoughts that you think may be from a spirit being but you only think you are thinking you own thoughts. We send and receive signals from cell towers and we send infrared transmissions through our television remotes, these are energy transmissions and are not far removed from thought transmissions since they both operate through energy. The Holy Spirit guides men through righteous thoughts. Satan guides men through unrighteous thoughts but the choice of what to believe is left to the man through his free will.

"But when **Jesus perceived their thoughts**, he answering said unto them, What reason ye in your hearts?"
… Luke 5: 22

"And again, **The Lord knoweth the thoughts** of the wise, that they are vain."
… 1 Corinthians 3: 20

"Above all, taking the shield of faith, wherewith **ye shall be able to quench all the fiery darts [thoughts, ideas and suggestions] of the wicked** [Satan and his demons]."… Ephesians 6: 16

136.
The speed of light can be manipulated!

"Scientists break the speed of Light"
"Scientists claim they have broken the ultimate speed barrier: the speed of light. In research carried out in the United States, particle physicists have shown that light pulses can be accelerated to up to 300 times their normal velocity of 186,000 miles per second. The work was carried out by Dr. Lijun Wang, of the NEC Research Institute in Princeton who transmitted a pulse of light towards a chamber filled with specifically treated Cesium gas."
…..United Kingdom Sunday Times, June 4, 2000, by Jonathan Leake, also in the N.Y. Times, May 30, 2000

"Researchers say they have slowed light to a dead stop, stored it and then released it as if it were an ordinary material particle. The achievement is a landmark feat that, by reigning in natures swiftest and most ethereal form of energy for the 1st time, could help realize what are now theoretical concepts for vastly increasing the speed of computers and the security of communications.
……. www.nytimes.com/2001/01/18/science/18 light, by James Glanz

The speed of light is slowing over time based on published reports of 164 different measurements over the last 300 years. The speed of light in our time with earths present conditions is not an absolute constant and probably never has been. "The speed of light has apparently decreased so rapidly that experimental error cannot explain it!"
….. Astronomer Barry Setterfield
…… cited from Dr. Kent Hovinds Creation Seminar, 2005

Today, men only know about 5% of the make-up of the universe and that applies to both matter (mass) and energy. That means that there is about 95% of both matter and energy in the universe that is unknown to Physics. I believe the unknown aspect of the universe includes Gods invisible extra-dimensional realm. Due to the following evidence, I believe the spirit world is reliant upon the use and manipulation of electricity or electromagnetism. For some time, various types of electronic equipment have been used to detect electronic fields and anomalies in those fields while researchers were actively searching for spirits. As mentioned earlier in the UFO research segment; these electronic sensors often fail or are interrupted due to a sudden, premature draw down of battery power or interference presumably by the very beings they are looking for. UFO investigators report automobiles that suddenly lose power while being driven and anything electronic; headlights, car radios etc. suddenly experience interference or they shut down completely. The same sort of anomalous activity happens to aircraft; compasses, radios and navigational equipment malfunction. After the UFO or spirit leaves everything electronic returns to normal, sometimes the interference manifests within the human investigator themselves (missing time and missing memories).

Are the Spirits of Men electric?

When men die their spirit and soul leave the body and the electrical component associated with life function leaves with the spirit. There is an absence of electrical impulses in the brain, heart or nervous system that would be sufficient to be considered conducive to life and the body is powered down, the energy has moved out with the spirit and soul.

Low Light Imaging Technologies

There are 2 basic types of night vision imagers;
First, Diffused light from the atmosphere is amplified and the environment is distinguishable in low light conditions.
Secondly, Infrared light is emitted at the sub-atomic level and Infrared imaging can see that light emission. In other words, all matter is giving off light at the atomic level all the time. Not only living matter but rock, dirt etc. There is an electrical source in all

matter in the universe. These imagers can see heat but they are not limited to heat, in an environment of total darkness when everything in the environment is the same temperature, these imagers can differentiate the objects in the environment solely on each objects light emissions. The human eye can see only about 1% of the light spectrum, there is 99% more light energy around us that we can't detect with our eyes. If we could see in the infrared spectrum we could see in pitch blackness based on the amount of light given off by the characteristics of the matter observed.

One of the forms of energy from Einsteins equation was electricity. Lightning is electricity, electricity is plasma. Plasma is one of the 4 fundamental states of matter in physics; solid, liquid, gas and plasma, so energy is matter. Plasma is everywhere in the universe. When ionizing gases we increase or decrease the number of electrons in the gas and it becomes plasma. Applying electronic fields to some gases will turn them into plasma. Some plasmas are electrically conductive and can be manipulated by an electromagnetic field. Of all the matter in the universe plasma is the most common. Since lightning is plasma and plasma is matter, maybe after Satan's exile from heaven he literally was sent to the earth in an electrical discharge:

"And he [Jesus] said unto them, I beheld Satan as lightning fall from heaven."
...Luke 10: 18

Every day around the globe there are between 4 and 8 million lightning strikes on the earth. Could the spirit world move back and forth as Satan may have- on a plasma discharge? Lightning also shoots straight up from the cloud tops out into the heavens. In 1989 "Sprite Lightning" was discovered that did exactly that, its fires off of the earth into outer space. Sprite lightning is visible between 40 and 55 miles above the cloud tops as it heads into the heavens.

139.
The first recorded photo of a 'Sprite' can be seen at www.universetoday.com/On the Hunt for High Speed Sprite's.

The Bible records several instances where lightnings or electrical discharges occurred, the first one is from the craft that God used to visit Ezekiel in:

"As for the likeness of the living creatures, there appearance was like burning coals of fire, and like the appearance of lamps [glowing]: it went up and down among the living creatures; and the fire was bright and out of the fire went forth lightning [electrical discharges]. And the living creatures ran and returned as the appearance of a flash of lightning [possibly jumping from one place to another in arcs of electrical discharge]."
... Ezekiel 1: 13- 14

Daniel speaking:... "Then I lifted up mine eyes, and looked, and behold a certain man clothed in linen, whose loins were girded with fine gold of Uphaz: His [the angels] body also was like the beryl, and his face as the appearance of lightning, and his eyes as lamps of fire, and his arms and his feet like in colour to polished brass, and the voice of his words like the voice of a multitude. And I Daniel alone saw the vision: for the men that were with me saw not the vision; but a great quaking fell upon them, so that they fled to hide themselves."
... Daniel 10: 5- 7

"And, behold, there was a great earthquake: for the angel of the Lord descended from heaven, and came and rolled back the stone from the door, and sat upon it. His countenance was like lightning, and his raiment white as snow: And for fear of him the keepers did shake, and became as dead men."
... Mathew 28: 2- 4

"And out of the throne proceeded lightnings and thunderings and voices: and there were seven lamps of fire burning before the throne, which are the seven Spirits of God."... Revelation 4: 5

"And the temple of God was opened in heaven, and there was seen in his temple the ark of his testament: and there were lightnings, and voices, and thunderings, and an earthquake, and great hail."
... Revelation 11: 19

Describing Jesus:..."And was transfigured [changed] before them: and his face did shine as the sun, and his raiment was white as the light."
... Mathew 17: 2

"Behold, I show you a mystery; We shall not all sleep, but we shall all be changed [raptured], In a moment, in the twinkling of an eye [a fraction of a second], at the last trump: for the trumpet shall sound, and the dead [who have received Jesus] shall be raised incorruptible, and we shall be changed...and this mortal must put on immortality [eternal life – we are going to live forever]." ... 1 Corinthians 15: 51- 53

Nicola Tesla theorized that the ark of the covenant was a electrical capacitor due to its building materials and the stories associated with it. The priests of the temple claimed that God would appear in a cloud that would materialize above the ark and the ark was where God lived in the temple. The ark killed men that got to close to it due to its electrical discharges.

Tesla was working on a system to provide free electricity to the entire world wirelessly. All a person needed was a receiver in his home or business and the electricity would be drawn straight out of the atmosphere. It would have worked basically the same way a radio works today; just turn it on and pull radio signals directly from the atmosphere only in this case, electricity would take the place of radio signals. Tesla's financial backer, J.P. Morgan, withdrew his support for what I believe was a lack of foreseeable profit and Tesla's 'electricity towers' and free electricity for all never came to fruition.

A Swedish born Nobel Prize winner in Physics and electrical engineer, Hannes Alfven discovered that all of space is electromagnetically divided up into 3-dimensional grid-like structures, **invisible structures** that are made from electricity. Hannes writes:

"From the cosmological [study of the universe] point of view, the most important new space research discovery is probably the cellular structure of space. As has been seen in every region of space accessible to in situ [natural or original positioning] measurements, there are a number of 'cell walls', sheets of electric currents, which divide space into compartments with different magnetization, temperature, density, etc."
… Hannes Alfven, Cellular Structure of Space, Cosmic Plasma, Dordrecht, sect. VI. 13. 1. 1981

"The Big Bang was a myth devised to explain creation"
… Hannes Alfven

"For by him [God] were all things created, that are in heaven, and that are in earth, visible and invisible,…"
…. Colossians 1: 16

Our solar system has a heliosphere which is an enormous magnetic bubble that contains our solar system, the suns solar wind, and the entire solar magnetic field. Earth has a magnetosphere which is an asymmetrical bubble extending out from the earth thousands of miles and it encapsulates the earths magnetic field which flows out from the North and South Poles and follows the curvature of the earth and joins together. The earth also has a gravitational field from within that draws mass towards the earth's core. Lastly the earth has another electromagnetic field that encapsulates the surface of the earth; the world grid or ley lines, this is what I believe Tesla was going to use in his power distribution system. Today the world grid is fairly weak but I believe in the not so distant past it may have been energized by men. The ley lines are theorized to be about as wide as a two lane highways and they originate and terminate in 'hubs' that look like the spokes on a bicycle wheel. Just picture a mesh net of triangular shapes that envelopes the globe and it's electrically charged. I believe Tesla's plan was to send his amplified electrical charges out into the grid and it would flow around the world to be picked up by anyone with a receiver anywhere. Could the spirit world use the grid system as a superhighway, it's all interconnected worldwide and out into the heavens. Interestingly, researchers have reported a higher incidence of UFO reports the closer you get to the grid lines. There seems to be a direct correlation between spirit activity on the world grid and building activity sites by men on the earth. Here is a list of some of the man made sites that are extremely close to, if not right on top of, ley lines or grid intersections;

The Statue of Liberty .... The Nazca Lines in Lima Peru
Mohenjo Daro......................... Maralinga Atomic Test Sight
The Great Pyramid of Giza ..... Easter Island
Nan Madol, Micronesia .... Ankor Wat Temple, Cambodia
Dragons Triangle, Japan........... Luxor Egypt Temple
Sedona Arizona .... Teotihuacan
Bermuda Triangle .... Stone Henge
Baalbek Lebanon .... Axum Coptic Christian Center
Marfa Texas, (Marfa Lights) ...Petra
Machu Picchu .... Lake Baikal USSR
Xiam Pyramid .... Bimini Road
Nebuchadnezzar's or Hussein Palace
Black Rectangle in Alaska....62.193766,-141.262196

My hypothesis; The spirit world influenced men to build on or close to these energy lines. I believe the pre-flood civilization had the technology to send power on the world grid and receive power off of the world grid in the distant past. I also believe that today there are spirits that dwell all along the grid and, as in the past, have been using the power in the grid.
An engineer named Christopher Dunn hypothesizes that the Great Pyramid in Egypt was theoretically a power plant; 'The Giza Power Plant'. The Great Pyramid is sitting right in the middle of a ley line which would be perfect positioning to transmit power from.

He found chemical residues inside the pyramid that, when mixed, would generate hydrogen gas. What did the hydrogen gas power? Could it have been used to generate electricity to power the grid back then as Tesla was trying to achieve in the last century? You may be **wondering** where all of the technological evidence went besides the residue and the pyramid itself. Anything that was not built to last, extremely robust such as the pyramids, was swept away by Noah's **flood 4400 years ago.** During the **flood,** the Bible records the mountains being moved from their places and flowing (liquefaction during an earthquake would cause a mountain to flow) and their were massive underwater earthquakes causing tsunamis. All of the pulverized rock that came out of the earth when the fountains of the deep broke open also added to the mud and debris that eventually settled out and buried everything, some deeper than others. I would estimated that the earths pre-flood surface was buried between 0 [Mountaintops] and 14,000 feet of mud and organic debris in the basins; **today** the deposits of organic debris have turned into today's coal seams and the water from the flood itself is today the worlds oceans.

"Gulf of Mexico oil rig worker Dan Gunter drilled through a tree 60 feet tall that was 14,000 feet below the sea floor.
……….Chevron Oil Company"
……... Kent Hovind Seminar 2005

There was a time when that tree was alive and growing in the sun and the birds were nesting in its branches. It may have been just another tree in a forest or it may have been a tree in someones front yard. 14,000 feet is 2.65 miles of washed in dirt and debris which could only have been caused by a huge flood and that's why there are over a thousand flood legends worldwide. When Noah and his family departed from the ark and repopulated the world the story of the flood was passed down from generation to generation even until today – the flood is still being talked about and its evidence is still visible worldwide in the floods hydrologically sorted rock strata [not Lyell's guess of a geologic record]. Sir Edmund Hillary commented on 100's of thousands of sea shells and clams that he found when he ascended to 26,000 feet on Mount Everest. Mountains are formed when 2 tectonic plates collide against each other or when magma from beneath pushes its way to the surface. Evolution claims this happens over millions of years but this could have happened within one year if enough force and earthquake activity is present. During the flood of Noah mountains were both destroyed and built up by the earthquakes, tsunamis and water that was overflowing the globe. When the fountains of the deep were broken up by earthquakes or the possible combination of an asteroid and earthquakes- that emptied the water reservoirs underneath the ground and the ground level sank to where the bottom of the water reservoirs (aquifers) once were. The Bible records earthquakes and tsunamis that occurred when they collapsed. Tsunami's are formed by landslides or a sudden increase or decrease in sea floor level during an earthquake. In Psalms 104 the Bible records that the water "goes up by the mountains" which is exactly what a tsunami does. The Christmas 2004 Indian Ocean tsunami that hit Sumatra was caused by an undersea earthquake that caused water to "go up onto the land" 98 feet high. This one earthquake and tsunami killed 230,000 people and it also triggered other earthquakes, one as far away as Alaska. If Everest was indeed formed during the flood of Noah there had to be an enormous amount of energy released in the earths crust to cause a mountain to go from the level of the sea bed to 5 miles high. If there was tsunamic activity equal to the earthquake activity then the chances of survival would be very slim. The Bible records that not one living thing that has the breath of life in its nostrils [reptiles, mammals, amphibians] survived outside of what was aboard the ark.

"[God] Which moveth the mountains, and they know not: which overturneth them in his anger. Which shaketh the earth out of her place, and the pillars thereof tremble."
... Job 9: 5- 6

"He putteth forth his [Gods] hand upon the rock; he overturneth the mountains by the roots."   ... Job 28: 9

"When thou [God] didst terrible things which we looked not for, thou camest down, the mountains flowed down at thy presence." ... Isaiah 64: 3

"Thou [God] **coverest** it [**the** earth] with the deep [today's ocean water] as with a garment: The waters stood above the mountains. At thy [Gods] rebuke they fled; at **the** voice of thy thunder they **hasted** away. **They go up by the mountains**: they go down by the valleys unto the place which though hast founded for them [today's oceans]. Thou hast set a bound [shorelines] that they may not pass over; that they turn not again to cover the earth.
.... Psalms 104: 6-9

"Whereby the world that then was, being overflowed with water, perished:" ... 2 Peter 3: 6

EVIDENCE THAT GODS WORD IS TRUE

For the Christians that think evolution is true and has to be worked into the Bible;

On day 3 of Creation--- God made grass, herbs, **fruit trees 'yielding' fruit**

On day 4 of Creation--- God made 2 great lights – Sun and Moon

On day 5 of Creation--- God made the insects to pollinate

If God made the grass, herbs, **fruit trees 'yielding' fruit** on the 3rd day did they have to wait thousands or millions of years for the sun to shine on them or multiple thousands and multiple millions of years before insects were present to pollinate them? **The fruit** trees were not dormant – they were already yielding fruit on the 3rd day.
..... **Cited from** Dr. Hovinds Creation Seminar 2005

146.
The Angkor Wat Temple Stegosaurus

A 12th Century Cambodian Khmer King named Suryavarman II built the largest Hindu temple in the world at Angkor Wat Cambodia. Carved on a pillar within the temple is a clear depiction of a Stegosaurus. The evolution religion claims that dinosaurs died out 62.5 million years ago and apes evolved into men 3 million years ago. The Stegosaurus population was supposedly extinct 59.5 million years prior to mans arrival. The earliest fossil remains of a Stegosaurus was not discovered and assembled until 1877 (the Temple was built in the 1100's). Men had to be on the earth at the same instance as dinosaurs because of this depiction on the Angkor Wat temple pillar. The carving on this temple pillar is not the only ancient artwork created by men that depict dinosaurs.

Dinosaurs depicted on the Ica Stones in Peru

The Ica stones depict Dinosaurs interacting with men. Thousands of these stones have been unearthed with dozens of different species of dinosaurs. Below are excerpts from the book; "Secrets of the Ica stones and Nazca Lines" by Dennis Swift,

"Over thirty years ago, I began investigating the incredible Ica stones found in Pre-Colombian Indian tombs in the desert of Southern Peru. Many of the strange engraved stones were acquired by Dr. Javier Cabrera, who converted large rooms in his mansion into a museum. The museum of the engraved stones sits on the corner of the Plaza de Armas in Ica, Peru. Carera's mansion has become known as the museum that scares scientists. What is frightening to the scientists is the advanced medical knowledge etched on the stones. The engraved stones show Indians performing complex brain, heart, and caesarian surgeries predating modern operations by thousands of years. Equally scary is the startling sight of stones with men dressed in loincloths and headgear and looking through telescopes at the planets. That is impossible; we all know Galileo invented the telescope, or did he? The most disturbing images on the stones are those of dinosaurs with man together: men riding dinosaurs, even attacking them with axes, spears, bows, and arrows......

I would have dismissed the Ica stones on the basis that dinosaurs and man missed each other by at least sixty-three million years. However, I couldn't explain why the Ica, Peru Regional Museum had a collection of engraved stones that had been discovered by Peruvian archaeologist in official excavations at Pre-Colombian Indian cemeteries. Among the stones is one with a pterosaurs engraved on it with outstretched wings, serpentine neck, flamboyant cranial crest, and other features unmistakably associated with our modern knowledge of a pterosaurs looks like....."

Dennis Swift later asked Dr. Cabrera:

"What other proof do you have that men lived with Dinosaurs? " You said that dinosaur and human fossils have been found together. He ceremoniously handed me a copy of his book. Emphatically, he pointed at a page and exclaimed, "Here's the proof." Translated from the Spanish it reads that

'…..a Colombian anthropologist, Homero Henao Marin, a professor at the University of Quindo, Colombia in April, 1971, excavated in a place called Tel Boquero in the State of Tolima, Columbia and uncovered a fossilized skeleton of a dinosaur Iguanodon twenty metres long next to a human skull. The fossilization process had turned the skull into gray calcareous stone with whitish striations.. This find was a tremendous paleontological significance for several reasons. For one, it is the first time a human fossil has been found anywhere in the world next to that of a dinosaur.... which permits us to conclude by association that they lived at the same time.'....."

"Some 11,000 of these strange engraved stones are in a museum in Ica, Peru. Dr. Javier Cabrera Darquera has turned two rooms of his magnificent mansion into a private museum…….
The first mention of these incredible stones is from a Spanish priest journeying to the Ica region in 1535. Father Simon, a Jesuit missionary, accompanied Pizarro along the Peruvian coast and recorded his amazement upon viewing the stones. In 1562, Spanish explorers sent some of the stones back to Spain."
…… Dennis Swift, "Secrets of the Ica Stones and Nazca Lines"pg. 9-10, 16, 28-29

Dinosaurs depicted on Moche Pottery

The Moche Indians of Peru pre-dated the Ica's and they also had encounters with dinosaurs and depicted dinosaurs on their pottery instead of carving them on stone as the Ica's later did. Again, an excerpt from Dennis Swifts book;

"The Moche Indians inhabited the North Coast of Peru from roughly 100 A.D. To 800 A.D. The Moche are distinguished by their pottery. They are famous for their singular mastery and realism in recording a variety of animals, portraits of people, and scenes of daily life, all captured in ceramic……masterfully done portrait jars: animals, plants, musical instruments, people with different diseases, and Moche warriors fighting dinosaurs....The significance of the Moche vases with dinosaurs fighting warriors directly relates to the Ica Stones. Some of the same kinds of dinosaurs with dermal spines are engaged in battle with Indian warriors...

The descriptions of dragons in cultures around the world fit well-known dinosaurs. In the first century, Pliny recorded the following account.

'Africa produces elephants, but it is India that produces the largest as well as the dragon, who is perpetually at war with the elephant, and is itself of so enormous a size as to envelope the elephants with its folds, and encircle them in it coils. The contest is equally fatal to both'....

Before modern man called them dinosaurs, they were well known to our predecessors as dragons."
.... Dennis Swift, "Secrets of The Ica Stones and Nazca Lines", pg. 77-80

Because of their interactions with so many species of dinosaurs I believe that the Moche and the Ica civilizations of Peru may have both been pre-flood civilizations which would place them at least 2350 B.C.(flood year) and dating back further from that point. Also, as an unfortunate consequence of evolutionists protecting their religion, any find similar to the above where a human skull is found with a dinosaur will be covered up by any evolutionist in order to preserve the evolution theory. How many amazing discoveries have been made that never saw the light of day in order to protect their religion?

The Acambaro Statues- Dinosaurs and mixed species of animals

In Acambaro, Mexico in 1944, 33,500 ceramic and stone statues were unearthed. Some of these statues look like long necked, heavy bodied dinosaurs. The following is an excerpt from Charles Hapgoods book "Mystery in Acambaro";

"In 1944 an accidental discovery of an extremely controversial nature occurred in Acambaro, Mexico. The find eventually yielded over 33,500 objects of ceramic and stone (including jade), and knives of obsidian (sharper than steel and still used today in heart surgery). Startling representations of Negros,

Orientals, and bearded Caucasians were included as were motifs of Egyptians, Sumerian and other ancient non-native American civilizations. There were portrayals of Big Foot and aquatic monster type creatures, **weird human-animal mixtures, and a host of other inexplicable creations.** In addition, statues of great reptiles measuring from less than an inch to 4 feet high or 6 feet long were discovered, some of them in active association with humans. The reptiles were generally eating the humans, but in some bizarre statuettes, a friendly, or even erotic, association was indicated. One famous statue, of a woman with arms outstretched to embrace a long-snouted animal, is probably of a pre-historic anteater mammal, but most of the other featured creatures were distinctly reptilian. To observers, many of these reptilian creatures resembled dinosaurs! Many scenes of reptiles and humans having sexual intercourse were thought to represent scenes out of various myths and legends, not necessarily depicting actual sexual relations between humans and animals. Sexual relations between humans and animals does occur, however, no matter how repellant this may seem. In the ancient Hittite Empire of Asia Minor, Circa 3000 B.C., only two crimes carried the punishment of death: Murder and Sodomy. Apparently, this was a serious crime in the ancient world, as it continues to be today. The figurines at Acambaro are particularly strange in this regard."
..... Charles H. Hapgood, "Mystery in Acambaro", 2000

The book of Jasher is an extra-Biblical account that ties into the old testament of the Bible. It gives more details about certain events that happened in the Bible, the Flood account and Noah's Ark, the formation of Israel as a nation are but 2 of many. The book of Jasher is mentioned in the Bible twice; in Joshua 10 and 2 Samuel 1;

"And the sun stood still, and the moon stayed, until the people had avenged themselves upon their enemies. Is not this written in the book of Jasher"
.... Joshua 10 :3

"(Also he bade them teach the children of Judah the use of the bow: behold, it is written in the book of Jasher.)"
…... 2 Samuel 1: 18

In the book of Jasher and in the book of Genesis God makes it clear that he is not happy with 'man' because they are not obeying his commandments. **Men are mixing species with species... evil is continually in their hearts, the world was corrupt and filled with violence.** The book of Jasher creates a more complete picture of the reason God destroyed the world with a flood. In the above account of Acambaro; they unearthed evidence of what God claimed men were doing prior to their destruction by the flood. They were sexually immoral, **they were mixing species of animals** and they knew that God hated what they were doing yet they did it partly just to mock God. In Acambaro we see the **'weird human-animal mixtures'**; some of these 'mixtures' could be depicted on some of the stone carvings in the Middle East and in abundance in Egypt, possibly not all creatures of myth as previously thought.

The Griffon:............. ½ lion ½ eagle
The Centaur …..........½ man ½ horse
The Minotaur ….........½ man ½ bull
The Satyr …..............½ man ½ goat
In Egypt ; Men with heads of birds or having wings
In the Book of Jasher there is an account of 2 other mixtures;
The Yemim …............½ man ½ bear
Other Yemim ….........½ **man ½ keephas**, ???

The following is an account from the Book of Jasher concerning some of these strange animal mixtures;

"And the sons of Shobal were Alvan, Manahath, Ebal, Shepho, and Onam, and the sons of Zibeon were Ajah, and Anah, this was that Anah who found the 'Yemim' in the wilderness when he feed the asses of Zibeon his father. And whilst he was feeding his

fathers asses he led them to the wilderness at different times to feed them. And there was a day that he brought them to one of the deserts on the sea shore, opposite the wilderness of the people, and whilst he was feeding them, behold a very heavy storm came from the other side of the sea and rested upon the asses that were feeding there, and they all stood still. And afterward about 120 great and terrible animals came out from the wilderness at the other side of the sea, and they all came to the place where the asses were, and they placed themselves there. And those animals, from their middle downward, were in the shape of the children of men, and from their middle upward some had the likeness of bears, and some the likeness of the **keephas,** with tails behind them from between their shoulders reaching down to the earth, like the tails of the **ducheephath**, and those animals came and mounted and rode upon these asses, and led them away, and they went away unto this day. And one of those animals approached Anah and smote [struck] him with his tail, and then fled from that place. And when he saw this work he was exceedingly afraid of his life, and he fled and escaped to the city. And he related to his sons and brothers all that had happened to him, and many men went to seek the asses but could not find them, and Anah and his brothers went no more to that place from that day following, for they were greatly afraid of their lives."
….. Jasher 36: 28-35

Could this be the result of the **mixing** of species that God was angry about? Yes, I believe so -

Chapter 6

THE ANUNNAKI, BIG FOOT [HAIRY MEN] AND THE BOOK OF JASHER

As previously mentioned, the evolution religion set the stage for an 'imagined alien invasion' from possible hostile intergalactic marauders looking for resources that they can take advantage of. To recap; The earth was created randomly through the evolutionists version of the 'Big Bang'. Life randomly, by chance, supposedly emerged out of a primordial soup and evolved into what we see today. Also, life may have randomly, by chance, emerged on other planets and that life evolved into what it is today, only far more advanced technologically, and they are now searching the cosmos as marauders; some scientists who think like Steven Hawking are afraid that they are as mean and hostile as men on the earth and they may destroy or enslave us.

The story of the Anunnaki begins with the premise that aliens came here to extract gold from the earth to restore **their planet's atmosphere.** They got tired of mining for themselves so they took the primitive hairy cave men types that were already here on the earth and reworked their DNA and made modern, slightly more intelligent and hairless men out of them, then used them as slaves to mine gold for them. Today's modern men are what remains. The story is laid out in Zachariah Sitchens series of books called "The Earth Chronicles". Mr. Sitchen translated a collection of Sumerian cuneiform tablets and relayed this story through his books. **Some believe that a random alien chance encounter with men on earth is what led to today's man rendering Gods creation claim an out-dated and meaningless legend.** I have a few concerns and questions for those who believe the story of the Anunnaki's creation of modern man.

Question 1: Did the Anunnaki claim to create the heavens and the earth?
Answer........No, according to the story, they found the earth already in existence, fully created.

Question 2: Did the Anunnaki claim to create men or any living organism?
Answer........No, they claim to have found men in a less evolved state; hairy, brutish or unintelligent, they reworked their DNA sequencing to make a more intelligent, trainable, hairless man – close to the men that we see today on the earth.

In fact, according to the story; the Anunnaki were present and witnessed God's 6 days of creation and they witnessed God creating in a 'creation chamber' and beyond that they themselves claim to have been created by God. They were using a creation chamber of their own to rework the DNA of men.
This may account for mans ability to 'mix one species with another species', which God despised!

Question 3: Were all ancient men hairy, brutish and unintelligent? No!

There are accounts in the King James Bible and the Book of Jasher that show hairy men walked hand in hand with hairless men. In one account, there was one of each, hairy and hairless, born as twins in the same hour.

In the Book of Jasher:

"And the Lord heard the prayer of Isaac the son of Abraham, and the Lord was entreated of him and Rebecca his wife conceived. And in about 7 months after the children struggled together within her, and it pained her greatly that she was weary on account of them, and she said to all the women who were there in the land.

Did such a thing happen to you as it has to **me**? And they said unto her, no.....

And they all inquired of the Lord concerning this matter, and they brought her word from the Lord and told her, two children are in thy womb, and two nations shall rise from them: and one nation shall be stronger than the other, and the greater shall serve the younger. And when her days to be delivered were completed, she knelt down, and behold there were twins in her womb, as the Lord had spoken to her. And the first came out red all over like a hairy garment, and all the people of the land called his name Esau [meaning: Hairy], saying, that this one was made complete from the womb. And after that came his brother, and his hand took hold of Esau's heel, therefor, they called his name Jacob. And the boys grew up to their 15th year, and they came amongst the society of men. Esau was a designing and deceitful man, and an expert hunter in the field, and Jacob was a man perfect and wise, dwelling in tents, feeding flocks and learning the instructions of the Lord and the commandments of his father and mother.

….. Book of Jasher 26: 8-9, 12-15, 17, pg. 69-70

Years later there is this account of the twins in the King James Bible:

"And Jacob said to Rebekah his mother, behold, Esau my brother is a hairy man, and I am a smooth man: My father [who is blind] peradventure will feel me, and I shall seem to him as a deceiver; and I shall bring a curse upon me, and not a blessing. And his mother said unto him, upon me be thy curse, my son; only obey my voice, and go fetch me them [goat kids]. And he went, and fetched, and brought them to his mother: and his mother made savory meat, such as his father loved. And Rebekah took goodly raiment [clothes] of her eldest son Esau, which were with her in the house, and put them upon Jacob her younger son: And she put the skins of the kids of the goats upon his hands, and upon the smooth of his neck: And she gave the savory meat and the bread, which she had prepared, into the hand of her son Jacob. And he

came unto his father, and said, 'My Father': and he said, 'Here am I'; who art thou, my son? And Jacob said unto his father, I am Esau thy firstborn: I have done according to as thou badest me: Arise, I pray thee, sit and eat of my venison, that thy soul may bless me. And Isaac said unto his son. How is it thou hast found it so quickly, my son? And he said, because the Lord thy God brought it unto me. And Isaac said unto Jacob, come near, I pray thee, that I may feel thee, my son, whether thou be my very son Esau or not. And Jacob went near unto Isaac his father; and he felt him, and said, the voice is Jacobs voice, but the hands are the hands of Esau. And he discerned him not, because his hands were hairy, as his brother Esau's hands; so he blessed him."
….. Genesis 27: 11- 23

There is another account in the Book of Jasher where I believe a hairy man was mistaken for an animal and shot.

"And Lamech was old and advanced in years, and his eyes were dim that he could not see, and Tubal Cain, his son, was leading him and it was one day that Lamech went into the field and Tubal Cain his son was with him, and whilst they were walking in the field, Cain the son of Adam advanced towards them; for Lamech was very old and could not see much, and Tubal Cain his son was very young. And Tubal Cain told his father to draw his bow, and with the arrows he smote Cain, who was yet afar off, and he slew him, for he appeared to them to be an animal. And the arrows entered Cains body although he was distant from them, and he fell to the ground and died. And the Lord requited Cains evil according to his wickedness, which he had done to his brother Abel, according to the word of the Lord which he had spoken. And it came to pass when Cain had died, that Lamech and Tubal Cain went to see the animal which they had slain, and they saw, and behold Cain their grandfather was fallen dead upon the earth. And Lamech was very much grieved at having done this, and in clapping his hands together he struck his son and caused his death. And the wives of Lamech heard what Lamech had done,

and they sought to kill him. And the wives of Lamech hated him from that day, because he slew Cain and Tubal Cain, and the wives of Lamech separated from him, and would not hearken to him in those days."
…... Book of **Jasher** 2: 26-33, pg. 5

Adams son Cain was probably a **hairy** man as was Esau and from a distance you may not have been able to tell them apart from an ordinary animal. In this **account,** Tubal Cain is described as being very **young. Keep** in mind that men in those days lived to be 700, 800 or 900 + years old and a 50–100 **year** old would seem like a very young man **to** them. The book of Jasher records when Abraham took Isaac up to a mountain in the land of Moriah to give him as a sacrifice, Isaac was 37 years old at the time according to the book of Jasher - 22: 53, pg.58.

ARE BIGFOOT IN THE "MAN" CLASS?

In research **done by** the **B.F.R.O.** – Big Foot Research Organization, they have compiled several attributes of Big Foot, based on eye witness testimony, that are comparable to descriptions of Isaac's sons in the book of Jasher.

Big Foot capabilities and attributes:
Run extremely fast
Leap extremely far
Yell or roar, extremely loud
Cause terror in men
Have the same color hair as men have: Red, blonde, brown and black and it turns gray as they age
Speak a language, sounds like a chattering sound
Throw Rocks, tree branches
Use tools
Look alarmingly like men in the face
Family group oriented

The Seminole Indians of Florida view Big Foot or Sasquatch as

"Other peoples" or "Men" and their tribal traditions record that the Seminoles and the "Big Foot people" joined together to fight their enemies.

The ratio of hairy men to smooth men in earths early history is unknown today and I am not claiming that Big Foot are their descendants but the possibility exists. Keep the above attributes in mind as you read the following accounts:

"And all the sons of Jacob shouted with a loud voice, and they all ran toward the inhabitants of Arbelan, and with a great and tremendous voice, and the inhabitants of Arbelan heard the noise of the shouting of the sons of Jacob, and **their roaring like the noise of Lions** and like the roaring of the sea and its waves. And fear and terror possessed their hearts on account of the sons of Jacob, and they were terribly afraid of them, and they retreated and fled before them into the city....
…… Jasher 39: 6-8

"And Judah, seeing that the men of Gaash were getting to heavy for them, **gave a most piercing and tremendous shriek and all of the men of Gash were terrified at the voice of Judah's cry**, and men fell from the wall at his powerful shriek, and all those that were from without and within the city were greatly afraid for their lives....
And he [Judah] ran at a distance with all his might, with his drawn sword in his hand, **and he sprang from the earth and by dint of his strength, mounted the wall**, and his sword fell from his hand. **And Judah shouted upon the wall, and all of the men that were upon the wall were terrified, and some of them fell from the wall into the city and died, and those who were yet upon the wall, when they saw Judah's strength, they were greatly afraid and fled for their lives into the city for safety.......**

Dan, Judahs brother, **leaped onto the wall....**
Naphtali, Judahs brother, **leaped onto the wall...**

And the inhabitants of the city had all descended into the city, and the sons of Jacob came to them in different directions, and the battle raged against them from the front and the rear, and the sons of Jacob smote them terribly, and slew about 20,000 of them men and women, not one of them could stand up against the sons of Jacob...."
..... Jasher 39: 19, 29-30, 41, 47,50

Isaac is dying so he summoned all of his children and grandchildren;

"And Isaac said unto Jacob, bring me hither thy sons and I will bless them; and Jacob brought his eleven children before his father Isaac. And Isaac placed his hands upon all the sons of Jacob, and he took hold of them and embraced them, and kissed them one by one, and Isaac blessed them on that day, and he said unto them, May the God of your fathers bless you and increase your seed like the stars of heaven for number. **And Isaac also blessed the sons of Esau,** saying, May God cause you to be a dread and a terror to all that will behold you, and to all your enemies. And Isaac called Jacob and his sons, and they all came and sat before Isaac, and Isaac said unto Jacob. The Lord God of the whole earth said unto me, unto thy seed will I give this land for an inheritance if thy children keep my statutes and my ways, and I will perform unto them [Israel] the oath which I swore unto thy father Abraham. Now therefor my son, teach thy children and thy children's children to fear the Lord, and to go in the good way which will please the Lord thy God, for if you keep the ways of the Lord and his statutes the Lord will also keep unto you his covenant with Abraham, and will do well with you and your seed all the days.
.... Book of Jasher 47: 4-8

The Sumerians who wrote the story of the Anunnaki either didn't know the fulness of Gods creation or they were trying to create doubt in the minds of readers concerning Gods creation. The story of the Anunnaki was written after the flood since it references the flood which happened approximately 4400 years ago or 2350 B.C.... Anunnaki researchers W.G. Lambert and A.R. Millard date the writing of the story at 1650 B.C. which was 700 years post flood. A story this amazing, if it were true, would also have had an enormous amount of corroborating literature surrounding it from other eye witnesses to back up the claim but there is very little available.

For arguments sake, lets say the Anunnaki did come to the earth and they did alter the DNA of men and animals prior to the flood. Perhaps they taught men how they can alter or mix the species of one animal with another or maybe men figured it out on their own; either way, its recorded in the book of Jasher that men did! Just prior to their destruction:

"And all the sons of men departed from the ways of the Lord in those days as they multiplied upon the face of the earth with sons and daughters, and they taught one another their evil practices and they continued sinning against the Lord. And every man made unto himself a God, and they robbed and plundered every man his neighbor as well as his relative, and they corrupted the earth and **the earth was filled with violence**. And their judges and rulers went to the daughters of men and took their wives by force from their husbands according to their choice, and the sons of men in those days took from the cattle of the earth, the beasts of the field and the fowls of the air, **and taught the mixture of animals of one species with the other, in order therewith to provoke the Lord**; and God saw the whole earth and it was corrupt, for all flesh had corrupted its ways upon earth, all men and all animals."
….. Book of Jasher 4: 16-18

Some today believe that the Cheetah could be a mix between and cat and a dog; it has the claws of a dog, the light colored fur is coarse like a dog, the black spots are soft like a cat. They are virtual clones of each other.

161.

Today we, mankind, are right on the same threshold as the pre-flood world; world wide violence (Islams mandate to deliver the world to Allah through violence if necessary), the moral decay of society, men publicly mocking God and being purposefully disrespectful to God and his laws, mixing species, creating devastating viruses through gene splicing and weaponizing them, tampering with genetics (Plum Island). Science and academia replacing God in the minds of men with a false religion and pseudo science created straight from their imaginations.

NOAHS ARK AND THE FLOOD OF THE JUDGEMENT OF MEN

The Book of Jasher has a detailed account of what God did to the pre-flood civilization for the things they did against God and his creation.

"And the Lord said, I will blot out man that I created from the face of the earth, yea from man to the birds of the air, together with cattle and beasts that are in the field for I repent that I made them."
…….. Book of Jasher 4: 19

"In his 595th year Noah commenced to build the Ark, and he made the Ark in 5 years as the Lord commanded. Then Noah took the three daughters of Eliakim, son of Methuselah, for wives for his sons, as the Lord had commanded Noah....
At that time, after the death of Methuselah, the Lord said to Noah, Go thou with thy household unto the ark; behold I will gather to thee all the animals of the earth, the beasts of the field and the fowls of the air, and they shall all come and surround the ark. And thou shalt go and seat thyself by the doors of the ark, and all the beasts, the animals, and the fowls, shall assemble and place themselves before thee, and such of them as shall come and crouch before thee, shalt thou take and deliver into the hands of thy sons, who shall bring them to the ark, and all that will stand

before thee thou shalt leave. And the Lord brought this about on the next day, and animals, beasts and fowls came in great multitudes and surrounded the ark. And Noah went and seated himself by the door of the ark, and of all flesh that crouched before him, he brought into the ark, and all that stood before him he left upon earth. And a lioness came, with her two whelps, male and female, and the three crouched before Noah, and the two whelps rose up against the lioness and smote her, and made her flee from her place, and she went away, and they returned to their places, and crouched upon the earth before Noah. And the lioness ran away, and stood in the place of the lions. And Noah saw this, and wondered greatly, and rose and took the two whelps, and brought them into the ark. And Noah brought into the ark from all living creatures that were upon earth, so that there was none left but which Noah brought into the ark. Two and two came to Noah into the ark, but from the clean animals, and clean fowls, he brought seven couples, as God had commanded him. And all the animals, and beasts, and fowls, were still there, and they surrounded the ark at every place, and the rain had not descended till seven days after. And on that day, the Lord caused the whole earth to shake, and the sun darkened, and the foundations of the world raged, and the whole earth was moved violently, and the lighting flashed, and the thunder roared, and all the fountains in the earth were broken up, such as was not known to the inhabitants before; and God did this mighty act, in order to terrify the sons of men, that there might be no more evil upon earth. And still the sons of men would not return from their evil ways, and they increased the anger of the Lord at that time, and did not even direct their hearts to all this. And at the end of seven days, in the six hundredth year of the life of Noah, the waters of the flood were upon the earth and all the fountains of the deep were broken up, and the windows of heaven were opened, and the rain was upon the earth forty days and forty nights. And Noah and his household, and all the living creatures that were with him, came into the ark on account of the waters of the flood, and the Lord shut him in. And all the sons of men that were left upon the earth, became exhausted through evil on account of the rain, for the waters were coming more violently upon the earth, and the animals and beasts were still surrounding the ark. And the sons of men assembled together, about seven hundred thousand men and women, and they came unto Noah to the ark. And they called to Noah, saying, open for us that we may come to thee in the ark – and wherefore shall we die? And Noah, with a loud voice, answered them from the ark, saying, Have you not all rebelled against the Lord, and said that he does not exist? And therefore the Lord brought upon you this evil, to destroy and cut you off from the face of the earth.

Is not this the thing that I spoke to you of one hundred and twenty years back, and you would not hearken to the voice of the Lord, and now do you desire to live upon earth? And they said to Noah, We are ready to return to the Lord; only open for us that we may live and not die. And Noah answered them, saying, behold now that you see the trouble of your souls, you wish to return to the Lord; why did you not return during these hundred and twenty years, which the Lord granted you as the determined period? But now you come and tell me this on account of the troubles of your souls, now also the Lord will not listen to you, neither will he give ear to you on this day, so that you will not now succeed in your wishes. And the sons of men approached in order to break into the ark, to come in on account of the rain, for they could not bear the rain upon them. And the Lord sent all the beasts and animals that stood round the ark. And the beasts overpowered them and drove them from that place, and every man went his way and they again scattered themselves upon the face of the earth. And the rain was still descending upon the earth, and it descended forty days and forty nights, and the waters prevailed greatly upon the earth; and all flesh that was upon the earth or in the waters died, whether men, animals, beasts, creeping things or birds of the air, there only remained Noah and those that were with him in the ark. And the waters prevailed and they greatly increased upon the earth, and they lifted up the ark and it was raised from the earth. And the ark floated upon the face of the waters, and it was tossed upon the waters so that all the living creatures within were turned about like pottage in a caldron. And great anxiety seized all the living creatures that were in the ark, and the ark was like to be broken. And all the living creatures that were in the ark were terrified, and the lions roared, and the oxen lowed, and the wolves howled, and every living creature in the ark spoke and lamented in its own language, so that their voices reached to a great distance, and Noah and his sons cried and wept in their troubles; they were greatly afraid that they had reached the gates of death. And Noah prayed unto the Lord, and cried unto him on account of this, and he said, O Lord help us, for we have not strength to bear this evil that has encompassed us, for the waves of the waters have surrounded us, mischievous torrents have terrified us, the snare of death have come before us; answer us, O Lord, answer us, light up thy countenance toward us and be gracious to us, redeem us and deliver us. And the Lord hearkened to the voice of Noah, and the Lord remembered him. And a wind passed over the earth, and the waters were still and the ark rested. And the fountains of the deep and the windows of heaven were stopped, and the rain from heaven was restrained. And the waters decreased in those days, and the ark rested upon the mountains of Ararat. And Noah then opened the windows of the ark, and Noah still called out to the Lord at that time and he said, O lord, who didst form the earth and the heavens and all that are therein, bring forth our souls from this confinement, and from the prison wherein thou hast placed us, for I am much wearied with sighing. And the Lord hearkened to the voice of Noah, and said to him, when though shalt have completed a full year thou shalt then go forth. And at the revolution of the year, when a full year was completed to Noah's dwelling in the ark, the waters were dried from off the earth, and Noah put off the covering of the ark. At that time, on the twenty-seventh day of the second month, the earth was dry, but Noah and his sons, and those that were with him, did not go out from the ark until the Lord told them. And the day came that the Lord told them to go out, and they all went out from the ark. And they went and returned every one to his way and to his place, and Noah and his sons dwelt in the land that God had told them, and they served the Lord all their days, and the Lord blessed Noah and his sons on their going out from the ark.

And he said to them, 'Be fruitful and fill all the earth; become strong and increase abundantly in the earth and multiply therein'.
.... Book of Jasher 5: 34 -36 and Chapter 6: 1 – 42

The Bible records that the next time God has to judge men in this way he will not use a flood again, he will use fire!

"Whereby the world that then was, being overflowed with water, perished: But the heavens and the earth, which are now, by the same word are kept in store, reserved unto fire against the day of judgment and perdition of ungodly men."
..... 2 Peter 3: 6-7

If the Anunnaki did exist, did they have a hand in corrupting men? If so, men were still held accountable to Gods law concerning what's required of them on the earth. The story of the Anunnaki says that they knew the flood was coming so they just abandoned the earth and left men to perish, supposedly their own improved upon creations. If they did exist, their story unfolds like another one of Satan's plots to destroy men.

UFO craft, spirits, ghosts, apparitions, Big Foot and other crypto-zoological animals could all very easily fit into the realm of the spirit world; appearing or disappearing in our three dimensional realm. I believe we have been shown the spirit realm so we may believe that there is a spiritual realm and that realm is much more than what evolution or science is capable of explaining. Their explanation lies outside of this 3 dimensional plane and, as of this writing, science has not cracked that particular code yet. A lack of physical evidence does not equate to nonexistence. I can't show you a television or radio wave yet we all know they exist because most of us have listened to the radio or watched a television program at some point in our lives. UFO's, spirits and cryptids have been witnessed by millions of people worldwide throughout human history including myself and I don't know a soul that can bring forth conclusive proof of

what they saw as I can't prove what I witnessed.
Spirit beings are not necessarily always non-physical. UFO's leave impressions in the earth when they land, Big Foot leave footprints in the earth. There is an instance in the Bible where Jesus, shortly after he died on the cross and was resurrected by God, suddenly materialized in the middle of a room full of disciples and one of the disciples, Thomas, who doubted the resurrection of Jesus was instructed to touch Jesus's wounds to confirm that he actually was the resurrected Jesus;
"And after eight days again his disciples were within, and Thomas with them: then came Jesus, the doors being shut, and stood in the midst, and said, peace be unto you. Then saith he to Thomas, reach hither thy finger, and behold my hands; and reach hither thy hand, and thrust it into my side: and be not faithless, but believing."
….. John 20: 26-27

At this point, if you are still thinking we may be invaded by aliens from another planet I can tell you beyond a shadow of a doubt that we have and are now in their midst, daily.

"Be not forgetful to entertain strangers: for thereby some have entertained angels unawares."
…….. Hebrews 13: 2

Angels are not born on the earth, rather, they came straight from heaven #3, sent here from God. Angels, both the visible and invisible, are walking among us and the ones that are visible you can't tell they are angels by looking at them or by talking to them. They wear clothes as you do, they eat as you do, they talk as you should talk, you can shake their hand and you won't be able to tell the difference between them and a man. We look like them because we were made after their image. Add that to what the Bible records about our spirits coming from and returning to God in heaven and I have concluded that the earth has always had a large population of extra-dimensional and extraterrestrial beings.

Especially when you consider that each of us have our own personal guardian angels that stay with us throughout our lives. There are 7 billion men and women so there are 7 billion guardians on the earth presently. The Bible records that when Satan was exiled from heaven #3 1/3 of the angels that had followed him were cast out with him and most are probably here on the earth. We are as much citizens of the heavens as we are citizens of the earth. We are as much citizens of the Spirit world as we are citizens of the physical world.

Chapter 7

THE DEVICE THAT FLOATED STONES.
THE SAPHIRE STICK - GOD USED IT, ABRAHAM USED IT, MOSES AND OTHERS USED IT

The maximum capacity that the largest crane on earth can lift today is about 20,000 tons. The ancient builders had no modern machinery that history is aware of that enabled them to lift monolithic stones or transport them, yet they did. Here are some of the larger quarried stones that were used in ancient construction:

20,000 tons or 40,000,000 lbs in Peru
16,250 tons or 32,500,000 lbs in Nanjing China
1242 ...tons or 2,484,000 lbs in Baalbek Lebanon
1100 ...tons or 2,200,000 lbs in Assuan Egypt
1000 ...tons or 2,000,000 lbs in Thebes Egypt
1000 ...tons or 2,000,000 lbs in Baalbek Lebanon
520 ....tons or 1,040,000 lbs in Axum Ethiopia
517 ....tons or 1,034,000 lbs in Jerusalem Israel
400 ....tons or 800,000 lbs in Giza Egypt
285 ....tons or 570,000 lbs in Alxandria Egypt
200 ....tons or 400,000 lbs in Saqqara Egypt

Nine of the stones listed above are in close proximity to Israel-- While the entire nation of Israel was in captivity to Egypt for over 400 years they did most of the construction in Egypt, and later they built for the Roman empire. Lebanon shares a border with Israel and Axum Ethiopia is where Solomon's son reportedly took the ark of the covenant, (also on the world grid).

"And all the cities of store that Solomon had, and cities for his chariots, and cities for his horsemen, and that which Solomon desired to build in Jerusalem, **and in Lebanon**, and in all the land of his dominion."..... 1 Kings 9: 20

169.
ED LEEDSKALNIN'S CORAL CASTLE

The next time you're in Florida, if time permits, drive South down Highway 1 or the South Dixie Highway about 25 miles south of Miami. There is a tourist attraction there at 28655 S. Dixie Highway called the 'Coral Castle'. The Castle was built entirely by **one man working by himself**. His name was Edward Leedskalnin - Ed weighed in at about 100 lbs.; he was a Latvian immigrant arriving in the United States in 1907. Ed purchased land to begin work on his Castle in 1918 and, for the most part, finished it, until he decided to move - buildings and all. Eds original site was in Florida City but he wound up moving everything he built, again, by himself, with the exception of a truck driver he hired to do the actual driving. His new site is in Homestead Florida where it's open to the public today. The reason Ed is so interesting is because of his chosen building material; Ed quarried rock from his property to use in the construction of his Castle. The largest stone he quarried weighed in at 30 tons and the average weight is 15 tons. It took Ed 22 years all total, including the move time, to finish it in 1940. The following is and excerpt from 'Southfloridaonline.com';

"Ed never allowed anyone to watch him work and he had an eerie 6th sense when anyone tried. He would immediately stop working until they left. However, Ed seemed to not care if children were sometimes present. It is surmised that Ed felt no one would believe them anyway. It has been reported that one night some children witnessed Ed "floating stones like hydrogen balloons"... There are a couple of credible accounts of adults witnessing strange occurrences as Ed worked. The man who Ed hired to move the stones with his truck stated that he had forgotten his lunch box one morning and went back to the Castle to get it. He had only been gone for a half hour and when he arrived Ed already had several of the monolithic stones stacked on the rails of the trailer like cordwood. He never saw how Ed loaded them, just that Ed had absolutely no heavy machinery that should have been necessary to manipulate such heavy stones; especially that

fast. Another story stated that Ed was seen singing to the stone with his hands placed on it. Oddly enough, legend has it that the "Magician"
Merlin moved the Stonehenge stones (about 40 tons each) by singing to them.... When anyone asked Ed how he cut and moved the huge stones, Ed would state that he knew the secrets of the master stone cutters of Egypt, Peru, the Yucatan, Etc. He also said that he understood the laws of weight and leverage. Ed actually wrote and published a small booklet on magnetism, which is believed to have something to do with Eds ability, but it is too difficult for most to comprehend."
....www.southfloridaonline.com/article-coral-castle

There are those who have tried to discredit Ed over the years. They published photos of Ed with large wooden tripods and chains with a block and tackle, they claim anyone can use this type of equipment with a 3 to 1 mechanical advantage to move any of the stones he used. The person that wrote that particular article should have spoken to a heavy equipment rigger prior to writing. The heaviest stone on the site is 30 tons or 60,000 lbs. His claim of Eds 3 to 1 mechanical advantage works out to be; 60,000: 20,000 lbs, Ed would have to hoist 20,000 lbs to lift 60,000 lbs. Even the average size blocks at 15 tons is 30,000 lbs to 10,000 lbs. Ed only weighed 100 lbs. Ed would have needed a mechanical advantage of 600 to 1 to begin to budge the heaviest stone.

Ed didn't want publicity in that regard, he didn't want anyone to observe him as he moved anything. He probably permitted the photos with block and tackle to throw inquisitive minds off. He went to great lengths to keep people away while he moved the stones and those who did get close reported something other than the normal mechanical means we employ today. "Floating stones like hydrogen balloons" was their terminology. Ed had his driver's trailer nearly loaded in a half an hour with no equipment present.

ED LEEDSKALNINS BOOK - "ELECTRIC CURRENT"

The entirety of Eds book is based upon electricity and electromagnetism and Ed explains how to make magnets – electromagnets and energy captive magnets. **Ed** equates electricity with magnetism as **magnetic currents that flow freely through** the air, **metals**, **rocks**, etc. Ed explains;

"The reason I call the results of north and south **pole** magnet's or functions magnetic currents and not electric currents or electricity is connected too much with those non-existing electrons. If it had been called **magneticity** then I would accept it. **Magneticity** would indicate that it has a magnetic base and so it would be all right....The real magnetic is the substance that is circulating in the metal...Each attractive particle within a magnet is a magnet itself, with north and south poles."

Mr. Leedskalnin does not explain overtly how to make an anti-gravity **device**, but you do come away with the sense that he is using electricity and magnetism when he is moving objects. Back in 1945 when Ed wrote his book he was not aware that the moon had lost its magnetic field and he claimed that the reason the moon did not get pulled down by earths gravity was because the earths magnetic field and the moons magnetic field were positioned as repellant forces pushing each other away as magnets do on the earth when you align their opposing poles. I am not totally convinced that what the **scientific** community is saying about "inertia" alone holding the moon in place is totally accurate either. There are 170 moons orbiting planets in our solar system alone, Jupiter by itself has 62 moons. They all would **have** needed to be perfectly set in orbit so their inertia's would hold them in place. **If they are being held in place by only inertia then God gets the credit for the precision that keeps them suspended in place.**

Ed proved in one of his experiments in his book that magnetism or electromagnetism does interact with the earths gravity. Below is an excerpt from Eds book that talks about his experiment; "Now take a three-foot long soft steel welding rod. It is already magnetized as a permanent magnet [magnetized earlier in preparation for this experiment]. Hang it in a fine thread so it is level [suspend it from above at its equilibrium or balance point]. Now measure each end [from the equilibrium point to each end] and you will see the south end is longer [Ed is in Florida which is well north of the equator] in my location at Rock Gate, between twenty-fifth and twenty sixth latitude and eightieth and eighty first longitude west. In the three-foot long magnet the South pole end is about a sixteenth of an inch longer. Farther north it should be longer yet, but at the equator both ends of the magnet should be equal in length. In earth's south hemisphere the north pole end of the magnet should be longer."

Ed has discovered that gravity, and thus, weight is altered magnetically! Ed shows that the weight of a magnet is altered by the interaction between the magnet itself and the earths magnetic field and earths gravity depending upon your location on the face of the planet. The question remains; How did Ed amplify this result and go from a few grams on a steel rod to 30 tons of rock?

Like Nicola Tesla, Ed had an intimate understanding of the way electricity flowed all around us and that it could be directed or captured. Ed viewed the earth differently as most of us do today, he claimed the earth and moon were a giant magnets and were made that way through electricity or, to borrow his terminology, magneticity. Ed tells how alternating current stays active in a wire between starts and stops:

"You have been wondering why alternating currents can run so far away from their generators. One reason is between every time the currents start and stop there is no pressure in the wire so the magnets (Current) from the air run in the wire and when the run starts there already are magnets (Current) in the wire which do not have to come from the generator, so the power line itself is a small generator which assists the big generator to furnish the magnets (electric current) for the currents to run with. I have a generator that generates currents on a small scale from the air without using any magnets around it."

There was a more recent article written on the effects of earths magnetic field on gravity similar to what Ed discovered and these researchers are also talking about the existence of extra dimensions. Keep Eds magnetic steel rod experiment in mind as you read the following article.

EARTHS MAGNETIC FIELD 'BOOSTS GRAVITY'
By **Michael Brooks, Porto Portugal**

"Hidden extra dimensions are causing measurements of the strength of gravity at different locations on earth to be affected by the planet's magnetic field, French researchers say.

This is a controversial claim because no one has ever provided experimental evidence to support either the existence of extra dimensions or any interaction between gravity and electromagnetism. But lab measurements of Newton's gravitational constant G suggest that both are real.

Newton's constant, which describes the strength of the gravitational pull that bodies exert on each other, is the most poorly determined of the constants of nature. The two most accurate measurements have experimental errors of 1 part in 10,000, yet their values differ by 10 times that amount. So physicists are left with no idea of its absolute value.

Now Jean-Paul Mbelek and Marc Lachieze-Ray of the French Atomic Energy Commission near Paris say they can resolve the contradiction by taking into account the location of the labs where the experiments were carried out. The pair suggest that electromagnetism and gravity influence one another enough for gravity's pull to be noticeably affected by the earth's magnetic field.

String Theory

Their work is based on theories such as string theory that try to unify all the forces, including electromagnetism and gravity, by invoking the existence of several extra spatial dimensions.

In a paper submitted to Classical and Quantum Gravity and presented at a meeting of the European Astronomical Society in Porto, Portugal, the researchers calculated the values they would expect G to have at different locations around the world. They say it should be greater where the earth's magnetic field is stronger, with the highest measurements at the north and south magnetic poles.

The values of G measured so far seem to fit with that idea. But the researchers say the best way to test their theory would be to take accurate measurements of G at locations such as the magnetic poles and particular longitudes on the equator, and then check those values against the predictions....

Exotic Physics

But other researchers are not convinced. Clifford Will, a gravity theorist at Washington University in St Louis, Missouri, believes improvements in terrestrial experiments will eventually do away with the need for explanations that rely on such exotic physics.

"In many ways it's a scandal that we don't have an agreed value for G, but if you look at the experiments, the values have been converging," he says. "In five years or so, we'll have an agreed value."

But Mbelek does not think so. Although the precision of individual measurements is improving, he says, the values are not converging. "
…. newscientist.com/article/earths magnetic field, Michael Brooks

Maybe each latitude will need its own value for "G". There is a story similar to Ed moving huge stones in the book of Jasher. The back story of this event begins with the nation of Israel being freed from Egyptian bondage through Moses. When Moses originally left Egypt decades prior he served under King Kikianus of Cush. When King Kikianus died Moses became the King of Cush for 40 years. God sent Moses back to Israel to free Israel from slavery and take them into the land God promised Abraham he and his descendants would live in forever. Moses, by Gods power, took Israel out of Egypt and led them into the wilderness area between Egypt and what is today Israel. The Israelites were not alone in the wilderness, there were other Kingdoms already present and Moses had to get permission to cross their lands, some said yes and some said no – go around, 40 years later they made it to Israel. The results of some of these encounters follow;

The children of Esau, the Mt. Seir region ………….. free passage
The kingdom of Moab, King Sihon …………….. free passage
The kingdom of Edom ……………………………….. no passage
The wilderness of Sin ………………………… they stayed for a ……………………………………………….. season in Kadesh
The southern Canaanite region, King Arad …Israel destroyed all
Back to Moab, King Sihon, the Amorites ….Israel took the cities ………………………………………………. from Aram to Jabuk

The region of Ammom	Israel took the land from them
King Og in the land of Beshan	Israel slew King Og

....and there were others but it was when Israel encountered King Og in the land of Bashan that an extremely large monolithic stone was hoisted off of the ground by a single man, King Og. Here is the 'book of Jasher' account of this event:

"And the children of Israel turned and went up by the way of Bashan to the land of Og, King of Bashan, and Og the King of Bashan went out to meet the Israelites in Battle, and he had with him many valiant men, and a very strong force from the people of the Amorites. And Og King of Bashan was a very powerful man, but Naaron his son was exceedingly powerful, even stronger that he was. And Og said in his heart, behold now the whole camp of Israel takes up the space of three parsa [12 miles], now will I smite them at once without sword or spear. And Og went up Mount Jahaz, and took there from one large stone, the length of which was three parsa [12 miles], and he placed it on his head, and resolved to throw it upon the camp of the children of Israel, to smite all the Israelites with that stone. And the Angel of the Lord came and pierced the stone upon the head of Og, and the stone fell upon the neck of Og that Og fell to the earth on account of the weight of the stone upon his neck. At that time the Lord said to the children of Israel, be not afraid of him, for I have given him and all his people and all his land into your hand, and you shall do to him as you did to Sihon."
…... Book of Jasher 85: 21 -26

A 12 mile long stone would weigh millions of tons depending upon thickness but if you had a device that cancels gravity then you could 'float it like a hydrogen balloon'.

There is another device recorded in the book of Jasher that has even greater power than the anti-gravity device. It was used by God himself! This device was passed down from generation to generation and eventually fell into the hands of Moses and he had it with him when he went back to Egypt to free Gods people and then all through the wilderness on the way to the promised land. From the book of Jasher:

"And God heard the voice of the children of Israel in their cry, in those days, and God remembered to them his covenant which he had made with Abraham, Isaac and Jacob. And God saw the burden of the children of Israel, and their heavy work in those days [building Egypt]. And he determined to deliver them... And afterward Moses went into the Garden of Reuel which was behind the house, and he there prayed to the Lord his God, who had done mighty wonders for him. And it was that whilst he prayed he looked opposite to him, and behold a sapphire stick was placed in the ground, which was planted in the midst of the garden. And he approached the stick and he looked, and behold the name of the Lord God of Hosts was engraved thereon, written and developed upon the stick. And he read it and stretched forth his hand and he plucked it like a forest tree from the thicket, and the stick was in his hand. And this is the stick with which all the works of God were performed, after he had created heaven and earth, and all the host of them, seas, rivers and all their fishes. And when God had driven Adam from the Garden of Eden, he took the stick in his hand and went and tilled the ground from which he was taken. And the stick came down to Noah and was given to Shem and his descendants, until it came unto the hand of Abraham the Hebrew. And when Abraham had given all he had to his son Isaac, he also gave to him this stick. And when Jacob had fled to Padan-Aram, he took it into his hand, and when he returned to his father he had not left it behind him. Also when he went down to Egypt he took it into his hand and gave it to Joseph, one portion above his brethren, for Jacob had taken it by force from his brother Esau. And after the death of Joseph, the nobles of Egypt came into the house of Joseph, and the stick came into the hand of Reuel the Midianite, and when he went out of Egypt, he

took it in his hand and planted it in his garden. And all the mighty men of the Kinites tried to pluck it when they endeavored to get Zipporah his daughter, but they were unsuccessful. So that stick remained planted in the garden of Reuel, until he came that had the right to it and he took it. And when Reuel saw the stick in the hand of Moses, he wondered at it, and he gave him his daughter Zipporah for a wife."
..... Book of Jasher 77: 38-51

Later:
Moses had the stick with him at the burning bush …….. 79:3
Moses used it to tame two lions at Pharaohs palace …... 79:22
Aaron, Moses's brother cast the stick in front of Pharaoh
and it turned into a snake, then back to a stick ………... 79:36,40
Moses stretched it over the Red Sea …........................... 81:36

The God that created the heavens and the earth is a 'high tech' God;
He supplied Israel and others with an anti-gravity device so they could move huge stones.
He gave the Sapphire stick to his patriarchs throughout time to exercise his will over the earth with.
(God, Noah, Shem and his descendants, Abraham, Isaac, Jacob [Israel], Joseph, Reuel stored it, Moses used it)
He has high tech craft that his messengers use and/or God himself.
He created all of the scientific disciplines on earth and those not on the earth.

P.S.: Pharaoh survived the Red Sea incident! Right after the host of Pharaoh pursued the Israelites into the Red Sea and just prior to their destruction by the "separated waters" crashing down on them;

"And the Lord ordered an angel to take him [Pharaoh] from amongst the Egyptians, who cast him upon the land of Ninevah

and he reigned over it for a long time."
….. Jasher 81: 40-41

I also found it interesting that the account of the sapphire stick that was implanted in the ground in Reuel's garden unfolds similarly to the Sword in the Stone or Excaliber.

The stick and the sword were both stuck in place
One who is worthy to take it may remove it
A great reward, a bride, is had by removing it
Many tried to remove it but failed
They both wield great power
They both had specific purposes

THE HIDDEN CODE WITHIN THE BIBLE

There is an encrypted code embedded within the pages of the Bible that speaks of people and events all throughout history. Specific events that were recorded in the Bible centuries ago concerning specific future dates throughout earth history unfolded with astonishing accuracy. Some researchers have found events that had not happened as of yet and eventually did happen as described in the code.
The code is embedded in both the Hebrew script and the English translated script. Researchers count equal numbers of letters, ' Equidistant Letter Sequencing', paying no attention to punctuation or spaces between the words or sentences. They record each letter as they find it, according to the number of letters skipped, then they begin their search in the text for messages or words that pertain to a certain event or person.
Prior to the invention of the computer all of this was done laboriously by hand; counting and recording each letter then scanning for words within. Today there are computer programs that have been developed specifically for this purpose and what previously took years to accomplish takes only minutes today. There are some that argue that you could take any substantial

text and do the same thing with it. The problem with that is they are only looking for identifiable words anywhere in their resulting text, be it on page 1 or on page 250. Finding individual words is not the issue, its the clustering of words together in one small area that collectively have meaning concerning a particular person or event that is significant. In Bible Code research, all pertinent information is assembled collectively together in close proximity usually within a few verses of text. It's the close proximity of pertinent information that has the statisticians scratching their heads and wondering how this could have been written without the aid of a computer so many centuries ago.

There was a man, Yacov Rambsel, that God gave a gift to discern these codes without the use of a computer. He said every so many letters equally spaced within the script would just stand out from the page, a 3-D effect, as he was reading the Torah and he could read the encoded message as he followed the normal text. Mr. Rambsel wrote 2 books full of the messages that he discovered in the Torah as he poured over the scriptures; "Yeshua", and "His Name is Jesus". His second book tells about the "Rabbis Experiment" which was an experiment done on behalf of a group of skeptical observers or researchers. In my mind, this proves beyond a shadow of a doubt that the Bible was written with encoded messages by a being of amazing intelligence; A.K.A. – The Supreme Being or God. The following is an excerpt concerning the 'Rabbis Experiment' from Yacov Rambsel's book, "His Name is Jesus";

"But that was only the beginning of the story, in a 1994 follow-up paper, the team of researchers recorded the results of their search for pairs of encoded words that relate to **events that occurred long after the time when Moses wrote the Torah**. They selected the names of thirty-four of the most prominent Rabbis and Jewish Sages who lived during the last 200 years. The process was simple, the researchers simply selected the 34 Sages with the longest biographies in the Encyclopedia of 'Great Men of Israel', a well-respected Hebrew reference book. They asked the computer program to search the text of the Torah for close word pairs coded at equally spaced intervals that contained the names of the famous Rabbis paired with the dates of their birth or death (using the Hebrew month and day). The Jewish people celebrate the memory of their famous Sages by commemorating the dates of their deaths. Incredibly, the computer program found every single one of the 34 names of these famous Rabbis embedded in the text of Genesis, paired at significantly close proximity with the actual date of birth or the date of death. The odds against these particular names occurring by chance were calculated by the Israeli mathematicians as only one chance in 775,000,000! The scientists and editors at the Statistical Science Journal who reviewed the experimental data were naturally astonished. They demanded that the Israeli scientists run the computer test program again on a second sample. This time they searched for the next 32 most prominent Jewish Sages listed in the 'Encyclopedia'. To the astonishment of the skeptical reviewers, the results were equally successful with the 2nd set of famous Sages. The staggering result of the combined test revealed that the names and dates of birth or death of every one of the 66 most famous Jewish Sages were coded in close proximity within the text of Genesis.

Despite the fact that all of the reviewers held previous beliefs against the inspiration of the scriptures, the overwhelming evidence and the integrity of the data were such that the Journal reluctantly agreed to publish the article in its August 1994 issue under the title 'Equidistant Letter Sequences in the Book of Genesis'."..............

Robert Kass, the editor of Statistical Science, wrote this comment about the study:

"Our referees were baffled: their prior beliefs made them think the book of Genesis could not possibly contain meaningful references to modern day individuals, yet when the authors carried out additional analysis and checks the effect persisted. The paper is thus offered to Statistical Science readers as a challenging puzzle."........

An article in Bible Review Magazine by Dr. Jeffrey Satinover, in October 1995, reported that the mathematical probability of these 66 names of Jewish Sages and their dates of birth or death occurring by chance in an ancient text like Genesis was less than 1 chance in 2 ½ billion!
"Interestingly, the researchers attempted to reproduce these results by running the computer program on other religious Hebrew texts outside the Bible, including the Samaritan Pentateuch, the Samaritans developed their own variant text of the 5 books of Moses, called the Samaritan Pentateuch, which differs in many very small textual details from the standard Hebrew Bible (Known as the Masoretic Text). Despite the surface similarity of the 2 texts, the researchers could not detect word pairs in the Samaritan Pentateuch or any other Hebrew text outside the Bible".
.... Dr. Jeffrey Satinover"
…….. cited from Yakov Rambsels book "His Name is Jesus" 1997, pg. 19

It is apparent that the Masoretic text is the most accurate divinely inspired version of the first 5 books of the Bible [Torah]; as men re-wrote it or re-translated the Bible the accuracy fell away. To have a version of the Bible that can be copyrighted - the new text has to be changed by at least 10% from the original and that pollutes Gods word after the 1st re-write much less the dozens and dozens of new translations we have today.

The following is a list of some of the interesting messages Yakov Rambsel found encoded in the Old Testament, each found in just one verse of the Bible;

Jonah ...... 3 : 10 ... Equidistant sequence a sign
Jonah ....4 : 7 ..... A breastplate for upright Jesus
Jonah ....2 : 8 ..... To distinguish set apart the Shepard Lord
Esther ......4 : 7 ...... Shiloh (Messiah) Jesus
Esther ......6 : 3 ...... From the Soul of Jesus my sin offering
Jeremiah .23 : 9 ...... Jesus Lord
Joshua .....6 : 4 ...... My Lord Jesus
Isaiah .....58 : 12 .... Prince Jesus
Ruth ....4 : 4 ...... Messiah from Israel
1 Kings .....8 : 20 ... My Name is Jesus
Ezra ....7 : 11.... Jesus our Messiah ark of rescue
1 Samuel ...2 :8 ...... Jesus Lamp stand Menorah
1 Samuel ...2 : 18 ... Punctured bread Jesus Lord
1 Samuel ...17: 32 ... I prey thee feel the Love he is Jesus
Zachariah ..6: 15 .... And you shall know Jehovah has sent me to you
Zachariah ..3: 8 ..... Jehovah fathered Jesus Virgin Mary

Encoded messages in the Bible that were found prior to the event happening:

October 1994 – Dr. Eliyahu Ripps discovered; "Yitzak Rabin assassin will **assassinate**"
---November 1995 – Rabin was assassinated

May 1994 – Michael Drosnin discovered; "Shoemaker–Levy will pound Jupiter July 16 1994"

July 16 1994, The comet broke up into a string of pearls and they, one by one, pounded the surface of Jupiter a total of 21 times.

184.
And the final pre-event discovery;

October 1994 – Dr. Elyahu Ripps discovered; "From Feb. 25 1996 all his people to war"
---Feb. 25 1996 – This was the first day of an onslaught of bombings that lasted 9 days. Tel Aviv and Jerusalem suffered 61 fatalities which drove Israel back into a 'State of War'.

Michael Drosnin found a message encoded about the Oklahoma City bombing;

Genesis 29 :25 Oklahoma
Genesis 30 :20 Death
Genesis 35 :3 ..Murrah Building
Genesis 35 :3 ..Desolated Slaughtered
Genesis 35 :3 ..Killed torn to pieces
Genesis 35 :5 ..There will be terror
Genesis 37 : 8 .McVeigh
Genesis 37 :12 Timothy

I personally found the following messages concerning the father of the "evolution religion" encoded within 8 verses in the book of Ezekiel chapter 34 : 22 – 29;

Darwins Trap ….. Men fell from Darwins lies ….. Anti Hero

I also searched some of the other names and words used in the characteristics of Big Foot according to the B.F.R.O., The Big Foot Research Organization;

Habakkuk 3: 5-15, within 11 verses;
…..."Big Foot Roar Yeti Foul Odor Chit Chat"

Song of Solomon 4: 11 – 5: 9, 13- 14 within 17 verses;
……."Big Foot Ohmah Almos Yowie Lion Roar Eats Fish Frog
……...Deer Boar Hog Elk Pig"

185.
Ezekiel 40: 40–48, within 9 verses;
…......"Big Foot Yeti Snow Man Hairy Man Forest Men"

Chapter 8

SCIENCE IN THE BIBLE: SOME MODERN SCIENTIFIC DISCOVERIES WERE RECORDED WITHIN THE PAGES OF THE BIBLE CENTURIES AGO

Flat earth or round earth; Megellan and Elcano's expeditions of 1519-1521

"It is he the sitteth upon the circle of the earth"
….. Isaiah 40: 22

Quarantine a person with an infectious disease;

"All the days wherein the plague shall be in him he shall be defiled; he is unclean: he shall dwell alone; without the camp shall his habitation be."
……. Leviticus 13: 46

The Hydrologic Cycle;" rain – evaporation – cloud formation"; repeat

"He bindeth up the waters in his thick clouds; and the cloud is not rent [torn] under them."
…... Job 26: 8

"For he maketh small the drops of water: they pour down rain according to the vapor thereof: Which the clouds do drop and distil upon man abundantly."
…... Job 36: 27-28

"To make the weight for the winds; and he weigheth the waters by measure. When he made a decree for the rain, and a way for

the lightning of the thunder."
...... Job 28: 25-26

"All the rivers run into the sea; yet the sea is not full; unto the place from whence the rivers **come, thither** they return again."
..... Ecclesiastes 1: 7

The second Law of Thermodynamics; by French Scientist Sadi Carnot in 1824
(Everything tends toward decay)

"And, thou, Lord, in the beginning has laid the foundation of the earth; and the heavens are the works of thy hands. They shall perish, but thou **remainest**; and they all shall wax old as doth a garment."
..... Hebrews 1: 10-11

Trade Winds and Meteorology; 1st Century Portugal

"The wind **goeth** toward the south, and **turneth** about unto the north; it **whirleth** about continually, and the wind **returneth** again to his circuits."
...... Ecclesiastes 1: 6

Giant Human Skeletons; even though evolutionary scientists are hiding them

"There were giants in the earth in those days; **and also after that**, when the sons of God came in unto the daughters of men, and they bare children to them, the same became mighty men which were of old, men of renown."
...... Genesis 6: 4
Notice the phrase in the above verse; **"and also after that"**, possibly today

"And there we saw the giants, the sons of Anak, which come of the giants: and we were in our own sight as grasshoppers, and so we were in their sight."
……… Numbers 13: 33

Hydrothermal Vents in the oceans, discovered in 1977

"Hast thou entered into the springs of the sea? Or hast thou walked in the search of the depth?"
…… Job 38: 16

Dinosaurs;
Terminology first coined in 1841 by Sir Richard Owen - the 1611 Bible translation records them as Dragons, Behemoth and Leviathan.

"Behold now Behemoth, **which I made with thee**; he eateth grass as an ox. Lo now, his strength is in his belly. He moveth his tail like a cedar: the sinews of his stones are wrapped together. His bones are as strong pieces of brass; his bones are like bars of iron. He is the chief of the ways of God: he that made him can make his sword to approach unto him. Surely the mountains bring him forth food, where all the beasts of the field play. He lieth under the shady trees, in the covert of the reed, and fens. The shady trees cover him with their shadow; the willows of the brook compass him about. Behold, he drinketh up a river, and hasteth not: **he trusteth that he can draw up Jordan into his mouth**. He taketh it with his eyes: his nose pierceth through snares. "
……. Job 40: 15 – 24

"In that day the Lord with his sore and great and strong sword shall punish leviathan the piercing serpent, even leviathan that crooked serpent; and he shall slay the dragon that is in the sea."
…….. Isaiah 27: 1

"Thou didst divide the sea by thy strength: thou **breakest** the heads of the dragons in the waters. Thou **breakest** the heads of Leviathan in pieces, and **gavest** him to be meat [food] for the people inhabiting the wilderness."
…... Psalms 74: 13– 14

"Therefor I will wail and howl, I will go stripped and naked: I will make a wailing like the dragons, and mourning as the owls."
…... Micah 1: 8

"Which I made with thee" -- In Job 40 :15 above, **God said he made Dinosaurs with men**. Some have claimed that behemoth was a modern animal such as a hippopotamus (river horse) but the description of behemoth said he moves his tail like a cedar tree. I take that to mean his tail is large and it has very little articulation to it when he moves. Hippopotamus's probably just open their mouths and gulp water down when they drink, **a long necked dinosaur would have to 'draw up' water** similar to a Giraffe.

Shipping Lanes using Oceanic currents; Mathew Maury – 1800's

"The fowl of the air, and the fish of the sea, and whatsoever passeth through the paths of the seas."
…... Psalms 8: 9

Psychosomatics; late 1900's

"A merry heart doeth good like a medicine, but a broken spirit drieth the bones."
…... Proverbs 17: 22

"The spirit of man will sustain his infirmity; but a wounded spirit who can bear?"
….. Proverbs 18: 14

The Placebo Effect or 'science based' faith healing – related to Psychosomatics. The doctor deceives the patient by allowing and encouraging them to think they are receiving a medically proven cure when they are receiving a treatment that has no basis in truth. Doctors are relying on the faith of the patient in 'believing' they will be cured.

The Red Shift (Gods Big Bang or stretch); – shows an expanding universe; Walter Adams, 1908

"It is he that sitteth upon the circle of the earth, and the inhabitants thereof are as grasshoppers; **that stretches out the heavens as a curtain**, and spreadeth them out as a tent to dwell in."
…... Isaiah 40: 22

"Who coverest thyself with light as with a garment: **who stretchest out the heavens like a curtain**:…who maketh the clouds his chariot: "
... Psalms 104: 2-3

"He hath made the earth by his power, he hath established the world by his wisdom, **and hath stretched out the heavens by his understanding.**"
... Jeremiah 51: 15

Planet Formation in the vacuum of space;
NASA space shuttle experiment – small dust sized particles were placed in clear bottles for observation and the particles stuck together as if they were magnetized when beyond earths gravity;

"...who can stay the bottles of heaven, when the dust **groweth** into hardness, and the clods cleave fast together?"
..... Job 38: 37-38

Water exists in outer space; 2nd and 3rd heavens

"Praise Him, Ye heavens of heavens, and ye waters that be above the heavens."
...... Psalm 148: 4

[The New Jerusalem coming down from heaven to earth] "And he [God] showed me a pure river of water of life, clear as crystal, proceeding out of the throne of God and of the Lamb [Jesus]. In the midst of the street of it, and on either side of the river, was there the tree of life..."
.... Revelation 22: 1-2

Iron and brass tools or weapons, **Metallurgy; Science guesses first used between 1300-1800 B.C.**

Lamech was born 874 years after Adams creation or approximately 5100 years ago in about 3100 B.C.
Lamech had a son that was a metallurgist; Tubal-Cain,(Tubal-Cain died a very young man, perhaps between 50 and 100 years old, probably before his 100th birthday); Remember, people lived much longer back then, Noah-lived 930 years, Methuselah – 969, Lamech - 777

"And Zillah [Lamechs Wife], she also bare Tubal-Cain, an instructor of every artificer [metal worker] in brass and iron: and the sister of Tubal-Cain was Naamah."
.....Genesis 4 :22

Lamech was born in approximately ...3100 B.C.
Perhaps 200 at Tubal-Cains birth?? ...-200

Tubal-Cain died young?? ....-100
~ **Date of first Iron and Brass** ....**2800 B.C.***
*Tubal-Cain had to first learn it and master it before he could be an instructor in metallurgy and for this reason brass and iron most likely pre-existed Tubal-Cain.

Teleportation – Transfiguration – Translation – Transformation;

Men have not cracked the code on these as of yet but some theories in mathematics make translation or teleportation possible.

"By faith Enoch was translated that he should not see death; and was not found, because God had translated him for before his translation he had this testimony, that he pleased God."
..... Hebrews 11: 5

"And no marvel; for Satan himself is transformed into an Angel of light. Therefor it is no great thing if his ministers also be transformed as the ministers of righteousness; whose end shall be according to their works."
.... 2 Corinthians 11: 14– 15

"And after 6 days Jesus taketh Peter, James, and John his brother, and bringeth them up into a high mountain apart, and was transfigured before them; and his face did shine as the sun, and his raiment [clothing] was white as the light. And behold, there appeared unto them Moses and Elias [both physically dead for centuries but their spirits were alive] talking with him."
...... Mathew 17: 1 – 3

GOD KNOWS ALL ABOUT MEN – PAST, PRESENT, AND FUTURE - THAT INCLUDES YOU!

There are trillions of stars and planets in the universe!

"He [God] telleth the number of the stars; he called them all by their names."
..... Psalms 147: 4

God knows all 7 billion people that are alive on the earth today by name. God also has individual plans for each of our lives. Not only us but also all that have been and gone and those that are to come.

"Thus saith the Lord, thy redeemer, **and he that formed thee from the womb.**"
..... Isaiah 44: 24

"For I know the thoughts that I think toward you, saith the Lord, thoughts of peace, and not of evil, to give you an expected end."
.... Jeremiah 29: 11

"**Before I formed thee in the belly I knew thee**; and before thou camest forth out of the womb I sanctified thee, and I ordained thee a prophet unto the nations."
..... Jeremiah 1: 5

God knows how many hairs are on each of our heads!
There are 7 **billion** + men alive today- plus the millions before us.

"But the very hairs of your head are all numbered."
..... Mathew 10: 30

194.
God knows the specific DNA sequence that makes up your body that you are 'living in' upon the earth!
Those past, the present (7 billion +) and the future millions.

"Forasmuch then as we are the offspring of God,..."
.... Acts 17: 29

"For I am fearfully and wonderfully made."
….. Psalms 139: 14

God made time, space, matter, science, life, mathematics, music, art, language and everything else!

"... I am the Lord that maketh all things; that stretcheth forth the heavens alone; that spreadeth abroad the earth by myself."
….. Isaiah 44: 24

God wrote the number 1 bestselling book (by far) in the history of the world; The Bible!
*Who said Jesus never wrote a book!

"All scripture is given by inspiration of God [God placed the thoughts into each writers mind], and is profitable for doctrine, for reproof, for correction, for instruction in righteousness."
….. 2 Timothy 3: 16

Chapter 9

EVIDENCE THAT PROVIDES OVERWHELMING "REASONABLE DOUBT" ABOUT THE EVOLUTION RELIGION

In 1912, at the Municipal Electric plant in Thomas Oklahoma, workers found a cast iron pot in an unmolested coal seam that evolutionary scientists claim is 250,000,000 years old. How can an iron pot get inside of a 250,000,000 year old coal bed that has never been dug into, drilled into, blasted into or had any other means of access into. The evolution "story" that evolutionists are guarding so closely states that men did not evolve from monkeys until 3,000,000 years ago, either monkeys were educated in metallurgy or their story is, as you are finding out, incorrect! Rule number 5 of the Scientific Method states that "If there is one shred of evidence that falsifies the hypothesis then the hypothesis is false, form another hypothesis." This is but one of a thousand shreds of evidence that falsifies the evolution hypothesis. The cast iron pot wasn't the only thing found in coal deposits over the decades; another was a long handled intricately detailed brass bell, another was a gold chain and I am assuming that there have been dozens of others that never were reported and recorded. How did these artifacts get into the coal layers that we see today? When God caused the flood he was fully aware that men would use anything they could find to keep themselves afloat. They probably attempted to preserve some of their personal belongings as they clung onto floating debris. The Bible records that the mountains were being effected by earthquakes during the flood which would cause tsunamic activity that would scour and wash away and bury cities, perhaps 14,000 feet or more. It rained for 40 days and nights but the water covered the earth for over a year. Organic material would sink forming today's coal seams, anything dropped or washed onto this organic material while the seam was forming would be trapped inside. The seams of coal are not millions of years old, they were formed during the flood 4400

years ago and the man-made artifacts trapped inside proves it. Evolutionary science claims that coal was formed 250,000,000 years ago.
Carbon 14 has a half life of 5770 years and is still barely measurable at 50,000 years. All Carbon 14 radiation should have dissipated from the coal seams around the world 250,000,000 – 50,000 years ago. Today Carbon 14 is still measurable in coal and diamonds.

Earths atmosphere gains 21 pounds of Carbon 14 each year. The atmosphere will reach Carbon 14 equilibrium when the production rate of Carbon 14 and the destruction rate of Carbon 14 are equal. At the current production rate of 21 pounds a year it calculates that the earth should reach the point of equilibrium in 30,000 years. Radio Carbon or Carbon 14 is still forming 28 – 37% faster than it is decaying away which means the earth is not in Carbon 14 equilibrium yet and the earth is less than 30,000 years old.
….. cited from Kent Hovinds creation seminar, 2005

THE SHRINKING SUN

"Since 1836, more that 100 different observers at the Royal Greenwich Observatory and the U.S. Naval Observatory have made direct, visual measurements that suggest that **the sun is shrinking** at a rate of 0.1% each century or **about 5 feet an hour.**"
…..Dr. John "Jack" Eddy and Aram Boornazian, Bulletin of the American Astronomical Society, Vol. 11.

The sun is losing 5,00,000 tons of matter per second, it's **shrinking at the rate of 43,800 feet or 8.29 miles a year.** It makes sense then, if we went back in time you would expect the sun to be larger than what we see today. There is a problem with applying the current rate of shrinkage to the sun over the last 3.8 billion years, which is , according to evolutionary scientists, when life on earth emerged and most life would need the light from the sun to live; animals eat plants, plants use photosynthesis to make their own food and that requires sunlight. Sunlight would also be required for eyes to evolve, finding a mate or looking for food, etc. The rate of shrinkage of a sphere as you go back in time diminishes because the volume of a sphere increases or decreases exponentially as size increases or decreases.

Example: If you have ten 10 **foot** spheres full of water would their volumes equal one 100 foot sphere full of water? No
One 10 foot **sphere** would contain 523.5987 cubic feet of water, multiplied by 10 and the combined cubic feet of water is 5235.987 cubic feet of water for the 10 smaller spheres.

One 100 foot **sphere contains** 523,598.70 cubic feet of water or 100 times more water than the 10 - 10 foot spheres combined.

For illustration purposes; To account for the higher volume of matter burning inside the sun and slowing the shrinkage rate as we go back in time we are going to use an average shrink rate of just one one hundredth of one mile per year in our calculation instead on today's current shrink rate of 8.29 miles a year:

Todays shrink **rate**; (3,800,000,000 X 8.29 miles/year [today's average] = a crazy number)

1 **One** hundredth of a mile per year shrink rate; 3,800,000,000 X .01 = 38,000,000 miles

Today the sun is about 860,000 miles in diameter. Even at this miniscule average shrink rate of .01 **miles** a year that would still be an enormous sun 3.8 billion years ago. Add 38,000,000 miles to 860,000 miles and you have a sun with a diameter of at least 38,860,000 miles back when life supposedly first began on the earth.

On average, Mercury is only 36 million miles from today's sun; Venus is 67 million miles from today's sun and the earth is 93,000,000 miles away from the sun. At some point in the past all of the water on earth would have boiled off and the earth would have been more Venus like. Then there is the gravity issue, the closer planets would have been drawn in or slung off into space. There would not have been granite on the earth because granite can only form in a non-molten state and if you heat granite to its molten state and allow it to cool it will no longer be granite; it will be rhyolite.

The burn rate of the sun in not an issue for Gods Creation Model based on the Bible. God records in Genesis the creation of the Sun and Moon:

"And God said let there be lights in the firmament of the heaven to divide the day from the night; and let them be for signs, and for seasons, and for days, and years: And let them be for lights in the firmament of the heaven to give light upon the earth: and it was so. And God made two great lights; the greater light [Sun] to rule the day, and the lesser light [Moon] to rule the night: he made the stars also. And God set them in the firmament of heaven to give light on the earth,"
…… Genesis 1: 14 - 17

The Bible records that **the earth is about 6000 years old** today and using today's burn rate we can get a close estimate of the original size of the sun at creation:

6000 x 8.29 = 49,740 miles (burn off since creation)

49,740 + 860,000 = 909,740 miles in diameter at the creation. The sun is about 5 ½ % smaller since creation.

If we go further into the future and divide the entire diameter of today's sun by today's burn rate:
860,000 miles divided by 8.29 miles/year = 103,739 years approximately*

*Probably much less since the volume of matter inside of a sphere becomes exponentially less as it shrinks in size as pointed out above. Also, if science is correct in their hypothesis of Super Nova's then the sun will expand and it will go out with a bang and shoot off across the galaxy instead of slowly burning out. (My question: What mechanism would cause it to shoot off across the galaxy?)
The 'Wise Wise' men of the evolution religion want you to believe that the sun is going to burn for millions and millions more years to come as is has been supposedly burning for millions or billions of years in the past. It is theorized that when the sun burns out it expands larger than our Solar System and engulfs everything in its path. Perhaps that will cleanse the earth of unwanted microbes and diseases and radioactive waste that men have been accumulating for the last century.

"Lift up your eyes to the heavens, and look upon the earth beneath: for the heavens shall vanish away like smoke, and the earth shall wax old like a garment, and they that dwell therein shall die in like manner; but my salvation shall be forever, and my righteousness shall not be abolished."
….. Isaiah 51: 6

"But the Day of the Lord will come as a thief in the night; in the which the heavens shall pass away with a great noise, and the elements shall melt with fervent heat, the earth also and the works that are therein shall be burned up. Seeing then that all these things shall be dissolved, what manner of persons ought ye to be in all Holy conversation and Godliness, looking for and hastening unto the coming of the Day of God, wherein the heavens being on fire shall be dissolved, and the elements shall

melt with a fervent heat. Nevertheless we, according to his promise, look for new heavens and a new earth, wherein dwelleth righteousness."
…... 2 Peter 3: 10– 13

"And I saw a new heaven and an new earth: For the 1st heaven and 1st earth were passed away; and there was no more sea, and I John saw the Holy City, New Jerusalem, coming down from God out of heaven, prepared as a bride adorned for her husband. And he [Jesus] that sat upon the throne said, Behold, I make all things new. And he said unto me, Write: For these words are true and faithful. And he said unto me, It is done, I am Alpha and Omega, the Beginning and the End. I will give unto him that is athirst of the fountain of the Water of Life freely. He that overcometh shall inherit all things: And I will be his God, and he shall be my son."
….. Revelation 21: 1 -2, 5 -7

"For as many as are led by the Spirit of God, they are the Sons of God."
…... Romans 8: 14

SUPER NOVA

Astronomers have observed that about every 30 years a star 'dies' and explodes into a 'Super Nova'.
If our universe is billions of years old, there should be several hundred million Super Nova's out there but there are fewer than 300. The only conclusion is that the universe is only a few thousand years old.
…….. Cited from Dr. Kent Hovinds Creation Seminar, 2005

Do Super Novas really destroy the solar system when they die? Some say yes, some say no.
In 1992, the "Line of Sight" technique or Doppler Effect was used to discover the first motion detected planets in the universe. The very first planets detected orbited around a Pulsar (The remains of

an exploded Super Nova) #PSR-B1257 +12. The planets that once orbited the Sun prior to the Suns death are still intact and now orbiting the Pulsar.
...Citation: Dr. Danny Faulkner, "Universe by Design"

The conclusion has to be that when Super Novas explode they are energetic but not energetic enough to destroy the planets in their respective Solar Systems. The Bible says that one day the earth will no longer have a sea. Perhaps our Sun is going to expand into a giant fireball engulfing the Solar System and burn off the surfaces of each planet, including our sea.

Dr. John "Jack" Eddy, a U.S. Naval Academy educated **astronomer who worked at the High Altitude Observatory at the National Center for Atmospheric Research and later NASA** stated:
"There is no evidence based solely on solar observations that the sun is 4.5 to 5 billion years old. " He continued: "I suspect that the sun is 4.5 billion years old. However, given some new and unexpected results to the contrary, and some time for frantic recalculation and theoretical readjustment, I suspect that we could live with Bishop Usher's value for the age of the earth and sun [4004 B.C.]. I don't think we have much in the way of observational evidence in astronomy to conflict with that."
…..Dr. John Eddy, author of "The Maunder Minimum",1978

An Alaskan Mammoth was unearthed in the early 1970's **and 2 different parts of the same Mammoth were sent to 2 different laboratories** for Carbon dating:

"One part of the Vollosovitch mammoth carbon dated at 29,500 years old and another part at 44,000."
…..Troy L. Pewe, Quaternary Stratographic Nomenclature In Unglaciated Central Alaska, Geographic Survey Professional Paper 826 (U.S. Government Printing Office, 1975, pg. 30)

The worldwide Flood of Noah happened about 4400 years ago in about 2350 B.C.

The oldest Desert on earth today ------The Sahara; it's about 4000 years old
The oldest Tree ------------------------- Brisclecone Pine; it's about 4300 years old
The oldest Oceanic Reef --------------- Great Barrier; it's about 4200 years old

EVOLUTIONIST DEVOUR THEIR OWN!

Kay Behrensmeyer is a geologist who was studying and attempting to date volcanic ash layers by using the Potassium Argon (K-Ar) dating technique. Kay concluded that a particular ash layer, the KBS Tuff, which was named after her, was 212 – 230 million years old.
…... Cited from Nature, April 18, 1970, pg. 226

In 1972, Richard Leakey was digging under the KBS Tuff and found a normal human skull. This skull, #KNM-ER 1470, was dated and found to be 2.9 million years old. "It's important to note that there were no disturbances in the layers of soil around the skull meaning it was not a burial site after the volcanic ash deposit."
….. Bones of Contention, Roger Lewin, pg. 257

How did a supposedly young 2.9 million year old human skull end up underneath a supposedly 212 -230 million year old unmolested ash layer? According to the evolutionists religion the evolutionists could not date the skull more than 3 million years because that is the outer limit of the age of a human skull in their religion (their religions imaginary story-line) and men have supposedly only been de-apenized for 3,000,000 years. [De-apenized; a fantasy word that means; evolutionarily advanced beyond the DNA of apes].

After all of Kays hard work, publicity and agreement from the scientific community from around the world the evolutionists were forced to go back and "re-test" the ash layer. Ten new samples were taken and now the ash layer dates from .52 – 2.64 million years old which **"conveniently"** falls within the outside parameters of a human skull in the evolution claim of **mans de-apenizement** 3,000,000 years ago. Evolutionists make up or 'select' any number that they need so it fits into their religious beliefs. The ash layer went from an outside estimate of 230 million years down to .52 or one half of one million years old [4600% error] just to make room for a skull that can't be over 3 million years old. (Our tuition and tax dollars at work)

…. The above events were cited in part through Bones of Contention, Roger Lewin, and Dr. Kent Hovinds Creation Seminar, 2005

Not only does the evolution religion or 'Science' force itself upon and victimize the whole world but it also victimizes its own.

Today's scientists consider Potassium Argon dating (used in the above story) to be the most trusted and reliable method available to date volcanic ash deposits. The theory; When a volcanic eruption occurs all of the Potassium Argon that is present gets released and that 'resets' the clock for Potassium Argon decay in volcanic ash.

When a scientist dates an ash deposit the number that they derive would be the number of years since the last eruption. Dr. Andrew Snelling works as a geologist and he points out a few problems with Potassium Argon dating; there have been several volcanic eruptions in the past that the date of the eruption was known and when scientists dated the ash layers from the known eruptions the numbers that they got did not match the years since the eruption as the 'Theory' or supposed science suggests:

POTASSIUM ARGON DATING WITH KNOWN ERUPTION DATES- The numbers don't match

Mt. Etna in Sicily **erupted in 1972** - Potassium Argon dated to have erupted 210,000-490,000 years ago.

Mt. Saint Helens, Washington, **1986** – Potassium Argon dated to have erupted 2,800,000 years ago.

Kilauea, Hawaii **erupted in 1959** – Potassium Argon dated to have erupted 1.7–15.3 million years ago.

"These and other examples raise a critical question, if Radiometric dating fails to give an accurate date on something of which we do know the true age, then how can it be trusted to give us the correct age for rocks that had no human observers to record when they formed? If the methods don't work on rocks of known age, it is most unreasonable to trust that they work on rocks of unknown age."
…….. article above cited from "answersingenesis/article/2007/05/30/how old is the earth"

ONTOGENY RECAPITULATES PHYLOGENY- Proven to be false in 1875

During the 1860's and 70's, there was an embryology professor at the University of Jena in Germany named Earnst Haeckel. Earnst read Darwins book and he decided to help Darwin and Darwin's hypothesis by creating a model of embryonic man that was going through the various stages of evolutionary development while inside the womb of its mother. Earnst came up with the Biogenic Law. The Law states that a human embryo supposedly goes through 4 evolutionary phases in the mother's womb:

F – Fish
A – Amphibian
R – Reptile
M – Mammal

Earnst gave the 4 Phases of development names that were as "Scientific" as he could make them sound in the hope that his audience would believe his claim;

Ontogeny Recapitulates Phylogeny

Ontogeny.......... Staged Growth of the Baby
Recapitulates ... Goes through the 4 phases again
Phylogeny .... Evolutionarily Sequence

Earnst Haeckel's claim is that the baby starts out with gills like a **fish, that**'s what Earnst wanted everyone to believe when he pointed at the skin folding up like an accordion at the inside **bend** of the neck. The embryo then turns into an amphibian, then a reptile and finally a man or mammal before its ever born. It turns out Earnst was engaged in his own "Career Building" agenda so by helping Darwin with evidence for his evolution hypothesis he was also helping himself, Earnst faked his embryonic drawings to make it look like they were, as Darwin supposed, evolving. By adding false claims to his faked subject matter in his embryonic drawings Earnst had a mutiny on his hands with the other **professors** at the University at Jena. **Earnst** made giant posters of his fake **embryonic transformative** stages of humans and dogs each showing the same **evolutionarily** development. **Earnst** toured Germany giving lectures on "Ontogeny Recapitulates Phylogeny". Earnst also wrote books; **'The Wonders of Life'**, ' The History of Creation', based on Darwins **theory** and his false claim of evolution happening in the womb and 'The Dual State' which added more fuel to Hitlers murderous plan.

206.
In 1875, The University of Jena held an "In House" trial for Earnst Haeckel concerning the falsifying of his embryonic developmental stages and was found guilty by 6 of his fellow professors and fired from the university. After Earnst was fired he gave this statement in defense of himself:

"A small percent of my embryonic drawings are forgeries; those namely, for which the observed material is so incomplete or insufficient as to fill in and reconstruct the missing links by hypothesis and comparative synthesis......
I should feel utterly condemned... were it not that hundreds of the best observers, and biologists lie under the same charge."
.... Earnst Haeckel, Trial Records, University of Jena, 1875

Darwins Book........................... 1859
Earnst Haeckel's Drawings 1869
Earnst was guilty of fraud 1875
Earnst's fraud still in use ....2014 – 15 - 16 – 17 -???

Earnst was a proven liar and forger over 135 years ago. It's time to remove Mr. Haeckel's forgeries and fraud from today's science books. Earnst was trying to show missing links or latent progressions that did not exist, he openly confesses that 100's of the best observers are liars when it comes to manipulating their work to achieve an outcome that they desire.
... The above article is cited in part from Dr. Hovinds Creation Seminar, 2005

"**As thou knowest not** what is the way of the spirit, nor **how the bones do grow in the womb of her that is with child**: even so thou knowest not the works of God who maketh all."
... Ecclesiastes 11: 5

I have included a couple of 'quotes' from Earnst Haeckel so you may have a more complete picture of the racist mind set that he shared with Darwin and Hitler:

"The lesser races [of men] were both inferior and worth less: "Woolly-Haired" peoples are incapable of a true inner culture or of a higher mental development........ no woolly haired nation has ever had an important history."
..... Earnst Haeckel, The History of Creation; Or the Development of the Earth and its inhabitants by the Action of Natural Causes, 1876, pg. 10

"Since the lower races – such as the Veddahs or Australian Negroes [both are men]– are psychologically nearer to the mammals – apes and dogs – than to the civilized European, we must, therefore, assign a totally different value to their lives."
..... Earnst Haeckel, The Wonders of Life, 1905, pg. 390---
(Germanies tax and tuition dollars at work)

We know that Darwin, Earnst and Hitler all thought this way- placing different values on human life. Thinking themselves favored more than other men because they were evolved more than other men which, they supposed, afforded them a higher status and value than other men.

As mentioned previously; men are 3 part beings: Spirit, Soul and Body. Our bodies are just temporary vessels that we need to live on the earth. The color of the body that we dwell in makes absolutely no difference to God, he made us and when he finished with his creation he looked at it and he said; "It is good", and the color of a body shouldn't make a difference to men either. There is no such thing as a 'lower race' of man or a 'higher race', we are all "men" in the eyes of the Lord. We are Gods most cherished creation, he made the entire universe just for us.

In the following article – soft tissue, fresh not fossilized, was found in a layer of rock that science claims is 350,000,000 years old. Like the Kay Behrensmeyer article earlier, it looks like scientists are going to have to re-think their estimation of the age of the layer from 350,000,000 to something much younger to 'allow it to exist' in their religion;

"According to an online story from 'Science Daily', February 18, 2013, "Ancient Fossilized Sea Creatures Yield Oldest Biomolecules Isolated Directly from a Fossil?", original organic materials (aka "soft tissue") called quinones were recently found in supposedly 350-million-year-old (myo) crinoid fossils found in the Midwestern U.S. However, studies have shown that cells and tissues from once-living things can only survive the animal's death—even under optimal conditions, like dry freezing conditions—for tens of thousands of years.

Much like original tissue found in supposedly 68 myo T.rex bones and a supposedly 80 myo mosasaur fossil, these original crinoid compounds, which often serve as pigments or as toxins to discourage predators, join a growing list of evidence that questions the age evolution assigns to such "primitive" fossils. Even worse for Darwinism, these findings are not coming primarily from creation science but from secular evolutionary science, which has yet to come to grips with the data.

Beyond the fact that such tissue can only survive for thousands of years, the Science Daily article also states that the crinoids in which the quinones were found "appear to have been buried alive in storms during the Carboniferous Period, when North America was covered with vast inland seas." It adds that they were "buried quickly and isolated from the water above by layers of fine-grained sediment... " So, to paraphrase, apparently these "sea lilies" were buried quickly in sediments by what must have been catastrophic ocean storms. If you didn't know better you might think it was referring to Noah's flood! But, of course, that's impossible because the flood took place roughly only 4,500 years ago. Either that or secular science has a lot of explaining to do.

In the face of such evidence, which strongly supports the Biblical time-frame for creation about 6,000 years ago, evolutionists

continue to cry "bacterial contamination" and/or mislead the public about the ability of anaerobic (oxygen free) conditions to preserve such tissue. In the meantime, they're hoping against hope to discover some magical natural mechanism to explain how such matter can last for hundreds of millions of years, contrary to their own facts. But hope isn't science and neither is magic. The obvious conclusion is that these crinoids are crying, "Flood, " as in the worldwide flood of the Bible."
... tisfortrex.com: Thomas, B. 2008. "Dinosaur Soft Tissue: Biofilm or Blood Vessels? Acts & Facts 37

This next article is about 3 different dinosaur specimens that are claimed to be 65-80 million years old. Again, evolutionists are going to have to go back and rewrite their religion to replace the unproven hopes of their imaginations with actual facts:

"March 24, 2005

NC State Paleontologist Discovers Soft Tissue in Dinosaur Bones

Conventional wisdom among paleontologist states that when dinosaurs died and became fossilized, soft tissues didn't preserve – the bones were essentially transformed into "rocks" through a gradual replacement of all organic material by minerals. New research by a North Carolina State University paleontologist, however, could literally turn that theory inside out.

Dr. Mary Schweitzer, assistant professor of paleontology with a joint appointment at the N.C. Museum of Natural Sciences, has succeeded in isolating soft tissue from the femur of a 68-million-year-old dinosaur. Not only is the tissue largely intact, it's still transparent and pliable, and microscopic interior structures resembling blood vessels and even cells are still present.
In a paper published in the March 25 edition of the journal

210.

"Science", Schweitzer describes the process by which she and her technician, Jennifer Wittmeyer, isolated soft organic tissue from the leg bone of a 68-million-year-old Tyrannosaurus rex.

Schweitzer was interested in studying the microstructure and organic components of a dinosaur's bone. All bone is made up of a combination of protein (and other organic molecules) and minerals. In modern bone, removing the minerals leaves supple, soft organic materials that are much easier to work with in a lab. In contrast, fossilized bone is believed to be completely mineralized, meaning no organics are present. Attempting to dissolve the minerals from a piece of fossilized bone, so the theory goes, would merely dissolve the entire fossil.

But the team was surprised by what actually happened when they removed the minerals from the T.rex femur fragment. The removal process left behind stretchy bone matrix material that, when examined microscopically, seemed to show blood vessels, osteocytes, or bone building cells, and other recognizable organic features.

Since current data indicates that living birds are more closely related to dinosaurs than any other group, Schweitzer compared the findings from the T.rex with structures found in modern-day ostriches. In both samples, transparent branching blood vessels were present, and many of the small microstructures present in the T.rex sample displayed the same appearance as the blood and bone cells from the ostrich sample.

Schweitzer then duplicated her findings with at least three other well-preserved dinosaur specimens, one 80-million-year-old hadrosaur and two 65 million-year-old tyrannosaurs. All of these specimens preserved vessels, cell-like structures, or flexible matrix that resembled bone collagen from modern specimens.

Current theories about fossil preservation hold that organic molecules should not preserve beyond 100,000 years. Schweitzer hopes that further research will reveal exactly what the **soft** structures isolated from these bones are made of. Do they consist of the original cells, and if so, do the cells still contain genetic information? Her early studies of the material suggest that at least some fragments of the dinosaurs' original molecular material may still be present.

"We may not really know as much about how fossils are preserved as we think", says Schweitzer. "Our preliminary research shows that antibodies that recognize collagen **react** to chemical extracts of this fossil **bone**. If further studies confirm this, we may have the potential to learn more not only about the dinosaurs themselves, but also about how and why they were preserved in the first **place**."
……..ncsu.edu/news/press-releases

In this next article, **it's** business as usual for the evolution religion. Once upon a time they all agreed that a **bone** would fossilize completely in about 100,000 years. 100,000 years **wasn't** enough time so they bumped it up to 1 million years. A million years wasn't enough time so today they are saying that **sequencable** proteins can survive for 68 million years. I am sure if they need more time they will give themselves a billion years in the near future, who knows, they may even go infinite. There are no boundaries for their claims and there is no basis in fact for their claims. **Their** guesses about the time it takes anything to do anything **are** not scientifically derived or proven and because they 'think so' does not make it ev**idence, their** religion needs more help to survive and that help comes in the form of time. Who can challenge it? They can't prove it took **any** amount of time and no one can prove it didn't! Survival of the fittest turned into survival of their religion; just add time. This thinking is exactly why evolution should be taught as a religion if taught at all.

"ANCIENT T.REX AND MASTODON PROTEIN FRAGMENTS DISCOVERED, SEQUENCED

68-million-year-old T.rex proteins are oldest ever sequenced

Ancient proteins have been found in bones like those of a 68-million-year-old T.rex fossil

April 12, 2007

Scientists have confirmed the existence of protein in soft tissue recovered from the fossil bones of a 68 million-year-old Tyrannosaurus rex (T.rex) and a half-million-year-old mastodon.

Their results may change the way people think about fossil preservation and present a new method for studying diseases in which identification of proteins is important, such as cancer.

When an animal dies, protein immediately begins to degrade and , in the case of fossils, is slowly replaced by mineral. This substitution process was thought to be complete by 1 million years. Researchers at North Caroline State University (NCSU) and Harvard Medical School now know otherwise.

The researchers' findings appear as companion papers in this week's issue of the journal Science.

"Not only was protein detectably present in these fossils, the preserved material was in good enough condition that it could be identified," said Paul Filmer, program director in the National Science Foundation (NSF) Division of Earth Sciences, which funded the research. "We now know much more about what conditions proteins can survive in. It turns out that some proteins can survive for very long time periods, far longer than anyone predicted."

213.

Mary Schweitzer of NCSU and the North Carolina Museum of Natural Sciences discovered soft tissue in the leg bone of a T.rex and other fossils recovered from the Hell Creek sediment formation in Montana.

After her chemical and molecular analysis of the tissue indicated that original protein fragments might be preserved, she turned to colleagues John Asara and Lewis Cantley of Harvard Medical School, to see if they could confirm her suspicions by finding the Amino acid used to make collagen, a fibrous protein found in bone.

Bone is a composite material, consisting of both protein and mineral. In modern bones, when minerals are removed, a collagen matrix—fibrous, resilient material that gives the bones structure and flexibility—is left behind. When Schweitzer demineralized the T.rex bone, she was surprised to find such a matrix, because current theories of fossilization held that no original organic material could survive that long.

"This information will help us learn more about evolutionary relationships, about how preservation happens, and about how molecules degrade over time, which could have important applications in medicine, " Schweitzer said.

To see if the material had characteristics indicating the presence of collagen, which is plentiful, durable and has been recovered from other fossil materials, the scientists examined the resulting soft tissue with electron microscopy and atomic force microscopy they then tested it against various antibodies that are known to react with collagen. Identifying collagen would indicate that it is original to T.rex—that the tissue contains remnants of the molecules produced by the dinosaur.

"This is the breakthrough that says it's possible to get sequences beyond 1 million years," said Cantley. "At 68 million years, it's still possible."

Asara and Cantley successfully sequenced portions of the dinosaur and mastodon proteins, identifying the amino acids and confirming that the material was collagen. When they compared the collagen sequences to a database that contains existing sequences from modern species, they found that the T.rex sequence had similarities to those of chickens, and that the mastodon was more closely related to mammals, including the African elephant.

The protein fragments in the T.rex fossil appear to most closely match amino acid sequences found in collagen of present-day chickens, lending support to the idea that birds and dinosaurs are evolutionarily related.

"Most people believe that birds evolved from dinosaurs, but that's based on the 'architecture' of the bones. " Asara said. "This finding allows us the ability to say that they really are related because their sequences are related."

"Scientists had long assumed that the material in fossil bones would not be preserved after millions of years of burial, " said Enriqueta Barrera, program director in NSF's Division of Earth Sciences. "This discovery has implications for the study of similarly well-preserved fossil material."....
.....nsf.gov- National Science Foundation News

Unless the thought enters their minds that these bones or fossils are not as old as they thought they were then they have no choice but to say these proteins and soft tissues can survive that long. Professor, these bones are not 60-80 million years old, they are less than 6000 years old. That's why they are still soft, pliable and sequencable in some circumstances.

"Ever learning, and never able to come to the knowledge of the truth."
... 2Timothy 3: 7

- Birds and Dinosaur's look to be related - because God used the same sort of DNA encoding.

Every living thing on the planet has DNA. The sequencing of one species may be close to the sequencing of another species and they may seem very similar. Most larger life forms on the planet have skeletal systems, circulatory systems with red blood coursing through their bodies, for the most part we all have immune systems, eyes to see with, ears to hear with, noses to smell with, teeth to bite with and we are all carbon based, it's plentiful. Not because we all evolved from one single organism but we were all created by one single triune God using a technology (DNA) that works for every living thing on the planet. As mentioned previously in chapter 4, DNA excludes the possibility for transformation to occur which eliminates any and all forms of evolutionary change. DNA itself is a design technology and God built limits into it to prevent species from trans-mutating or evolving from his original design. A living organism will not change to something different, it will die, thus preserving Gods original creation which was complete and perfect from day one. God created separate species in varying sizes and capabilities, both plant and animal, from His same DNA technology.

CARBON 14 IS STILL MEASURABLE IN COAL, DIAMONDS AND FOSSILS - ITS EVERYWHERE

All Carbon 14 should have decayed away from all remains of living organisms within 50,000 years after the organism's death, plant or animal. Why is Carbon 14 still 'Super Abundant' everywhere?

"Carbon 14 in dinosaurs at the American Geophysical Conference in Singapore:

On how to date a dinosaur;

'Real Science' radios Bob Enyart interviews Hugh Miller, a member of the international scientific team that presented at the 2012 AGU Geophysical Conference in Singapore, the Carbon dating results [from five respective laboratories around the world] of bone from 10 dinosaur's (from the Gobi Desert in China, from Europe, Alaska, Texas, and Montana). C-14 [Carbon 14] lasts only thousands of years, not millions. Yet each of these dinosaurs had plenty of radiocarbon (as expected in that virtually every relevant peer-reviewed paper on the topic confirms the presence of endogenous soft tissue in fossils; see dinosaursofttissue.com). With the scientific breakthroughs and discoveries coming in daily, this is a great time to be alive!"........
"Scientists are consistently finding C-14, as reported in 2011 in the Journal 'PLOS One' for an allegedly 80-million-year-old mosasaur, and as reported elsewhere in natural gas, limestone, fossil wood, coal, oil, graphite, marble, the 10 dinosaurs described above, and even in supposedly billion year old diamonds."
.... Cited from, 'kgov.com/carbon-14-and-dinosaur-bones'

Why are some dinosaur bones extremely radioactive? If dinosaur's died out 65 million-years-ago all C-14 radioactivity should have decayed away 65,000,000 – 50,000 years ago; all dinosaur bones should have a radiation level that's equal to their surroundings by now. The reason is that dinosaur's did not die out 65,000,000 years ago, they died out in the flood of Noah 4400 years ago.
I believe that certain dinosaur's such as the predatory or scavenger varieties received multiple doses of Carbon-14 and other radiation, because they ate other dinosaur's that had been accumulating their own levels of Carbon-14 throughout their lives

and when they were eaten, their Carbon-14 accumulation passed on to the predator or scavenger. That's not the only reason dinosaurs can be radioactive, a meteor can release radioactivity into the atmosphere. A meteor could have been used by God to shatter the earth's crust and break open the fountains of the deep as described in the Bible. Remember, it took months before life on earth was finally extinguished by the flood. Today, **some species of dinosaur's are so radioactive that museums cannot display them in public**. All types of radioactivity should have reached equilibrium by now, Carbon-14, uranium and thorium.

"The lead paint is used to protect museum visitors and staff when the specimen fossil has relatively low radioactivity. However, some dinosaur bones are so radioactive, museums can only display replicas."
…….. Quora.com

"Disturbance of Radioactive Equilibrium

"The difficulty of the quantitative determination of uranium and thorium in bones according to their y-activity is associated with the possible deviation from radioactive equilibrium. Since the age of the investigated bone, according to the data of the Paleontological Method, is about 70 million years, it can be considered with great probability that the time elapsed is sufficient for radioactive equilibrium to have been established between uranium and its products, [yet radioactivity is still present],regardless of whether all the uranium was in the bones from the very beginning (biochemical origin) or whether it accumulated over a long geological period (geological origin)."
….. Mongolia State University, Atommaya Energiya, 1973, Vol. 35, No. 2, pg. 130-132

Why do Comets exist?

Comets have a lifespan of about 10,000 years   If the universe is billions of years old as the evolution religion would have us believe then how can comets still be flying around since they are constantly sloughing off material.....
…... Cited from Dr. Kent Hovinds Creation Seminar, 2005

Why does the earth have granite today?
The earth should not have granite because granite had to form on a cool planet!
Evolutionarily science says the earth was a hot molten mass.

Dr. Robert Gentry wrote a book about his research into all the different granites found around the globe: "Creations Tiny Mystery", in his book Dr. Gentry talks about 'Radio Polonium Halos' which are found in every granite around the world. As Polonium decays, (164,000ths/sec) or .164 seconds = half-life, it fragments apart and looks like a tiny firework exploding in the night sky giving off the "Halo" effect. In a hot molten rock (As the theory of evolution states in its creation model of the earth), these halos would be lost within a minute. Dr. Gentry concluded that the earth was never a hot molten rock- it had to be cool in order to preserve these halos in the granite. Granite when melted and re-cooled is not granite any longer - its rhyolite. If the earth were ever a hot molten mass we would have never seen granite on the earth.

P.S. - When Dr. Gentry published his findings the university that employed him fired him! His research was doing damage to the evolutionarily religious system by proving that the earth was never a hot molten mass as their religion claims it was. (Our tuition and tax dollars at work – again)

Its not about the truth – its all about the "Religion" and the money that they receive to research it and teach it, even if they have to

destroy the lives of their students, fellow scientists and professors to protect it, they have and will!
..... Cited, in part, from Dr. Hovinds Creation Seminar, 2005

The 'Evolution Religion' or 'Humanist Model' of the world places today's man at the pinnacle of evolutionary development. Today's man is supposedly taller, stronger and **wiser**, Homo **Sapien Sapien**, or **wise wise man, thus** more evolved that any man prior. This way of thinking about themselves is probably the reason there is no mention, in today's textbooks, about the discoveries of extremely **tall** human skeletons. How can they claim to be taller and more evolved when there were men in the past that tower over today's man?

In 1883, Lompoc Rancho, CA – 12 foot long human skeleton
In 1925, 20 miles outside of South Bend IN - 8 skeletons all wearing copper armor – 8-9 feet long
In 1931, Humbolt Lake bed Nevada – 10 foot long skeleton
In 1902, Shreveport LA – 20 skeletons all 9 feet and over
The Government of Turkey has a 12 foot long human skeleton found at the base of Mt. Ararat they claim is the skeleton of Noah.
….. Cited from Dr. Kent Hovinds Creation Seminar, 2005

"There were giants in the earth in those days."
…... Genesis 6: 4

Scientific researchers also claim that there are no remains of a "Big Foot" on record; maybe there **are**!

For more accounts of **'Giant Human Skeletons'** go to www.stangrist.com/giants.

"No terrestrial rocks closely approaching an age of 4.6 billion years have yet been discovered. The evidence for the age of the earth is circumstantial, being based upon...**indirect** reasoning."
..... Dr. Stephen Moorbath, evolutionist, University of Oxford, 1977

"Fresh" Dinosaur bones that were found 'not' fossilized or; still in original calcified form
'Along the banks of the Colville River west of Prudhoe Bay, AK'. Frozen dinosaur bones were found that are "as light as balsa wood and look as fresh as yesterdays dog bones. "... "Their structure was porous and the fossils [bones] were not mineralized."
......Don Lessem, OMNI, Jan. 1990 pg. 32

Why are there only 7 billion people on the earth today?

Back up 2000 plus years to the year 0; there were about ¼ of a billion people on the earth when Jesus was here the first time. Back up to the **flood, 4400 years ago,** and there were 8 people on the earth to begin **repopulating**.

Year...0 there were ¼ billion people on the earth
In 1800 there were 1 billion people on the earth
In 1985 there were 5 billion people on the earth
In 1999 there were 6 billion people on the earth
In 2013 there were 7 billion people on the earth

From the **time** Jesus walked on the earth in the year 0 until the year 1800 there was an increase in population of ¾ of a billion people.
In the last 14 **years**, there has been an increase in population of 1 billion people and the previous 14 years prior to that there was also an increase in population of 1 billion people.
Evolutionarily science wants us to believe that men have been here for 3,000,000 years. In the past 2013 **years** our population went from ¼ billion to 7 billion.

Since the flood 4400 years ago it went from almost nothing, 8 people to 7 billion.
…….. Cited ,in part, from Dr. Hovinds Creation Seminar, 2005

David Derbyshire, Science correspondent of the "Weekly Telegraph" in the U.K.; wrote the following article which appeared on Sept. 30th, 2004.

"We are all related to man who lived in Asia in 1415 B.C." Every one in the world is descended from a single person who lived around 3500 y.a.[the flood was in 2350 B.C., or about 4400 years ago], according to a new study.
Scientists have worked out the most recent common ancestor of all 6,000,000,000 people alive today probably dwelt in Eastern Asia around 1415 B.C.
Although the **date** may seem relatively recent, researchers say the findings should not come as a surprise. Anyone trying to trace their family tree soon discovers that the number of direct ancestors doubles every 20-30 years. It takes only a few centuries to clock up thousands of direct ancestors. Using a computer model, researchers from the Massachusetts Institute of Technology (MIT) attempted to trace back the most recent common ancestor using estimated patterns of migration throughout history.
From a study done on Mitochondria **DNA this** report was filed in "**Nature**", "The Family Tree Way" 26 Sept. 2004.
"They calculated that the ancestors location in eastern Asia allowed his or her descendants to spread to Europe, Asia, remote Pacific Islands and the Americas. Going back a few thousand years **more, the** researchers found a time when a large fraction of people in the world were the common ancestors of everybody alive today – while the rest were ancestors of no one alive. That date was 5353 B.C., the team reports in Nature. The researchers, led by Dr. Steve Olson, stressed that the date was an estimate.
"Nevertheless, our results suggest that the most recent common ancestor for the worlds current population lived in the relatively

recent past – perhaps within the last few thousand years." he said. He added: "No matter the language we speak or the colour of our skin, we share ancestors who planted rice on the banks of the Yangtze, who domesticated horses on the steppes of the Ukraine, who hunted giant sloths in the forest of North and South America and who labored to build the great pyramid of Khufu." Although some groups of people may have lived in isolation from the rest of the world for 100's of years, the researchers say no one alive today had been untouched by migration."
…... The Weekly Telegraph, United Kingdom, by David Derbyshire, 2004

Noah's flood was not the only flood that God beset men with.

THE FIRST FLOOD THAT COVERED ONLY 1/3 OF THE EARTH

Paleontologists in China found a dinosaur nursery complete with hundreds of nests and hundreds of eggs fossilized in the nests. These nests had all been buried by flood sediment and a whole new dinosaur nursery was found below the first nursery within the rock layers. Of course the evolutionists thought this was absolute proof there was not a worldwide flood and they and Darwin were correct all along since what evidence that may have proved a flood happened was now in question because the dinosaurs lived through a flood to nest again and get buried again by another flood. It was the second flood that insured they would not be back to nest again. According to the book of Jasher, there was a precursor flood to the worldwide flood. This earlier flood only covered 1/3 of the earth;

"And the sons of men went out and they served other Gods, and they forgot the Lord who had created them in the earth; and in those days the sons of men made images of brass and iron, wood and stone, and they bowed down and served them. And every man made his god and they bowed down to them, and the sons of men

forsook the Lord all the days of Enosh and his children; and the anger of the Lord was kindled on account of their works and abominations which they did in the earth. **And the Lord caused the waters of the river Gihon to overwhelm them, and he destroyed and consumed them, and he destroyed a third part of the earth, and notwithstanding this, the sons of men did not turn from their evil ways, and their hands were yet extended to do evil in the sight of the Lord."** [Just like today]
….. Jasher 2: 4- 6

It amazes me how many humanists or evolutionists are on the Internet fervently arguing their cases about how they are correct and "the young earth creationists" are wrong. It's a competition with them to see who is the smartest and most "evolved" intellectually. What they don't realize is if they suddenly died they would find out they have 'lost' this particular debate by lifting up their eyes in hell and there will be nothing anyone can do to help them at that point.

Creationists are - NOT - trying to prove they are smarter than anyone else. Christian's are trying to keep you and future generations of human beings out of hell and born into Gods Kingdom where all men were destined to live originally. We love you and God loves you and we both desire that everyone finds their way to heaven! Join us and join God.

"Herein is Love, not that we loved God, but that he loved us, and sent His Son to be the propitiation [sacrifice] for our sins. Beloved, if God so loved us, we ought also to love one another."
……1 John 4: 10-11

PHARAOHS WAR MACHINES – A jet and a helicopter carved centuries before their inventions

Earlier than 1000 B.C. Pharaoh Seti I built the Temple of Osiris at Abydos Egypt. Ramesis II had the temple reworked and it is not clear which of the 2 Pharaohs had the depictions of a jet airplane and a helicopter carved inside the temple. Some think this was just an accident that happened during Ramesis II's re-carving of the Temple but maybe this unfolded similarly to John the Baptists revelation on the Isle of Patmos where he saw a prophetic vision of the future war that was going to take place just north of Jerusalem. John saw the "War of Armageddon" and all the machines of war used to fight it. Perhaps the Pharaoh had a similar vision and saw jets and helicopters and other war machines and he recorded part of his vision in stone on the Temple walls.

DO ALL SCHOLARS, PROFESSORS, DOCTORS, POLITICIANS AND GOVERNMENTS ALWAYS HAVE YOUR BEST INTEREST IN MIND AS THEY ARE LIVING THEIR OWN PERSONAL LIVES AND FOLLOWING THEIR OWN BELIEFS?

The following evidence and opinions are not here to degrade the entirety of higher education or all educators, doctors, professors, etc. My intent is to show that there can be hidden motives for some men to do the things they do because some do have only their own interests in mind. Having said that, there have also been advances made in medicine and scholarly endeavors that should be applauded for aiding mankind. If we are honest with ourselves, we should be able to admit that there are things in this world that we, collectively as men, just do not know yet. There was a time in the scientific and medical communities when, admittedly, we knew much less than what we know today and the evolution religion fits right in to this era of shortsightedness.

Today more that ever our world needs "True" science, moral doctors and honest educators:

Science used to say something different than what we now know today;

--"The world is flat" - the world is round

---The earth is the center of the universe – geocentricity. - The sun is the center

---Its unnecessary to wash your hands before surgery – believed to be true until the Civil War – to prevent infections

---If someone becomes ill, cut them open and let the illness drain out with the blood – Humors; blood letting – George Washington died from this

---Oxygen injected into the body would cure any disease, called Diaduction treatment

---A machine that vibrates a patient at a certain frequency can cure anything, called an Oscilloclast treatment

---Shining a multi-colored light on a patients skin to cure most diseases, called Spectro-Chrome therapy

---The "Electrometabograph" and its close cousin "The Magical Radio Wave Machine"

The patient would sit in front of the machine and get blasted with radio waves to cure disease. This machine "supposedly" also worked on patients thousands of miles away if needed. Send the doctor a check - the doctor would aim his Magical Radio Wave Machine in your direction and send your treatment out into the air.

---Severe the tissues of the brain (frontal lobe) to control patient behavior – Lobotomy

RADIOACTIVE PRODUCTS FOR EVERYDAY HOUSEHOLD USE

"When radiation was first discovered by Madame Curie, it was found that many of the popular 'healing' hot springs contained radon in the water. Logically, if radon in the water was good for you, then the radium itself would be even more effective. Ironically, Madame Curie's fingers had fallen off before her death, but **the gullible public** purchased these radioactive products anyway! In the 1920's and '30's, it was possible to buy radium-

containing products such as beauty creams and contraceptives. Heating pads containing radioactive ore were a popular item. Manufacturers claimed that their products would cure cancer, epilepsy, tuberculosis, high blood pressure, arthritis, kidney trouble, and numerous other diseases. Male wearers of the Radioencrinator, a gold-plated piece of refined radium, were advised to place it under their scrotum's at night for the health of the endocrine glands. Radioactive water was drunk with enthusiasm by the medical community and their patients. Some products allowed the consumer to infuse their water with radioactivity at home. The Revigataor, which was a crock lined with radioactive ore, produced water that was five times as radioactive as the maximum recommended for well water today. Eben Byers, wealthy tycoon and amateur golf champion, was an endorser of Radithor, a radioactive tonic water containing 2 mCi of radium. He drank over 1400 bottles until portions of his mouth and jaw were surgically removed, and died of radium poisoning in April 1932. With Eben Byers' death on the front page of the New York Times, proponents of the curative powers of radium began to rethink their theories."
…. h2g2.com/dna/h2g2/alabaster

Most of the above "Science and Scientific Treatments" took place less than 150 years ago - the scientific community has and continues to be wrong about certain issues even when they were all agreeing that it was true.

This article states;" **the gullible public**" inferring that it is the responsibility of each member of society to insure that what these paid, trusted, certified, professional experts are telling us and our children is the absolute truth. Basically, if we die it's our own fault - unfortunately, this is still a need in today's world! If we are being force-fed a religion against our will, that's also our own fault.

Continuing:

PHRENOLOGY:

The shape of the head indicates the nature of the individual.

If you went in to get a **'Phrenology Assessment'** the **doctor** would use a Psycograph. This is a helmet with 1954 **parts that** has adjustable rods sticking down and making contact with your head and from those measurements the **doctor** could determine 32 characteristics about your psychological makeup.
The first 6 characteristics are -

Personality
Intelligence
Spirituality
Suavity
Morality
Sexamity

Hitler, arguably, may have used a device like this on the Jewish people through his own **doctors**, Josef Mengele (The Angel of Death) and others. On Hitlers list 'The Evolutionary Progression of Man' he noted that the Jewish **people** had "Fiendish Skulls". Perhaps **Hitler** used this 'technology' and terminology as "supposed "-"Scientific **proof**" of his claim to the German Supreme Court that the Jewish people were not humans. This device is reportedly making a comeback outside of the U.S.A.

DEATH BY MEDICINE – A research paper done by 5 American Doctors

In 2001, Medical treatments unnecessarily prescribed or performed by doctors were the #1 killer of Americans

In 2003, a group of 5 doctors joined together to research the causes and costs of death and healthcare in America. The abstract of their findings is recorded below:

"A definitive review and close reading of medical peer-review journals, and government health statistics shows that American medicine frequently causes more harm than good. The number of people having in-hospital, adverse drug reactions (ADR) to prescribed medicine is 2.2 million. Dr. Richard Besser, of the CDC, in 1995, said the number of unnecessary antibiotics prescribed annually for viral infections was 20 million. Dr. Besser, in 2003, now refers to 10's of millions of unnecessary antibiotics. The number of unnecessary medical and surgical procedures performed annually is 7.5 million. The number of people exposed to unnecessary hospitalization annually is 8.9 million. The total number of Iatrogenic [Medical treatment] deaths shown in the following table is 783,936. It is evident that the American medical system is the leading cause of death and injury in the United States. The 2001 heart disease annual death rate is 699,697; the annual cancer death rate is 553,251."

.... Death by Medicine, Gary Null PhD, Carolyn Dean MD ND, Martin Feldman MD,

.... Debora Rasio MD, Dorothy Smith PhD, pg. 1

In the year 2001-
#1 killer of Americans –
Unnecessary treatments by U.S. Healthcare........ 783,936 deaths
#2 killer of Americans –
Heart Disease .... 699,697 deaths
#3 killer of Americans –
Cancer .... 553,251 deaths

What would motivate a doctor to perform a very expensive and life threatening operation on a patient that did not need the surgery? The love of money!......the root of all evil.
Thank you to the 5 brave doctors who honestly reported what is

apparently the truth about today's motivation of a percentage of the U.S. medical profession.

It's a Global issue
"A survey published in the Journal of Health Affairs pointed out that between 18% and 28% of people who were recently ill had suffered from a medical or drug error in the previous two years. The study surveyed 750 recently-ill adults in five different countries. The breakdown by country showed 18% of those in Britain, 25% in Canada, 23% in Australia, 23% in New Zealand, and the highest number was in the U.S. At 28%.
….. Death by Medicine, pg. 32

It's almost as if some **doctors** are purposefully creating illnesses in their patients so they will **insure** future office visits and a future income stream. Some doctors may think the same way Darwin, Hitler and Haeckel did and do not value certain people's lives as highly as they value their own lives or bank account's. Some of those in higher education and other members of the "Professional Community" may have an agenda that is in opposition to the Christian ethic. Not because Christianity is in error but they are just so intellectually beyond the idea of God that they don't need or desire him or his moral laws. Again, these are the "authorities that we trust and pay to help us and some are risking our lives and profiting on our trust in them. They do all they can to resist acknowledging Gods **existence** leaving themselves free to engage in immoral and unethical activities. (Made easier to do since our schools teach against the existence of God)

"And whosoever shall offend one of these little ones that believes in **me, it** is better for him that a millstone **were** hanged about his neck, and he **were** cast into the sea."
…... Mark 9: 42
Killing your patient, even accidentally, just to make a payment on your Mercedes qualifies as "Offend"

"For it is written, I will destroy the wisdom of the wise, and will bring to nothing the understanding of the prudent. Where is the wise? Where is the scribe? Where is the disputer of this world [Satan]? For after that in the wisdom of God the world by wisdom knew not God, it pleased God by the foolishness of preaching to save them that believe."
…..1 Corinthians 1: 19– 21

Have you noticed that the genealogies in the Bible 'end' at Jesus? - Gods children are being added to those genealogies today; one by one, as they receive Jesus as Lord. Even those who have not received him yet still have a place reserved and waiting for them. Every man, even the ones that drive a Mercedes.

Perhaps Darwin, Lyell, Haekel and other non-Christian educators that were in positions to influence the world views of so many students did not have a full understanding of the future effects of what they were teaching. Maybe they thought that they were only furthering the collective knowledge of the world and their own careers. The price the world paid was deceit heaped upon destruction heaped upon death. By learning evolution and not Gods Word we have reaped corruption and if we don't expel Satan's evolution from our schools that corruption will be absolute. Mans first judgment or punishment was destruction by water, the next is destruction by fire, as stated earlier from 2nd Peter:

"But the heavens and the earth, which are now, by the same word are kept in store, reserved unto fire against the day of judgment and perdition of ungodly men."
… 2 Peter 2: 3

THE NUMBERS DON'T LIE – The Statistics of Evolution

Since evolution was introduced back in the 1960's the morality of mankind has taken a nose dive in the U.S. and probably in every nation where its has been adopted over Gods Word. Measurable moral issues such as drug usage, pornography, rape, suicide, murder, theft, alcoholism, teen pregnancy, sexually transmitted diseases, divorce rates, child abuse and violent crimes have all skyrocketed since the removal of God and the introduction of the evolution religion in our schools. Research any statistical analysis done on any of the above categories and, in every case, the data shows a dramatic increase in incidence rates which are proof of the rampant moral decay in America since evolutions inception. Today our prisons are bursting at the seams with the product of evolutionary teaching in our school systems. Prisons are having to release non-violent offenders in order to make room for the violent offenders. As mentioned earlier; homosexuality was another 'Judgment' that our nation received from God by the teaching of 'Evolution' – worshiping the creation more than the creator. I found very little statistical information concerning homosexuality prior to 1980 that is meaningful. Just 30 years ago; homosexuality was not mentioned or celebrated as it is today. Back then the U.S. government had no classification for homosexuals in the government census but today the government does have a classification for homosexuals and lesbians in the census. Governmental laws have been changed to allow the marriage of homosexuals within the last decade. In only 50 years, the homosexual lifestyle went from virtually non-existent on the American landscape to open parades, public gatherings, legal marriage and broadcasters now celebrate homosexuality and homosexual unions through television programming promoting the homosexual lifestyle. Broadcasters have also increased television violence, sex and profanity well over 50% in each category since the 1960's. Public educators encourage tolerance for homosexuality because, supposedly, its a choice for anyone to live any life-style that they choose, some of those same educators taught evolution and helped to bring about that lifestyle to begin with. I am not against educators and I am not against homosexuals; I am against mans ignorance of the Satanic spirit behind evolution and homosexuality that is engaged in the destruction of men's souls. Take evolution out of our school systems and teach Gods creation model and homosexuality will diminish along with all of the other moral issues listed below:

The following statistics are from Dr. Kent Hovinds Creation Seminar, 2005:

From 1963–1985
10-14 year old girls giving birth
....100% increase
Pregnancies up 553% ---Difference were aborted

From 1963–1985
10–14 year old's Sexually Transmitted Disease
....385% increase

From 1963 – 1990
Teen girls premarital sex; 25% in 1963; 70 % in 1990
....45% increase

From 1963 – 1990
All unwed mothers giving birth; 6% in 1963; 33% in 1995
....27% increase

From 1963 – 1992
Unmarried couples living together
.... 725% increase

From 1963 – 1978
U.S. Divorce rate
.... 100% increase

From 1963 – 2000
Child Abuse
.... 2300% increase

From 1963 – 1995
Violent Crime
.... 995% increase

From 1963 – 2000
Illegal Drug usage
.... 6000% increase

From 1963 – 1980
High School SAT Scores
.... 90 point decrease

From 1963 – 1993
Suicide Rates for 15 – 24 year old's
.... 275% increase
.... Dr. Hovinds Creation Seminar, 2005

In a study by the CEPR, "Center for Economic and Policy Research " called "The High Budgetary Cost of Incarceration", they found the following:

"**Over** the same period [1990 – 2000], the U.S. population increased about 33% and the prison and jail population increased by more than 350%."

In 2012; The U.S. has the highest numbers of prisoners than any other nation:

1- United States -------2,019,000 --------- 715 prisoners per 100,000 people

2- China ---------------- 1,549,000 ---------- less than 420 prisoners per 100,000 people

3- Russia ----------------- 846,000 ---------- 584 prisoners per 100,000 people
….dailypaul.com, 2012

"In 1994, an obituary study revealed that the median age of death for homosexual males was 42 and for lesbians was 49."
…... Cameron, Playfair, Wellum, "The Longevity of Homosexuals: Before and after the Aids epidemic", "Omega Journal of Death and Dying", 1994

Economist Allen Freeman presented a speech to the "Historical Materialism Conference" in December of 2006. Mr. Freeman was not giving a speech on "The Effects of Evolutionary Teaching" or " The High Cost of Expelling God from The United States School System" but the numbers presented and the timing of the downturn exactly correlates with 'Evolution In' and 'God Out' of our public school systems. He writes:

"We find that the economy has, since Globalism [1980], been growing at approximately half the rate it was before, and that this trend shows no sign of reversing, to the contrary, the 2000 recession turns out to be one of the most serious since 1974, and the recovery from it is faltering, geographically uneven, and dominated by imbalances between the U.S. and the rest of the world. We also find that inequality under Globalism, measured as the ratio of GDP [Gross Domestic Product] per capita in the 'advanced' countries to those in the rest of the world, increased by a factor of between 2 and 3 times under Globalism, and this ratio too, shows no sign of reversing."
…. Alan Freeman, 2006

Mr. Freeman states that the U.S. economy has been growing at half the normal pace since **globalism, the** truth is, the decline of the U.S. economy began back in the 1960's; about the time America traded God's creation for Satan's **evolution**. Worldwide and domestically GDP dropped from 5.3 in the 1960's to 3.5 in 1982; Our economy has been hovering at this new lower pace ever since. The graph for the statistical data above can be seen at: www.countddownnet.info/archivio/analisi/world

The U.S. economy continues to falter; in 2008 the stock market plummeted and collectively we lost **billions** in a day. In Biblical prophesy; some researchers say that there is another financial crash that is going to happen to the U.S. in September of 2015 if we continue ignoring Gods word and continue our "business as usual" mindset. Is what has happened to America just part of the political and economic **climate** we are living in? Could it be just coincidence and just part of today's fast paced, survival of the fittest world. I **don**'t think so! Since the government sponsored **evolution** religion began, in earnest, in the early 1960's our economy has been teetering at 3.5 %, in one 10 year span 1990 – 2000 our prison population increased 350% and beyond that illegal drug usage increased 6000%, sexually transmitted diseases in teens increased 385%.. Why did any of these have to increase at all if **evolution was the truth and God didn't really exist**. Just prior to these increases every moral issue listed above was on a stable course. These things happened because when we kicked God out of our schools we kicked morality out of our schools. We have replaced Gods 'true moralities" of compassion, caring, giving, honesty, loving kindness, Godliness, correctness, chastity, temperance, Holiness and a strong work ethic with what the evolution religion dictates. Survive, be stronger, fight and conquer, take what you need, spread your genes like it's a competition, mating is just a product or our evolutionary past and natural and normal. **If it feels good, do it, even with members of the same sex, live any lifestyle that you choose and celebrate others that chose alternate lifestyles. After all, you're just a** product of chance and not God's greatest creation whom he loves. It amazes me why teachers and parents do not see where the bullying problems are stemming from- survival of the fittest. When a young child watches a video of 2 bull's fighting over which one gets to mate with the female and pass along their genes then children just might get the idea that it is required of them to fight to get what they want, be it sex or anything else. If America's children are taught that the fittest get to survive and pass their genes on to the next generation then **our school system creates a percentage of children** who believe that fighting is normal and dominating others is acceptable; case in point – Adolf Hitler, the supreme bully.

There is a spiritual reason for the American decline! Turning our back's on God and, by default, allowing Satan to lead America. Satan stepped in to fill the void left when God was expelled from school, both in the form of prayer in school and by replacing God's creation with Satan's evolution. Satan has gone out of his way to teach the opposite of what the Bible says about the universe and the life in it.

"If my people, which are called by my name, shall humble themselves, and pray, and seek my face, and turn from their wicked ways: then will I hear from heaven, and will forgive their sin, and will heal their land."
…… 2nd Chronicles 7: 14

Chapter 10

SATANIC LITERATURE- THE DOCTRINES OF DEMONS
SATAN AT WORK TO DESTROY MEN

THE CHURCH OF SATAN – Opposites don't attract

The Bible records that Satan has a position of limited authority on the earth and he has to use men to do his will, men have to contend with him; or serve him. There are only two final destinations for the spirits of men; "Heaven or Hell". The Bible also says that the Holy Spirit will help men discern spiritual things through comparisons.

"In whom the God of this world **[Satan], hath blinded the minds of them which believe not**, lest the light of the glorious Gospel of Christ, who is the image of God, should shine unto them."
…... 2 Corinthians 4: 4

"Which things also we speak, not in the words which man's wisdom **teacheth**, but which the Holy Ghost **teacheth**; **comparing spiritual things with spiritual**. But the natural man receiveth not the things of the Spirit of God: for they are foolishness unto him: neither can he know them, because they are spiritually discerned [understood]. But he that is spiritual **judgeth** all things, yet he himself is judged of no man."
…... 2 Corinthians 2: 13- 15

In 1966, Anton Lavey founded the Church of Satan so he and his followers could live the way they chose, they **lived** absolutely carnal, **unholy** lives and did what pleased them **on**- what they supposed - was their own terms, similar to the tolerance taught in our public schools today. According to the above verse; if you do not believe in the God of heaven, **the God of this world can blind your mind** and do with you anything he desires, cause people to kill people and write books [Origin of Species, etc.] that are not in line with Gods Word [the Bible], and start religions [evolution, Islam] that send millions to hell. Satan blinded the minds of Hitler, Stalin, Lavey, Mohammed, Darwin and thousands of others for his purposes; killing, stealing and destroying.

"The thief [Satan] cometh not, but for to steal, and to kill, and to destroy: I am come [Jesus] that they might have life, and that they might have it more abundantly."
.... John 10: 10

To become a member of higher status in Satan's Church a practitioner is required to break or do the opposite to each of the 10 commandments recorded in the Bible. They are required to renounce and absolutely pervert Gods Word.

BIBLE... **CHURCH OF SATAN**

1-You shall have no
other Gods
before me ....They confess Satan as their
....Lord and God, then **renounce**
....**and curse** the God of the Bible

2-You shall not make
for yourself an Idol .... They worship a horned goat
.... head idol

3-You shall not take the
name of the Lord your
God in vain .... They ceremoniously curse
.... Jehovah, Jesus, and the Holy
.... Spirit

4-Remember the Sabbath
and keep it Holy................................They worship Satan on the
.... Sabbath, (Saturday)

5-Honor your father
and mother ....They ceremoniously curse
.... their father and mother

6-You shall not murder ....They commit at least one
.... murder

7-You shall not
commit adultery ....They have public adultery
.... ceremonies

8-You shall not steal ....They steal

9-You shall not give
false testimony [lie] ....They lie

10-You shall not covet .... They covet the property of
.... others and have public
.... fornication ceremonies

"Ye are of your father the devil, and the lusts of your father ye will do. He was a murderer from the beginning, and abode not in the truth, because there is no truth in him. When he [Satan] speaketh a lie, he speaketh of his own: for he is a liar, and the father of it."…... John 8: 44

"And before Him [Jesus] shall be gathered all nations; and He shall separate them one from another, as a Shepard divideth His sheep [Christians] from the goats [Satan's], "......
…... Mathew 25: 32
Anton Lavey also published his list of Satanic guidelines or "Rules" to abide by in his church-

"The 11 Satanic Rules of the Earth" ….By Anton Lavey

1…Do not give opinions or advice unless you are asked.

2…Do not tell your troubles to others unless you are sure they want to hear them.

3…When in anothers lair [house], show them respect or else do not go there.

4…If a guest in your lair annoys you, treat them crudely and without mercy.

5…Do not make sexual advances unless you are given the mating signal.

6…Do not take that which does not belong to you unless it is a burden to the other person and they cry out to be relieved.

7…Acknowledge the power of magic if you have employed it successfully to obtain your desires. If you deny the power of magic after having called upon it with success, you will lose all you have obtained.

8...Do not complain about anything to which you need not subject yourself.

9...Do not harm little children.

10..Do not kill non-human animals unless you are attacked or for your food.

11..When walking in open territory, bother no one. If someone bothers you, ask them to stop. If they don't stop, destroy them.
….. Anton Lavey's book, "11 Satanic Rules of the Earth", 1967

In the 7th rule above "Acknowledge the Power of Magic" , this is the occult side of Satan's church, magic is the power that they acknowledge is from Satan. Satan is their God and he supplies power to his followers through what they call 'magic' but is actually a demonic manifestation. Satan's magic is not a harmless construct or sleight of hand as we normally consider magic to be. This magic is a supernatural and demonically controlled power over human beings as they, demons, work for and through men. Magic is also celebrated in "A Course in Miracles" which is another one of Satans inspired works, more later. The magic celebrated in the Harry Potter books is leading our children in the direction of the occult and some will wind up joining the ranks of Darwin, Haeckel, Hitler, Stalin and others.

THE BIBLE COMPARED TO EVOLUTIONARY SCIENCE – Direct Opposition

Anton Lavey took Gods 10 Commandments and perverted them by teaching his followers to do the exact opposite of what God commanded.

242.
Dr. Kent Hovind compiled a list of perversions from another religion that did the opposite of what God recorded in the Bible; Evolution compared to Gods creation model.

..... BIBLE (CREATION)......................... EVOLUTION ....

1...Earth before the Sun................................ Sun before the Earth

2...Oceans before land .... Land before oceans

3...Light before the Sun .... Sun before light

4...Land life first .... Marine life first

5...Fruit trees before fish .... Fish before fruit ....trees

6...Fish before insects .... Insects before fish

7...Plants before the Sun .... Sun before plants

8...Marine mammals before .... Land mammals ....land mammals...before marine ....mammals

9...Birds before reptiles ....Reptiles before ....birds

10..Atmosphere between 2 layers of water..... Atmosphere above ....the water

11..Man brought death into the world ....Death brought man ....into the world

12..God created man ....Man created God
.... Dr. Kent Hovinds Creation Seminar, 2005

Everything that God has done for men Satan twists and perverts it and claims the opposite happened. Satan wants mankind to fail in finding the "True" God of heaven. Satan is, temporarily, the God of this world and his number one goal is to destroy men; both body and soul by any form of deceit or destruction that he can cause one man to commit against another man.

"Lest Satan should get an advantage of us: For we are not ignorant of his devices."
…… 2 Corinthians 2: 11

"For such are false apostles, deceitful workers, transforming themselves into the apostles of Christ. And no marvel; for Satan himself is transformed into an angel of light."
….. 2 Corinthians 11: 13 – 14

"And he [Jesus speaking] said unto them, I beheld Satan as lightning fall from heaven, behold I give unto you power to tread on serpents [Satan's workmen] and scorpions, and over all the power of the enemy. And nothing shall by any means hurt you. Notwithstanding in this rejoice **not, that** the **spirits** are subject unto you; but rather rejoice, because your names are written in heaven."
….. Luke 10: 18– 21

"For the mystery of iniquity doth already work; only He who now restrains will restrain [the Holy Spirit with the body of Christ], until He [The Holy Spirit] be taken out of the way, And then shall the wicked be revealed, whom the Lord shall consume with the Spirit of his mouth, and shall destroy with the brightness of his coming. Even him [the Anti-Christ], whose coming is after the working of Satan with all power and signs and lying wonders. And with all deception of unrighteousness in them that perish; because they received not the **love** of the **Truth** [Jesus], that they might be saved, and for this cause God shall send them strong

delusion, that they should believe a lie [Islam, ACIM, evolution in part]."
..... 2 Thessalonians 2: 7– 11

"And I [John] saw an angel come down from heaven, having the key to the bottomless pit and a great chain in his hand. And he laid hold on the Dragon, that old Serpent, which is the Devil and Satan, and bound him 1000 years."
..... Revelation 20: 1– 2

SATANS FALSE RELIGIONS; HIS RULERSHIP OVER THE EARTH TO DESTROY THE SOULS OF MEN

"And the Devil, taking him [Jesus] up into a high mountain, showed unto Him all the kingdoms of the world in a moment of time. And the Devil said unto Him, all this power will I give thee, and the glory of them: for that is delivered unto me; and to whomsoever I will give it. If thou therefore wilt worship me, all shall be thine."
.... Luke 4: 5- 7

Satan attempted to entice Jesus into serving him by allowing Jesus to rule over the earths territories and kingdoms complete with their false religions. Satan, being the God of this present world, has power over all people and religions that do not belong to the one true [Triune] God; Jesus, Jehovah and The Holy Spirit. Satan has deceived men all over the world into believing in idols and false gods in an effort to keep men separated from the true"God" that exiled him from heaven and took back control of the men of the earth when Jesus went into Hell after His crucifixion. God created men with a built-in need to worship Him and Satan and his demonic angels have spent the past 6000 years perverting Gods plan by replacing God worship with idol worship and false god worship. Satan sets up principalities in countries around the globe and within those principalities he creates his own false religions where the people of the regions are worshiping anything other than the God that created them. Satan then sets his princes over these false religions to act like a caring benevolent God- this is what I believe Satan was offering Jesus, an overseer position over these false religions. Satan hijacked Gods 'plan of worship' for men and used God's overall design to create his own religions complete with his own Gods, prophets, offerings, worship, sacrifices, heaven, hell, places of worship,etc. For each false religion Satan found a man that he tempted as he tempted Jesus and those unwary men became the prophets of each false religion, ie. Mohammed.

"But I say, that the things which the Gentiles [non-Jews] sacrifice, they sacrifice to devils, and not to God: And I would not that you should have fellowship with devils. Ye cannot be partakers of the Lords table, and of the table of devils."
…...1 Corinthians 10: 20– 21

"As concerning therefore the eating of those things that are offered in sacrifice to idols, we know that an idol is nothing in this world, and that there is none other God but one. [the Trinity, the Triune God; Jehovah, Jesus and The Holy Spirit]"
….. 1 Corinthians 8: 4

"Their idols are silver and gold, the work of men's hands. They have mouths, but they speak not: Eyes have they, but they see not: They have ears, but they hear not: Noses have they, but they smell not: They have hands, but they handle not: Feet have they, but they walk not: Neither speak they through their throat, they that make them are like unto them; so is everyone that trusteth in them."
…... Psalms 115: 4– 8

"And the rest of the men which were not killed by these plagues yet repented not of the works of their hands, that they should not worship devils. And Idols of gold, and silver, and brass, and stone, and of wood: Which neither can see, nor hear, nor walk."
…... **Revelation 9: 20**

Every non-Christian religious organization on earth that has a statue or an idol or an ideology that is to be worshiped, revered, prayed to, defended, offered to- and or sacrificed to- is a false, dead Satanic religion. Satan used unwitting or purposefully disobedient men to set up his decoy religions for the sole purpose of destroying Gods plan for man-kind and stealing Gods greatest and most precious creation away from him; men.

"And the seventh angel sounded; and there were great voices in heaven, saying, The kingdoms of this world are become the Kingdoms of our Lord, and of his Christ [Jesus, when he returns to set up his Kingdom in Jerusalem to rule the earth]; and he shall reign for ever and ever."
…... Revelation 11: 15

"For there are three that bear record in heaven, the Father, the Word [Jesus], and the Holy Ghost: and these three are one."
… 1 John 5: 7

"No ideology (religion), existing today is going to last, none, only Christ will last as King of Kings and Lord of Lords. And He will come back in flaming fire taking vengeance on them that know not God and obey not the Gospel of the Lord Jesus Christ, they are going to be punished with everlasting destruction."

… Billy Graham, Houston Crusade, 1981

"All religions are perversions of Christianity"

… C.S. Lewis

A COURSE IN MIRACLES – WRITTEN BY SATAN

In this segment, the reader needs to pay close attention to detail because when Satan dictated this book he added a new dimension, an extra layer of confusion to add to his claims of 'Changes in the atonement process'. To set the stage for the writing of "A Course in Miracles" or ACIM, Satan, who was the true author, found an agnostic psychologist, Dr. Helen Schucman, and he dictated the entire book to her over a period of 10 years. She claimed that she did not hear an audible voice but an inner voice that fed her a 'rapid dictation' that she took down in shorthand. Satan used terminology that she was familiar with from her occupation as a psychologist: terms such as ego, illusion, sanity, insanity, interpersonal, planes of existence, vertical perception, reciprocal, etc. Satan also used terminology and doctrine from the Christian Bible that Dr. Schucman was not at all familiar with. I am going to lay out Satan's or ACIM's salvation plan for man without any references first then come back later and give references from ACIM and comparison references from the Bible. The 1394 pages of ACIM as a simplified overview follows:

ACCORDING TO ACIM; Everything that has to do with the earth is an illusion or delusion. Men are still in heaven today, they never left heaven, all men are having an illusion in their minds that the earth and our physical bodies exist. Our lives, in general, exist on a physical plane only as an illusion. In mans illusions, Jesus is falsely used only to shift the blame for mans incorrect thoughts (Satans replacement for evil and sin) onto Jesus. So, in effect, Jesus never existed as a physical man and he never went to the cross. Jesus did not die for mans sins since he wasn't really on earth in a flesh body but only existed as a scapegoat in the errant minds of men in heaven until their thoughts are corrected by miracles. Sin does not exist, just wrong thoughts. When men get their thoughts corrected by the use of miracle thoughts then Jesus is released for sins he never committed and **each man has atoned for his own "incorrect thinking" (sins).** God doesn't care about what men call sin, in fact, God encourages men to sin if we find it pleasurable because it has no effect on us.

Space, time, planets, rivers, houses, jobs, etc, are all illusions used only to teach men that they have been thinking incorrectly and incorrectly using Jesus as a scapegoat for their own shortcomings. Death is not real, sickness is not real, the physical world is not real, bodies are not real. So, as you can imagine, that negates the entire Bible since the Bible is based on a flesh man dying on a physical cross and resurrecting from the dead to save all of mankind from sins that, according to ACIM, don't really exist.

Dr. Shucman did not want her name associated with ACIM until after her death, I don't blame her but she missed out on a chance at correction. A normal psychologist would throw up a handful of red flags if someone walked into their office and said, "Nothing is really here, its all an illusion in my head, that's what the voice in my head keeps telling me". But not only did she finish her book, she had two colleagues, both Doctors, helping her. One by typing out her shorthand and the second by editing the book when it was finished. Out of fairness to the Doctor who edited Dr. Schucmans book, he made a comment about the book that I agree with 100% since Satan is the King of the Demons, the following is his conclusion:

"If the Bible were considered literally true, then the course would have to be viewed as demonically inspired."
... Dr. Kenneth Wopnick, Editor of 'A Course in Miracles'

Dr. Helen Schucman was a Psychologist and a Professor of Medical Psychology at Columbia University. Dr. Schucman began hearing "The Voice" or "A Voice" in the mid 1960's and in 1975 ACIM was published. Dr. Schucman describes in an interview her experience while hearing "The Voice":

Dr. Schucman: "A Voice... sounds as though it has something to do with hearing. And I don't hear anything. I think its the sort of hearing that you can't really describe. It doesn't have anything to do with ears...I don't really know...it was very rapid...if I didn't catch a phrase, I could say, "Would you mind doing that again."...It wasn't my voice. It couldn't have been because it talked about a whole area with which I am entirely unfamiliar...And it came very easily, very rapidly, very smoothly...I could stop anytime or pick it up anytime...The only curious thing that I do know, and this is curious, I am used to doing pretty much what I want to. And I do make my own decisions. But for some reason or other it never occurred to me not to do this,...I think the thing that I found upsetting about it was that it went against everything I believe, which is very hard to do... It talked about a system I don't know anything about, and confused me no end..."

… Dr. Helen Schucman interview, ACIM.org, Aug. 1976

In another interview with Dr. Schucman:

"The Voice made no sound, but seemed to be giving me a kind of rapid, inner dictation which I took down in a shorthand notebook. The writing was never automatic. It could be interrupted at any time and later picked up again. It made obvious use of my educational background, interests and experience, but that was in matters of style rather than content. Certainly the subject matter itself was the last thing I would have expected to write about."

Helen Schucman interview,"ACIM, About The Scribes"

According to Dr. Schucman in her interviews, the entirety of her book was taken down verbatim. Dr. Schucman asked "The Voice" to "do that again" which I take to mean repeat what he just said so she could record it accurately. Dr. Schucman was not a Christian but rather a confessed agnostic and was not familiar enough with the Bible to write about ACIMs content. Just as the Bible was inspired by the Holy Spirit in its writing so was ACIM inspired only not by Jesus or the Holy Spirit but by Satan.

"All scripture is given by inspiration of God, and is profitable for doctrine, for reproof, for correction, for instruction in righteousness."

… 2 Timothy 3: 16

Dr. Schucmans colleague, Dr. William Thetford, was present on many occasions when "The Voice" was speaking to Dr. Schucman. He became intrigued by the rapid dictation that she was taking and they worked together to produce the book. Dr. Thetford would type all of Dr. Schucmans dictations and encouraged her to keep going. Dr. Thetford did not add content to the book, he only typed it verbatim according to Dr. Schucmans writings. Below is an interview with Dr. Thetford nine years after the publication of 'A Course in Miracles':

Question: "Helen seemed to have much more difficulty embracing the course material than you did. Was there any kind of spiritual or religious background in your life, or anything else, that made this so?"

Dr. Thetford: "Well, it certainly wasn't due to any early religious background for me. I had gone to the Christian Science Sunday School until age 7, when my sister died suddenly and my parents lost all interest in all religion. Later in my youth I attended various Protestant Churches, but by the time I had finished my graduate work at the University of Chicago, I had certainly given up any interest in religion. Besides I recalled how the University of Chicago was often described as a Baptist University where atheist professors taught Jewish students Thomistic Philosophy! With that kind of background, I think its apparent that whatever religious beliefs I might had would simply have become more confused."

Question: "What would you say is your Philosophical or Spiritual outlook then?"

Dr. Thetford: "I would describe myself as agnostic. I was not really concerned with whether spiritual reality was a fact or not. **Freud regarded religion as an illusion**, and I think many of the graduate students and faculty with whom I associated at the time saw religion as something that lacked intellectual respectability."
... New Realities Magazine, September/October 1984

Satan knows all about Freudian Psychology and that every Psychology Professor knows Freud's views on Religion, it sounds as if Satan influenced Freud also. This is what Satan used, illusion, to model his attack on the Bible around. They both, Schucman and Thetford had a background that was predisposed to accept "Illusion" as a religious doctrine.

When Helen Schucman was a girl she attended Catholic and Southern Baptist Churches. Her family during her childhood were non-observant Jewish. In her adult life she claimed to be agnostic after ACIM and atheist prior to ACIM.

Bill Thetford attended four different denominational Churches into his teen years; Christian Science, Presbyterian, Methodist and Congregational. As an adult he claims to be agnostic where God is unknown and unknowable.

The Bible has something to say to men and women who preach and or teach things other than the doctrine recorded in the Bible. Drs. Schucman and Thetford were both confessed agnostics, they were not saved which meant that they were not led by the Holy Spirit of the Christian Bible. In short, God is bound by His word to mankind through the Bible. The Bible scripturally prohibits Gods use of an agnostic or atheist to rewrite the doctrine of atonement and salvation. ACIM completely opposes every doctrine in the Bible, the Bible says that God never changes and in ACIM there are wholesale changes to the most important scriptures in the Bible. The following scriptures speak directly to Drs. Schucman and Thetford and anyone else who follows and teaches or preaches this false doctrine from Satan;

The Bible "But the natural man [the unsaved; atheists, agnostics] receiveth not the things of the Spirit of God: for they are foolishness unto him: neither can he know them, because they are spiritually discerned [understood]."
...1 Corinthians 2: 14-15

The Bible "For many deceivers are entered into the world, who confess not that Jesus Christ is come in the flesh. This is a deceiver and and anti-Christ."
... 2 John 7

The Bible "Be sober, be vigilant: because your adversary the devil, as a roaring lion, walketh about, seeking whom he may devour."
.... 1 Peter 5: 8

The Bible "To the law and to the testimony: If they speak not according to this word [Gods inspired scriptures, the Bible], it is because there is no light in them."
... Isaiah 8: 20

The Bible "But if our Gospel be hid, it is hid to them that are lost [perishing], in whom the God of this world [Satan] hath blinded the minds of them which believe not, lest the light of the glorious Gospel if Christ, who is the image of God, should shine unto them. For we preach not ourselves, but Christ Jesus the Lord; and ourselves your servants for Jesus' sake. For God, who commanded the light [Jesus] to shine out of darkness, hath shined in our hearts, to give the light of the knowledge of the Glory of God in the face of Jesus Christ."
... 2 Corinthians 4: 3-6

The Bible "This I say therefore, and testify in the Lord, that ye henceforth walk not as other Gentiles [non Jewish people] walk, in the vanity of their mind. Having the understanding darkened, being alienated from the life of God through the ignorance that is in them, because of the blindness of their heart."
... Ephesians 4: 17-18

The Bible "For the time will come when they will not endure sound doctrine; but after their own lusts shall they heap to themselves teachers, having itching ears; and they shall turn away their ears from the truth, and shall be turned unto fables [legendary stories with supernatural circumstances]."
... 2 Timothy 4: 3

The Bible "Now the Spirit speaketh expressly, that in the latter times some shall depart from the faith, giving heed to seducing spirits, and doctrines of devils; speaking lies in hypocrisy; having their conscience seared with a hot iron [making themselves unable to hear the guidance of the Holy Spirit]."... 1 Timothy 4: 1

The Bible "Because the carnal [unsaved] mind is enmity against God: for it is not subject to the law of God, neither indeed can be. So then they that are in the flesh cannot please God. But ye are not in the flesh, but in the Spirit, if so be that the Spirit of God dwell in you. Now if any man have not the Spirit of Christ, he is none of his."
… Romans 8: 7-9

The Bible "(For many walk of whom I have told you often, and now tell you even weeping, that they are the enemies of the cross of Christ: Whose end is destruction, whose God is their belly, and whose glory is in their shame, who mind earthly things [including Satanic literature].)"
… Philippians 3: 18-19

The Bible "For such are false apostles, deceitful workers, transforming themselves into the apostles of Christ. And no marvel; for Satan himself is transformed into and angel of light. Therefore it is no great thing if his ministers [people who allow Satan to use them] also be transformed as the ministers of righteousness; whose end shall be according to their works."
… 2 Corinthians 11: 13-15

The Bible "But though we, or an angel from heaven, preach any other Gospel unto you than that which we have preached unto you, let him be accursed. As we said before, so say I now again, if any man preach any other Gospel unto you than that ye have received, let him be accursed. For do I now persuade men, or God? Or do I seek to please men? For if I yet pleased men, I should not be the servant of Christ. But I certify you, brethren. That the Gospel which is preached of me is not after man. For I neither received it of man, neither was I taught it, but by the revelation of Jesus Christ."
… Galatians 1: 8-12

The Bible "Now I beseech you, brethren, mark them which cause divisions and offenses contrary to the doctrine which ye have learned; and avoid them. For they that are such serve not our Lord Jesus Christ, but their own belly: and by good words and fair

speeches deceive the hearts of the simple."
... Romans 16: 17-18

As I mentioned earlier, these scriptures were also for anyone that followed, but not limited to, the doctrine of 'A Course in Miracles' and/or teach them, you can add the Koran, the Satanic Bible, Evolution to that list also. Some of the leading proponents of ACIM are Dr. Robert Schuller who is the X-pastor of the Crystal Cathedral. Dr. Schuller is also one of the leading proponents of Chrislam [detailed in the next section] which is a hybrid blending of the Christian Bible with the Koran. Another proponent of ACIM is Oprah Winfrey who, in times past, has had speakers and teachers of ACIM on her television show to teach ACIM to her studio and television audience. If you have heard that Oprah claims there are multiple ways to heaven without Jesus this is why!

The latest estimate on the circulation of ACIM is approximately 3 million copies to date. There are an estimated 1500 Christian Churches in the U.S. that use ACIM in their Sunday School classes or in Church Bible studies. Divide the 1500 Churches by 50 states and that's 30 Churches per state on average. It's little wonder that the U.S. is in crisis spiritually. Nowhere in ACIM do you find the name "Jesus". Our lawmakers don't allow the name of Jesus or the 10 commandments to exist in public any longer. Jesus has been taken out of our schools. Christ has been taken out of Christmas and Jesus is no longer spoken of in our government agencies. Our military chaplains are forced to not name the name of Jesus because our government has lost its way. Some Pastors are now saying we don't need Jesus or the cross, they are mixing Islam with Christianity, new supposedly Christian Bibles replace Jesus and Jehovah with Mohammed and Allah, more on this later.

In decades past Biblical scholars put together a list of the fundamental belief requirements for Christianity, they call it the Five Fundamentals of Faith:

1 … Jesus was God from eternity and became flesh

2 … Jesus was born of a virgin

3 … Jesus is the only way to salvation

4 … Jesus was crucified for the sins of all men

5 … Jesus will come again

Here are what happens to the Five Fundamentals of Faith when ACIM is taught:

1 … Jesus was never God in the flesh

2 … Jesus was never born

3 … Jesus saved no one, all men save themselves

4 … Jesus never died

5 … Jesus is not coming

According to ACIM the crucifixion and death of Jesus was an illusion in an imaginary world from mans ego for the purpose of projecting negative thoughts [incorrect thoughts] away from the errant thinking minds of men. Men are not held accountable for the "illusion of sin" because, according to ACIM, men can't sin so men correct their own incorrect thoughts and save themselves. All of ACIM is meant to do away with the need for salvation and the person who supplies that salvation, Jesus. Satan shifts the blame for sin, sickness and death over to the human ego where he claims that is where all errant thoughts [sins] originated from thus hiding himself and his own evil nature; in short, Satan is making himself and his evil works non-existent in the minds of men. Any Sin or evil is only in the mind and has no outward source and Satan is making men to blame for sin by calling sin and incorrect thought.

ACIM "It can indeed be said that ego made its world on sin." …ACIM, page 471

Lets recap Satans 'Fiery Darts', they are thoughts, ideas and suggestions. Men receive them like Dr. Schucman received her communication from Satan, inside her head but disguised as just a thought. Dr. Schucman did not recognize Satans presence because she had no instruction from the word of God about it. She had no idea Satan was using her to write such a destructive book, she had no idea that that was even possible.

The Bible "Put on the whole armour of God, that ye may be able to stand against the wiles [schemes, traps] of the devil...Above all, taking the shield of faith, wherewith ye shall be able to quench all of the fiery darts[thoughts, ideas, suggestions] of the wicked [Satan]."
... Ephesians 6: 11, 16

The characters Satan refers to in ACIM are the Father, Son, and Holy Spirit; only they are not who Satan hopes you believe they are. Satan plans on taking the Holy Spirits place and speak to every man or woman his own desires. He probably will not have them do anything outlandish, only keep them believing they don't need Jesus and have them work to correct their own thinking and they will go straight to Hell when they die, as planned. According to ACIM, God wants men to do their own will not his will:

ACIM "Do you not understand that to oppose the Holy Spirit is to fight yourself? He tells you but your will; He speaks for you... And all he knows is but your knowledge saved for you that you may do your will through him." ...ACIM page 727

ACIM "You cannot separate yourself from the truth by giving "autonomy" to behavior. This is controlled by me automatically as soon as you place what you think under my guidance. Whenever you are afraid, it is a sure sign that you have allowed your mind to miscreate and have not allowed me to guide it."
...ACIM page 48-49

Below are 3 examples where ACIM refers to Biblical scriptures and Satan is feigning (pretending) to be Jesus or the Holy Spirit.

ACIM "No man cometh to the Father but by me" does not mean that I am in any way separate or different from you except in time, **and time does not really exist.**" ...ACIM page 25

ACIM "A guide does not control but he does direct, leaving it up to you to follow; 'Lead us not into temptation' means' Recognize your errors and chose to abandon them by following my guidance." ... ACIM page 27

ACIM "God is not mocked" is not a warning but a reassurance, God would be mocked if any of his creations lacked holiness. The creation is whole, and the mark of wholeness is holiness." ...ACIM page 30-31

In the above statement Satan is saying that God created everything whole and sinless and in no need of being saved thus excluding Jesus, the savior of the world.

ACIM is literally re-writing Biblical concepts especially those concerning salvation and the true way to Heaven which in the end, for those who follow ACIMs doctrine, would usher men into Hell, its 100% anti-Jesus and anti-man. Illusionary world or not; ACIM is still planting the seeds of doubt about the Bible into the souls of men and the following accounts in ACIM are responded to with accounts in the Christian Bible;

ACIM "There is no life outside of Heaven. Where God created life, there life must be. In any state apart from Heaven life is illusion." ACIM page 574

The Bible Jesus speaking "Let not your heart be troubled, ye believe in God, believe also in me. In my fathers house are many mansions; if it were not so, I would have told you. I go to prepare a place for you. And if I go to prepare a place for you, I will come again, and receive you unto myself; that were I am [Heaven #3], there you may be also"...John 14: 1-3

ACIM Man created the world as an illusion in his mind- "Salvation is no more than a reminder this world is not your home...And nothing that you think you see in it is really there at all. This is seen and understood as each one takes his part in its

undoing, as he did in making it." ACIM page 615
.. Also.."It is as needful that you recognize you made the world you see." ACIM page 526

The Bible "For by Him [Jesus] were all things created, that are in Heaven, and that are in earth, visible and invisible, whether they be thrones, or dominions, or principalities, or power: all things were crated by him, and for him." ... Colossians 1: 16

ACIM God did not create mans body, the body is an illusion. "The body neither lives nor dies, because it cannot contain you who are life...God did not make the body, because it is destructible, and therefore not of the Kingdom." ... ACIM page 133,134

The Bible "And the Lord God formed man of the dust of the ground, and breathed into his nostrils the breath of life; and man became a living soul. ... Genesis 2:7
."For He [God] knoweth our frame [body], He remembereth that we are dust." ...Psalms 103 : 14

ACIM Sin is an illusion- "Forget not that the ego [within the mind] has dedicated the body to the goal of sin, and places in it all its faith that this can be accomplished." ACIM page 486

...Also... "Are not the frail entitled to believe that every stolen scrap of pleasure is their righteous payment for their little lives? Their death will pay the price for all of them, if they enjoy their benefits [sins] or not. The end of life must come, whatever way the life be spent. And so take pleasure in the quickly passing and ephemeral. These are not sins, but witness unto the strange belief that sin and death are real, and innocence and sin will end alike within the termination of the grave." ... ACIM page 656

The Bible "For all have sinned, and come short of the glory of God; being justified freely [without works] by his grace through the redemption that is in Christ Jesus." ... Romans 3: 23-24

... Bible... "But if we walk in the light, as He is in the light, we have fellowship one with another, and the blood of Jesus Christ his son cleanseth us from all sin. If we say that we have no sin, we deceive ourselves, and the truth is not in us."...1 John 1: 7-10

ACIM Fear is an illusion- "You can never control the effects of fear yourself, because you made fear, and believe in what you made." ACIM page 32

The Bible "The fear of the Lord is the beginning of wisdom: and the knowledge of the Holy is understanding." ... Proverbs 9: 10

The Bible records fear or a variation of fear; feared, feareth,etc., 518 times.

ACIM Truth is an illusion- "Illusion meets illusion; truth, itself." ... ACIM page 568

The Bible "**Jesus saith** unto him '**I am** the way, **the truth**, and the life: no man cometh unto the Father, but by me." .. John 14: 6

ACIM Sickness and death are both illusions- "Miracles enable you to heal the sick and raise the dead because you made sickness and death yourself." ... ACIM page 21

...Also... "The body cannot heal, because it cannot make itself sick. It needs no healing. It's health or sickness depends entirely on how the mind perceives it, and the purpose that the mind would use it for. " ... ACIM page 466

The Bible "How God anointed Jesus of Nazareth with the Holy Ghost and with power: who went about doing good, and healing all that were oppressed of the devil; for God was with him." ...Acts 10: 38

...Also... "And it is appointed unto men once to die, but after this the judgment." ... Hebrews 9: 27

ACIM Jesus' crucifixion was an illusion- "If a person identifies with the death of Jesus on the cross he is insane." ... ACIM page 119-120

...ACIM... The betrayal of the son of God [Jesus] lies only in illusions, and all his "sins" are but his own imaginings."
...ACIM page 413

The Bible "In Him [Jesus] was life; and life was the light of men. And the light shineth in darkness [on unredeemed men], and the darkness comprehended it not....And the word [Jesus] was made flesh [born a man on the earth], and dwelt among us, (and we beheld his glory, the glory as of the only begotten of the Father,) full of grace and truth." ... John 1: 4-5, 14

... Also... "Beloved, believe not every Spirit, but try the Spirits whether they are of God: because many false prophets are gone out into the world. Hereby know ye the Spirit of God: Every Spirit that confesseth that Jesus Christ is come in the flesh is of God: And every Spirit the confesseth not that Jesus Christ is come in the flesh is not of God: and this is the spirit of anti-Christ, whereof ye have heard that it shall come; and even now already it is in the world." ... 1 John 4: 1-3

ACIM The call for everyone to teach that Jesus never died!- "You will not find peace until you have removed the nails from the hands of Gods Son, and taken the last thorn from his forehead. The love of God surrounds his son whom the God of crucifixion condemns. Teach not that I died in vain. Teach rather that I did not die by demonstrating that I live in you." ...ACIM page 252

ACIM "You are not persecuted, nor was I [presumably Jesus speaking but actually Satan]." ... ACIM page 121

The Bible Jesus speaking "Blessed are you when men shall revile you, **and persecute you**, and shall say all manner of evil against you falsely, for my sake." ... Mathew 5: 11

ACIM   Man saves himself- "You do not have to seek far for salvation. Every minute and every second gives you a chance to save yourself." ... ACIM page 214

...Also... "Choose once again if you would take your place among the saviors of the world, or would remain in Hell, and hold your brothers there."... ACIM page769

The Bible "Jesus saith unto him, I am the way, the truth, and the life: no man cometh to the Father [or goes to heaven], but by me."...John 14: 6

...**Bible**... "Be it known unto you all, and to all the people of Israel, that by the name of Jesus Christ of Nazareth, whom ye crucified, whom God raised from the dead, even by him doth this man stand here before you whole. This is the stone[Jesus] which was set at naught of you builders [they disregarded Jesus as a false prophet], which has become the head of the corner! Neither is there salvation in any other: for there is none other name under Heaven given among men, whereby we must be saved." ... Acts 4: 10-12

...Also... "Even the righteousness of God which is by faith of Jesus Christ unto all and upon all them that believe: for there is no difference: for all have sinned, and come short of the glory of God; being justified freely by his grace through the redemption that is in Christ Jesus: Whom God has set forth to be a propitiation through faith in his blood, to declare his righteousness for the remission of sins that are past, through the forbearance of God; to declare, I say, at this time his righteousness: that he might be just, and the justifier of him that believeth in Jesus." ... Romans 3: 22-26

ACIM Jesus can be mistaken!- "The Son of God [Jesus] can be mistaken, he can deceive himself; He can even turn the power of his mind against himself." ... ACIM page 471

...Also... "In time, the Holy Spirit clearly sees the Son of God [Jesus] can make mistakes. On this you share His vision." ...ACIM page 473

The Bible "Then answered Jesus and said unto them, verily, verily, I say unto you, the Son can do nothing of himself, but what He seeth the Father do: For what things soever He doeth, these also doeth the Son likewise."... John 5: 19-23

...Bible... "I[Jesus] can of mine own self do nothing: As I hear, I judge: And my judgment is just; because I seek not mine own will but the will of the Father which hath sent me." ... John 5: 30

... Also... Jesus speaking "I and my Father are one."...John 10: 30

ACIM "God has but one son, there is but one God." ACIM page 226

...Also... " God has not many sons, but only one, who can have more, and who be given less?... ACIM page 719

The Bible "For the earnest expectation of the creature waiteth for the manifestation of the sons of God [The plurality of sons, many more than one son]." Romans 8: 19

ACIM "Swear not to die, you Holy son of God! You make a bargain you cannot keep. The son of life cannot be killed. He is immortal as His Father."... ACIM page 713

Satan is trying to convince men that the eternal Jesus could not die on the cross if he wanted to; Yes he is God and he is immortal. Nevertheless Jesus came and did just that, He died in the flesh body he was born in for you and me.

The Bible "Blessed be the God and Father of our Lord Jesus Christ, which according to his abundant mercy hath begotten us again to a lively hope by the resurrection of Jesus Christ from the dead. To an inheritance uncorruptible, and undefiled, and that fadeth not away, reserved in Heaven for you. Who are kept by the power of God through faith unto salvation ready to be revealed in the last time." ... 1 Peter 1: 3-5

...Also... "Jesus said unto her, **I am the resurrection**, and the life: he that believeth in me, though he were dead, yet shall he live. And whosoever liveth and believeth in me shall never die. Believest thou this?" ... John 11: 28-30

ACIM "If this were the real world, God would be cruel. For no Father could subject his children to this as the price of salvation and be loving. Love does not kill to save." ... ACIM page 283

The Bible "For God so loved the world, that he gave his only begotten son [Jesus], that whosoever believeth in him should not perish, but have eternal life." ... John 3: 16

...Also... Jesus speaking: "Greater love hath no man than this, that a man lay down his life for his friends."... John 15: 13

ACIM "The second coming is merely the return of sense... The second coming is the awareness of reality, not its return." ACIM page 208-209

The Bible "In my Fathers house are many mansions: If it were not so I would have told you. I go to prepare a place for you, and If I go and prepare a place for you, I will come again, and receive you unto myself; that where I am there you may be also." .. John 14: 2-3

ACIM "How wonderful it is to do your will [not Gods]; ...unless you do your will you are not free... He [God] joins with you in willing you be free. And to oppose Him is to make a choice against yourself, and choose that you be bound."...ACIM page 728

The Bible "And He [Jesus] said, Abba, Father, all things are possible unto thee; take away this cup from me: nevertheless not what I will but what thou wilt." ... Mark 14: 36

...Also... Jesus speaking "For whosoever shall do the will of my Father which is in Heaven, the same is my brother, and sister, and mother."... Mathew 12: 50

...Also... "Thy Kingdom come, thy will be done in earth as it is in Heaven." ... Mathew 6: 10

ACIM "For the world is the opposite of heaven, being made to be its opposite, and everything here takes a direction exactly opposite of what is true." ... ACIM page 402

The Bible "For thus saith the Lord that created the Heavens; God Himself that formed the earth and made it; He hath established it, He created it not in vain, He formed it to be inhabited: I am the Lord, and there is none else."... Isaiah 45: 18

...Bible... "And God made the firmament, and divided the waters which were under the firmament from the waters which were above the firmament; and it was so. And God called the firmament Heaven. And the evening and the morning were the second day...And God said let the waters bring forth abundantly the moving creature that hath life, and fowl that may fly above the earth in the open firmament of heaven."... Genesis 1: 7-8,20

Heaven #1 – Earths atmosphere [the firmament] where birds fly. Earth is not the opposite of heaven its part of the heavens. Hell would be the opposite of Heaven.

...Also... "Thou art worthy, O Lord, to receive glory and honour and power: for thou hast created all things, and for thy pleasure they are and were created."... Revelation 4: 11

ACIM "The Bible repeatedly states that you should praise God. This hardly means that you should tell him how wonderful he is, He has no ego with which to accept such praise, and no perception with which to judge it."... ACIM page 95

The Bible "I will call upon the Lord, who is worthy to be praised: so shall I be saved from my enemies."... Psalms 18:3

...Also... "But you are a chosen generation, a royal priesthood, an holy nation, a peculiar people: that you should shew forth the praises of Him who hath called you out of darkness into His marvelous light." ...1 Peter 2: 9

...Also..." Jesus speaking "Yea; have you never read, out of the mouths of babes and sucklings thou hast perfected praise?" ...Mathew 21: 16

ACIM "The journey to the cross should be the last useless journey...Do not make the pathetic error of clinging to the old rugged cross."... ACIM page 74

...Also... "The idea that the guiltless son of God can attack himself and make himself guilty is insane... Nothing can justify insanity, and to call for punishment upon yourself must be insane." ... ACIM page 312

...ACIM... "Sacrifice is a notion totally unknown to God."
...ACIM page 57

...Also... "The crucifixion did not establish the atonement; the resurrection did." ...ACIM page 56

...Also... "You do not have to seek far for salvation. Every minute and every second gives you a chance to save yourself."
...ACIM page 214

...Also... " And the pain in this [mans] mind is so apparent, when it is uncovered, that its need of healing cannot be denied. Not all the tricks and games you offer it can heal it, for here is the real crucifixion of Gods Son. And yet he is not crucified. Here is both his pain and his healing, **for the Holy Spirit is merciful and his remedy is quick.**" ...ACIM page 291

The last line is written in the same style as the Koran; **for Allah is merciful and his remedy quick.**

The Bible "But we speak the wisdom of God in a mystery, even the hidden wisdom, which God ordained before the world unto our glory. Which none of the princes of this world knew [Satan, Demons}: for had they known it, they would not have crucified the Lord of glory [Jesus]."... 1 Corinthians 2: 7-8

...Also... 'Be it known unto you all, and to all the people of Israel, that by the name of Jesus Christ of Nazareth, whom ye crucified, whom God raised from the dead...Neither is there salvation in any other: for there is none other name under heaven given among men, whereby we must be saved."... Acts 4:10,12

...Also... "For even the son of man [Jesus] came not to be ministered unto but to minister and to give his life a ransom for many."... Mark 10:4 5

...Also... "But this man [Jesus], after he had offered one sacrifice for sins forever [His crucifixion], sat down on the right hand of God...For by one offering He hath perfected forever them that are sanctified...And their sins and iniquities I will remember no more."... Hebrews 10: 12, 14, 17

...Bible... " Who in the days of his flesh [Jesus the man], when He had offered up prayers and supplications with strong crying and tears unto Him [Jehovah] that was able to save Him from death, and was heard in that He feared; though He were a son, yet learned He obedience, by the things which he suffered; And being made perfect, He became the author of eternal salvation unto all them that obey Him; called of God a high Priest after the order of Melchizedek."... Hebrews 5: 7-10

The Bible records that Satan is the God of this world!

"But if our Gospel [The recorded ministry of Jesus] be hid, it is hid to them that are lost [perishing]. In whom the God of this world [Satan] hath blinded the minds of them which believe not. Lest the light of the glorious Gospel of Christ, who is the image of God, should shine unto them."...2 Corinthians 4: 3-4

ACIM "There are no idolaters in the Kingdom but there is great appreciation for everything that God created, because of the calm knowledge that each one is part of him. Gods son knows no idols, but he does know His Father"... ACIM page 225

The Bible "Be ye not unequally yoked together with unbelievers: for what fellowship hath righteousness with unrighteousness? And what communion hath light with darkness? And what concord hath Christ [Holiness] with Belial [an unholy demonic]? Or what part hath he that believeth with an infidel? **And what agreement hath the temple of God with idols?** For ye are the temple of the living God; as God hath said, I will dwell in them [inside of our human bodies], and walk in them; and I will be their God, and they shall be my people."... 2 Corinthians 6: 14-16

...Also... "**Idolatry**, witchcraft, hatred, variance, emulations, wrath, strife, seditions, heresies, envyings, murders, drunkenness, revellings, and such like: of the which I tell you before, as I have also told you in time past, that they which do such things will not inherit the Kingdom of God."... Galatians 5: 20

ACIM "The first coming of Christ is merely another name for the creation, for Christ is the son of God. The second coming

Christ means nothing more than the end of the ego's rule and the healing of the mind."... ACIM pg. 88

The Bible "In the beginning God created the Heaven and the earth." ... Genesis 1: 1

Also .... "And God created great whales, and every living creature that moveth, which the waters brought forth abundantly after their kind, and every winged fowl after his kind: and God saw that it was good."... Genesis... 1: 21

The Bible continues: "I [God] have made the earth, and created man upon it: I, even my hands, have stretched out the heavens, and all there host have I commanded." ... Isaiah 45: 12

The second coming according to the Christian Bible:

"For if we believe that Jesus died and rose again, even so them also which sleep in Jesus will God bring with him. For this we say unto you by the word of the Lord, that we which are alive and remain unto the coming of the Lord shall not prevent them which are asleep. For the Lord himself shall descend from heaven with a shout, with the voice of the archangel, and with the trump of God: and the dead in Christ shall rise first: Then we which are alive and remain shall be caught up together with them in the clouds, to meet the Lord in the air: and so shall we ever be with the Lord." ...1 Thessalonians 4: 14 – 17

ACIM "The Holy Spirit forgives everything because God created everything." ... ACIM pg. 206

The Bible "Wherefore I say unto you, all manner of sin and blasphemy shall be forgiven unto men: but the blasphemy against the Holy Ghost shall not be forgiven unto men." ... Mathew 12: 31

ACIM "It is impossible to speak in an unknown tongue."
...ACIM pg. 198

The Bible "And these signs shall follow them that believe;...they shall speak with new [unknown] tongues. ... Mark 16: 17

I, personally, am a witness to Spiritual revelation that a Christian can receive from God based solely on speaking in tongues.

ACIM "Your insane laws were made to guarantee that you would make mistakes, and give them power over you by accepting their results as your just due, what could this be but madness? ... ACIM pg. 505

Before I give the Bible response to ACIM about the law I am going to give a brief overview of what Jesus did to redeem mankind.

The law of the old testament was given so that unholy and unrighteous men would know they are in opposition to Gods will.

Bible "Knowing this, that the law is not made for a righteous man, but for the lawless and disobedient, for the ungodly and for sinners, for unholy and profane, for murderers of fathers and murderers of mothers, for manslayers, For whoremongers, for them that defile themselves with mankind, for menstealers, for liars, for perjured persons, and if there be any other thing that is contrary to sound doctrine." ... 1 Timothy 1 : 9 – 10

Jesus came to fulfill the law!

Bible "Think not that I am come to destroy the law, or the prophets: I am not come to destroy, but to fulfill."
... Mathew 5: 17

Every law that was ever broken or ever would be broken [Biblically known as sins] Jesus took upon his body when He died on the cross. When a person, by faith, receives Jesus's work on the cross; His death, burial and resurrection that person's lawlessness is redeemed by the only person who ever kept the law and fulfilled the law. When father Jehova looks upon that person after they have received Jesus's redemption he sees only Jesus because that person became the embodiment of Christ on the earth and Christ is sinless which makes the Christian sinless also.

Bible "For we are members of his [Jesus'] body, of his flesh, and of his bones..... For this cause shall a man leave his father and mother, and shall be joined unto his wife, and they two shall be one flesh. ... For the husband is the head of the wife, even as Christ is the head of the church: and he is the savior of the body." ... Ephesians 5: 30, 31, 23

Also: "And He is the head of the body [Today known as Christians], the church: who is the beginning, the firstborn from the dead; that in all things he might have preeminence." ... Colossians 1: 18

Now for the response of ACIMs claim of "Insane Laws"

The Bible "Knowing that a man is not justified by the works of the law, but by the faith of Jesus Christ, even we have believed in Jesus Christ, that we might be justified by the faith of Christ, and not by the works of the law; for by the works of the law shall no flesh be justified."... Galatians 2: 16

Also "Not by works of righteousness which we have done, but according to His mercy He saved us, by the washing of regeneration, and renewing of the Holy Ghost; which He shed on us abundantly through Jesus Christ our Savior." ... Titus 3: 5 – 6

The Bible again: "But now we are delivered from the law,that being dead therein we were held: that we should serve in newness of Spirit, and not in the oldness of the letter [The Mosaic Law of the old testament]. What shall we say then? Is the law sin? God forbid. Nay, I had not known sin, but by the law; for I had not known lust, except the law had said, thou shalt not covet. But sin, taking occasion by the commandment, wrought [created] in me all manner of concupiscence [desire]. For without the law sin was dead. For I was alive without the law once: but when the commandment came, sin revived and I died...Was then that which is good [the knowledge of lawlessness or sin] made death unto me? God forbid. But sin, that it might appear sin, worketh death in me [the wages of sin is death for all mankind] by that which is good that sin by the commandment might become exceedingly sinful. [Given to man to avoid sin and avoid death]" ... Romans 7: 6-9, 13

God did not say that by the keeping of the law there is a remission of sin. He said that by the shedding of blood there is a remission of sin. Jesus shed His blood that all men may share in His redemption as sinless and righteous.

"And almost all things are by the law purged with blood; and without shedding of blood is no remission [forgiveness of sin]." ... Hebrews 9: 22

ACIM "God does not teach. To teach is to imply a lack, which God knows is not there." ... ACIM pg. 132

Bible "But the comforter, which is the Holy Ghost, whom the Father will send in my name, **He shall teach you all things**, and bring all things to your remembrance, whatsoever I have said unto you." ... John 14: 26

Also: "Now we have received, not the spirit of the world, but the Spirit which is of God [Holy Spirit]; that we might know the things that are freely given to us of God. Which things also we speak, not in the words which mans wisdom teacheth; **but which the Holy Ghost teacheth**; comparing spiritual things with spiritual. But the natural man receiveth not the things of the Spirit of God; for they are foolishness unto him: neither can he know them, because they are spiritually discerned." ... 1 Corinthians 2: 12 -14

Also in the Bible: " But the comforter, which is the Holy Ghost, whom the Father will send in my name, **He shall teach you all things**, and bring all things to your remembrance, whatsoever I have said unto you." ... John 14: 26

ACIM "After correction is complete, the Holy Spirit will depart from men." ... ACIM pg.129

The Bible "And I will pray the Father, and He shall give you another comforter, **that He may abide with you forever.**" ... John 14: 16

The above verse is another Biblical proof that God would not have used Drs. Schucman and Thetford to write a new atonement doctrine for mankind. By the wording in this verse something has to happen prior to receiving the Holy Spirit. According to the first word in the verse, "AND", then Jesus will pray to the father to send the Holy Spirit to them. The requirement is to keep Gods commandments first then He sends the comforter. Neither Schucman nor Thetford received Jesus's atonement for their sins so they never passed the first hurdle for the ministry of the Holy Spirit to move in and guide them throughout their lives. They had no Holy Spirit so they had no guidance which proves the spirit that they were hearing was not the Holy Spirit but Satan. They were both agnostics and atheists by their own admission. They neither loved God nor did they keep His commandments.

"If you love me, keep my commandments. And I will pray the Father, and He shall give you another comforter, that He may abide with you forever." ... John 14: 15- 16

ACIM "You are not two selves in conflict." ... ACIM pg. 396

The Bible "This I say then, walk in the Spirit and ye shall not fulfil the lust of the flesh. For the flesh lusteth against the Spirit, and the Spirit against the flesh: and these are contrary the one to the other: so that ye cannot do the things that ye would." ... Galatians 5: 16- 17

This harkens back to the two natures we each have in our souls, the sin nature from Satan and Gods law written on our hearts. Even after we are born again our souls have the old nature in operation to a degree, that is why we need to renew our minds or wash our minds with Gods scriptures so we know Gods heart and we don't fulfil our old natural way of thinking. It does not happen over-night but requires constant reading and hearing Gods word.

As you can clearly see, there is absolutely no agreement between the Holy Bible and "A Course in Miracles" and they are not written by the same God. It amazed me to learn that 1500 Christian Church's use this Satanic book inside Jesus's Church teaching Jesus's body that Jesus is no longer required for salvation. This is part of the falling away that the Bible speaks of, more on this in the next segment on "Islam". God said that Satan weakened the nations of the earth when he fell from heaven and ACIM has its own share of that weakening but even ACIM is nothing compared with Evolution and Islam where millions upon millions have been led astray.

"How art thou fallen from Heaven, O Lucifer [Satan], son of the morning! How art thou cut down to the ground, which didst weaken the nations. For thou [Satan] hast said in thine heart, I will ascend into Heaven, I will exalt my throne above the stars of God: I will sit also upon the mount of the congregation, in the sides of the North: I will ascend above the heights of the clouds: I will be like the most high. Yet thou shalt be brought down to hell, to the sides of the pit." ... Isaiah 14: 12- 15

... ACIM, cited from the 2007 edition by Barnes and Noble

Bible	**ACIM** (comparison)
Jesus came to save the lost	(Satan) is trying to keep the lost lost
Jesus came to destroy the works of Satan	(Satan) is trying to destroy the works of Jesus
Satan is the source of evil and corruption	Mans ego is the source of evil and corruption
The Bible was given by inspiration of God	A.C.I.M. was given by dictation of Satan
Jesus saves men	Men save themselves

Chapter 11

IS THE GOD OF THE CHRISTIAN BIBLE ALSO THE GOD OF THE KORAN OF ISLAM

So far we have compared the Bible to the church of Satan; then the Bible to the **evolutionists** or **humanists** model, then ACIM. Now **let's** compare the Bible to Islams Koran (Quran) to see if both of these religions share the same God as many today believe.

Let's compare certain verses in the Christian Bible to **verses** in the Koran to see if each **reflect** the same values, morals **and** directives for their followers. If the values, morals and directives are an exact match then we can say "Yes, they share the same God. If the values, morals and directives do not match then they would not share the same God. Before we begin, remember earlier about Satan's use **of** perverting everything that has to do with the one true Christian God to deceive man-kind. Keep that in mind when Mohammed [Allah's prophet and writer of the Koran] talks about certain attributes such as morality or God [which God is he referring to?], or any other descriptive words, they are aimed specifically at Muslim **religious** beliefs only.

The Roles are Reversed!

For **clarity,** I will tell you at the outset that the God that Mohammed **speaks of** is not the God of the Christian Bible and the Satan he **speaks of** is not the Satan of the Christian Bible. Looking at it from a Christian perspective, the God of Islam is the Christian Bibles Satan and the Satan of Islam is the Christian Bibles God. This is where all of the confusion has come from concerning Islam and the Western belief system. Everyone is using the same terminology but the personalities and **"offices" held,** (Gods, Satan's) behind them are opposites. The Christian God is absolutely not the Islamic god. Mohammed's morality is not the morality of the Christian Bible, Mohammed was inspired to write Satanic morality which in this case is Christian immorality. If Mohammed says that Allah says it's acceptable to own slaves and to solicit them out for prostitution then that is morally acceptable in Islam, not in Christianity. If Mohammed says to kill anyone that leaves the religion of Islam then murder is perfectly acceptable in the Islamic religion. When Muslims say that they adhere to a higher moral standard they are saying they adhere to what Mohammed's claims Allah commands them to do, murder, lie, own slaves or solicit prostitutes. etc.- and that, in their minds, is morally acceptable and hence, since Allah commanded it then it holds a greater morality than the morality of all other religions.

Islamic morality equates to Koranic commandments and the Koran disagrees with the Bibles Ten commandments! Eastern Muslim morality does not equate to Western Christian morality. Islam does not live by the Western Christian ethic, they live solely by what Mohammed said Allah said. Mohammed's only miracle in his life was writing down what he heard Allah say to him. Mohammed died nearly 1400 years ago and he didn't know where he was going when he died! (Why did Allah wait so long to send a prophet to write his word, the Koran?)

Mohammed speaking:
"When I am dead and buried in the ground, and go back to dust, is that all? What will happen to me?"
…….. Koran, Surah 19: 66

Jesus speaking:
"That whosoever believeth in him [Jesus] should not perish, but have eternal life. For God so loved the world, that he gave his only begotten son, that whosoever believeth in him should not perish, but have everlasting life."
…… Bible, John 3: 15 – 16

Jesus speaking:
"Verily, verily, I say unto **thee,** except a man be born again, [receive Jesus as Lord], he cannot see the **Kingdom of Heaven** [**he** will be imprisoned in hell]."
….. Bible, John 3: 3

Mohammed speaking:
…"But if they [**non-Islamists**] fight you, slay them. Such is the reward of those who reject faith
[of Islam]….**and** fight them on until there is no more persecution and **the religion** [Judaism , Hinduism or Christianity **etc.**] becomes Allah's"
….. Koran, Surah **2**: 191, 193

Jesus speaking:
"Ye have heard that it hath been **said, thou** shall love thy neighbor, and hate thine enemy. But I say unto you, love your enemies, bless them that curse you, do good to them that hate you, and pray for them which despitefully use you, and persecute you: That ye may be the children of your father which is in heaven; for he **maketh** the sun to rise on the evil and on the good, and **sendeth** rain on the just and on the unjust."
….. Bible, Mathew 5: 43- 45

Mohammed speaking:
"Fighting is prescribed upon you [Islam], and you dislike it. But it is possible that you dislike a thing that is good for you."
….. Koran, Surah **2**: 26

Mohammed speaking:
"Let those fight in the cause of Allah who **sell** the life of this world for the hereafter. To him who **fighteth** in the cause of Allah, -whether he is slain [**martyred**] or gets victory – soon shall we give him a reward of great (value)."
….. Koran, Surah **4**: 74

In the Islamic world, Muslim's fight and die for their God **Allah**. **What** does Satan desire for men? Death; Satan came but for to steal, to kill, and to destroy.
In the Christian world, God took on a human body and died for all of us so that we may each live!
What did Jesus come to the earth to provide? Abundant Life for all men that receive him.

As recorded earlier, Jesus speaking:

"The thief [Satan] cometh not, but for to steal, and to kill, and to destroy: I [Jesus] am come that they might have life, and that they might have it more abundantly."
... John 10: 10

"But [Jesus] made himself of no reputation, and took upon him the form of a servant, and was made in the likeness of men: And being found in fashion as a man, he humbled himself, and became obedient unto death, even the death of the cross. Wherefore God also hath highly exalted him, and given him a name which is above every name: That at the name of Jesus every knee should bow, of things in heaven [heavens 2 and 3], and things in earth [heaven 1], and things under the earth [hell, the lake of fire]: **And that every tongue should confess that Jesus Christ is Lord, to the Glory of God the Father.**"
…... Bible, Philippians 2: 7 – 11

As in "A Course in Miracles" Satan wrote the Koran specifically to drive men away from Jesus Christ as the savior of the world.

In 8 chapters in the Koran there are almost identical verses that all say the same thing:
Anyone that confesses that Jesus is the son of God is cursed and they will go to hell for believing it.

Sura's 4:165– 5:18– 6:101– 9:30– 17:111– 19:38– 23:91 – 88:92
Why would Allah [Satan] go to such extremes about Jesus?
Because Jesus is the Son of God and all who find him find eternal

life. Satan's main objective is to keep men from Jesus.

THE MADRASES - ISLAMIC SCHOOLS OF INTOLERANCE

There are schools in Islamic countries where the Korans intolerance of other religions and peoples are being taught to potential future Islamic terrorists by the millions. These schools push the verses in the Koran which pertain to taking over the world for Allah through compulsion (force), violence and death if necessary. Why would you teach intolerance to millions of your children? Perhaps you are a people preparing for war- why else.

Below is an excerpt from Don Richardsons book; "Secrets of the Koran":

"At least 40 million Muslim youth in the Muslim world's religious schools, called Madrases, are avidly memorizing the entire Koran plus a general extremest body of related traditions – the Hadiths [*]. In the hands of extremists – whether run by Saudi Wahabbists, Osama Bin Laden's followers or Indonesian Mullahs- these schools become breeding grounds for potential terrorists. Early in the training, Muslim teachers especially focus pliable young minds on dozens of the Korans extremely militant war verses, plus other texts that assure paradise for Muslim martyrs. Hatred for Jews and Christians (largely synonymous with Israel and America) and general disdain for all non-Muslims (defined by Muslim instructors as the House of War) are deeply instilled. The Bible is described as corrupted, separation of Islam from political control is despised."
…... Don Richardson, "Secrets of the Koran", 2003, pg. 69

*... The 'Hadiths' mentioned above are commentaries written, verse by verse on the Koran by Islamic scholars.

What are called Islamic Terrorists in the West are called obedient servants of Allah in the East. Their duty is service to Allah and Allah commands the conquering of the entire globe. That's why it seems absurd to the West that Islamic Terrorist groups like ISIS or ISIL can have a 400 page thick annual report that spells out and documents the previous years death and destruction perpetrated for Allah. Its an Islamic Business Report on death and destruction. There are several different denominations or sects that are under the umbrella of Islam including splinter groups within the different sects. The writers of the 'Hadiths' were the main reason for the splits in the Islamic religion. The Scholars who wrote the 'Hadiths' wrote their own independent collections of the 'Hadiths' and they did not agree with each other. This is the reason certain sects of Islam are fighting with other sects within Islam. They are basically engaged in a Civil War based on their religious beliefs that differ through each scholars Hadith collection, not on governmental policies or disputes. If you are a Christian, could you imagine the Catholics and the Baptists fighting and killing each other over differences in their denominational beliefs. This is yet another reason why there has not been nor will there ever be peace in the Middle East – until Jesus returns.

Below are a number of verses from the Koran that are probably being taught as part of the "House of War" teachings at the Madrases:

"It is he who has sent his messenger with guidance and the religion of truth. That he make it prevail over all religion [take over the world], even though the Pagans [Non-Islamists] may detest."
….. Koran, Surah 61: 9

"Remember thy Lord [Allah] inspired the angels (with the message): I am with you: give firmness to the believers [In Islam]: I will instill terror into the hearts of **the unbelievers [Non-Islamists- Christians, Judaism, etc]: Strike off their heads, strike off their fingertips."** *….. Koran, Surah 8: 12

*.....The Ali translation of the Koran in the English translation says: "Smite ye above their necks and smite all their fingertips off them. " instead of "Strike off their heads, strike off their fingertips"-
...The English Ali translation tries to diminish the vulgarity of the Koran for the western reader.

"And fight them on until there is no more persecution, and religion becomes Allah's in its entirety [control of the world by one religion – Islam]. But if they cease, verily Allah doth see all that they do."
…... Koran, Surah 8: 39

"When you travel through the earth, there is no blame on you if you shorten your prayers, for fear the unbelievers [Non-Islamics] may attack you; **for unbelievers [Judaism, Christianity, etc.] are to you open enemies**. When thou (O Messenger) art with them, and standeth to lead them in prayer, let one party of them stand up (in prayer) with thee, taking their arms [weapons] with them:..."
….. Koran, Surah 4: 101 – 102

"O ye who believe [in Islam]! Take not the Jews and the Christians for your friends and protectors. They are but friends and protectors to each other. And he amongst you that turns to them (for friendship) is of them. Verily Allah guideth not a people unjust."
…….. Koran, Surah 5: 51

"The punishment of those who wage war against Allah and his messenger, and strive with might and main for mischief through the land is; Execution, or Crucifixion or the cutting off of hands and feet from opposite sides, or exile from the land: That is their disgrace in this world, and a heavy punishment is theirs in the hereafter."
….. Koran, Surah 5: 33

280.

"**Never should a believer [of Islam] kill a believer; except by mistake**, and whoever kills a believer by mistake it is ordained that he should free a believing slave."
…… Koran, Surah 4: 92

"Not equal are those believers who sit (at home), except those who are disabled, and those who strive and fight in the cause of Allah with their goods and their persons. Allah hath granted a grade higher to those who strive and fight with their goods and persons than to those who sit (at home). Unto all (In faith of Islam) hath Allah promised good; **but those who strive and fight hath he distinguished above those who sit** (at home) by a great reward."
….. Koran, Surah 4: 95

"Then fight in Allah's cause- Thou art held responsible only for thyself- and rouse the believers [In Islam], It may be that Allah will restrain the fury of the unbelievers [Judaism, Christianity,etc.], for Allah is the strongest in might and in punishment."
….. Koran, Surah 4: 84

"O Prophet: Rouse the believers [In Islam] to the fight. If there are 20 amongst you, patient and persevering, they will vanquish 200 [Jews, Christians,etc.] : If a hundred, they will vanquish a thousand of the unbelievers [Non-Islamists]: for these are people without understanding."
…… Koran, Surah 8: 65

"Fight those who believe not in Allah nor the last day, nor hold that forbidden which hath been forbidden by Allah and his messenger [Mohammad], **nor acknowledge the religion of truth, from among the people of the book [the Torah, the Bible].** Until they pay the Jizya [tax] with willing submission, and feel themselves subdued."….. Koran, Surah 9: 29

Is Allah through Mohammad actually confessing that Islam is not a religion of "truth"; is he saying Islam is a false religion by saying "nor acknowledge the religion of **truth from the people of the book - which are the religions of the Jewish and Christian peoples.**" Mohammad was allowed by Satan to gain financially **by taxing** the other religions around him? And, to allow Muslims to have sexual intercourse with almost anyone he desired, up to four wives, according to the Koran.

"O ye who believe [in Islam]; What is the matter with you, that, when ye were asked to go forth in the cause of Allah, ye cling heavily to the earth [did not risk martyrdom]? Do you prefer the life of this world to the hereafter [why not die and reap a reward from Allah]? But little is the comfort of this life, as compared with the hereafter."
…… Koran, Surah 9: 38

"**Unless you go forth [and kill and risk your own death], He [Allah] will punish you** with a grievous penalty, and put another in your place; but him ye would not harm in the least, for Allah hath power over all things."
…… Koran, Surah 9: 39

"Those who believe in Allah and the last day ask thee for no exemption from fighting with their goods [paying their own way, using their own weapons] and **persons** [risking their lives]. And Allah **knoweth** well those who do their duty."
…….. Koran, Surah 9: 44

"Say: Can you expect for us (any fate) other than one of two glorious things – (Martyrdom or **victory**) [**our** own deaths or our enemies deaths]? But we can expect for you either that Allah will send his punishment from him or by our hands. So wait (expectant): we too will wait with you."…… Koran, Surah 9: 52

"O ye who believe [in Islam]! **Fight the unbelievers [Christians, Jews, etc.] who are near to you** and let them find harshness in you: and know that Allah is with those who fear him."
..... Koran, Surah 9: 123

"Therefore, **when ye meet the unbelievers [Christians, Jews, etc.], (In fight), smite at their necks [strike off their heads]."**
...... Koran, Surah 47: 4

"O **Prophet**: Strive hard against the unbelievers [Non-Islamists] and the hypocrites, and be harsh with them. Their abode [home] is Hell, - and evil refuge.".
...... Koran, Surah 66: 9

..... The primary source for the English translation of the Koran was:
The Custodian of the Two Holy Mosques:
King Faud Complex; The Kingdom of Saudi Arabia [A westernized Ali translation].

"Radical Islam claims authorization from the Koran to oppose not only Jews and Christians but also everyone who **does** not accept Mohammed as a prophet, The Koran is **divinely** inspired, Islam is the ultimate religion and Jihad is every Muslims sacred duty. Thus Hindus, Buddhist, Taoists, New Agers, Atheists, Agnostics, **Materialists**, Secular Humanists and even truly moderate Muslims also stand in radical Islams Ok-to-Kill **corral**. There can hardly be a more important concern in todays world. If **radical** Muslim views of the Koran are correct, there will always be Muslims answering the Korans call to violence."
.....Don Richardson, "Secrets of the Koran", 2003, Pg.25

283.

Below are a couple of examples of the 'Hadiths' mentioned earlier:

Mohammed speaking; "If anyone changes his Islamic religion, kill him"
... Hadith 9.57

"Promises that when a Muslim dies as a martyr [in this case, someone who dies while trying to murder someone that opposes his religion], you will go to the highest level [100] of heaven."
…... Hadith 1.35

The Christian Bible also records a great deal of bloodshed and killing in it! The Bible records these events that happened in a 'descriptive' aspect of a historical account. The Koran records its 'war verses' in a "prescriptive" aspect. In other words, the Koran is written in such a way as to constantly invoke Muslims to take action no matter what generation is reading it throughout time. To Islam, it apparently does not matter what religion a person believes in, they are all under the same threat. It is a doctrinal command in Islam to convert the entire world to Islam and deliver it to Allah. If a person does not convert to Islam within the prescribed time constraints, usually 3 attempts, then they are to be beheaded with a sword.
Satan's plan is to destroy men by using the Islamic religion by pitting religion against religion and in doing so man against man. His plan is mans destruction no matter what form that takes. In Islam, followers are required to convert non-Islamists one by one under the threat of death if necessary. If Christian's convert then Satan renders them useless in God's Kingdom. When the true God [Jesus] came to this earth as a man he never once caused bloodshed, he never made anyone sick, he never caused anyone's death, he never required one man to harm another. The complete opposite is true, Jesus went about destroying the works of Satan which, in part, are death, destruction, sickness, disease etc.

"For this purpose the Son of God [Jesus] was manifested, that he might destroy the works of the devil."
... 1 John 3: 8

"For the Son of Man [Jesus] is not come to destroy men's lives, but to save them."
... Luke 9: 56

Islam has a worldwide agenda and in implementing their agenda they are required to go out into the nations of the world and occupy and convert each country for Allah. They have been emigrating into the western countries for decades waiting for the day that they will have enough Muslims in place to vote their own Islamic believers into public office or into sensitive policy-making areas to give Islam a foothold for their eventual takeover.

"Those who believe [in Islam], and emigrate [to the non-Islamic nations- USA-France-Europe,etc.] and fight for the faith, in the cause of Allah, as well as those who give [fighters] asylum and aid, - these are all in very truth the believers [in Islam]: For them is the forgiveness of sins and a provision most generous."
...... Koran, Surah 8: 74

"Take my word, if 6 -8 million Muslims unite in America [Islams sworn enemy along with Israel], the country will come to us."
...... Siraj Wahhaj, from a speech he delivered, Muslim to Muslims in New Jersey, 1992

If you believed in the Korans teachings about destroying all religions for Allah's sake then when your number one enemy, Israel, suffers any form of catastrophic damage to its people, possibly up to 20,000,000 dead, then you would consider that a great victory for Allah instead of a holocaust.

"Today, they have created a myth in the name of holocaust."
…...Mahmoud Ahmadinejad, X-President of The Islamic Republic of Iran, from a speech given in the …..City of Zahedan

"The very existence of the Zionist regime [the Jewish people of Israel] is an insult to humanity.... The Zionist regime and the Zionists are a cancerous tumor... The nations of the region will soon finish off the usurper Zionists in the Palestinian land."
….. Mahmoud Ahmadinejad, Speech at the August 2012 Annual Protest Against the Existence of Israel Conference.

"Those who think they can revive the stinking corpse of the usurping and fake Israel regime by throwing a 60th Birthday party are seriously mistaken... and this regime is on its way to annihilation."
….. Mahmoud Ahmadinejad, from a speech concerning Israels 60th birthday in 2008

There are many other similar remarks from Ahmadinejad that are directed towards Israel, he also feels the same way about the United States and I believe he speaks for all of radical Islam.

"The anti-Defamation League released a statement saying the Iranian leader showed he "Is deeply infected with Anti-Semetism [Hatred for Israel]", and displayed "The true threat the Iranian regime poses to Israel, the United States and the West."
….. CNN.com, 9/23/2008

The "American Empire in the World is reaching the end of its road."
….. CNN.com, 9/23/2008, quote from Mahmoud Ahmadinejad

Many in the West desire to believe the best in people so when a nation's leader or a religious leader from another nation speaks about peace, they hope and believe they are hearing the truth. When the truth about any comment is wrapped up in another religions morality that proclaims "It's acceptable to lie when you absolutely have to" then there is a built-in conflict waiting to happen. Islamic followers can look a non-Muslim in the eye and lie to them and it's acceptable to the Islamic religion. Beyond that, an Islamic leader can look into a camera at a press conference and do the very same thing. Anything that brings Allah victory or preserves a Muslims life, including lying, is acceptable to a Muslim.

IS IT ACCEPTABLE TO LIE IN THE MUSLIM FAITH?... YES!

"Allah will not call you to account for thoughtlessness (vain) in your oaths, but for the intention of your hearts; and he is oft-forgiving, most forbearing."
…... Koran, Surah 2: 225

You can be forgiven by Allah if you tell someone one thing then do another concerning a Muslim or Islam in general when you know the truth is hidden inside your soul. In other words- its acceptable to tell a lie, Allah will not hold you accountable for lying!

"Allah will not call you to account for what is futile [useless or meaningless words] in your oaths, but he will call you to account for your deliberate oaths:"
…... Koran, Surah 5: 89

The following article is an excerpt from "islamicreview.com"; by Abdullah Al Araby:

"In the Hadith, Mohammed, emphasizes the same concept."
"From "Ehiaa Oloum al-Din, " by the famous Islamic scholar al-Ghazali, Vol. 3: PP.284-287:

One of Mohammed's daughters, Umm Kalthoum, testified that she had never heard the Apostle of God condone lying, except in these three situations:

1...For reconciliation among people
2...In War
3...Amongst spouses, to keep peace in the family.

"Unfortunately, when dealing with Muslims, one must keep in mind that Muslims can communicate something with apparent sincerity, when in reality they may have just the opposite agenda in their hearts. **Bluntly stated, Islam permits Muslims to lie anytime that they perceive that their own well-being, or that of Islam, is threatened.**

In the sphere of international politics, the question is: Can Muslim countries be trusted to keep their end of the agreements that they sign with non-Muslim nations? It is a known Islamic practice, that when Muslims are weak they can agree with most anything. Once they become strong, then they negate what they formerly vowed.

The principle of sanctioning lying for the cause of Islam bears grave implications in matters relating to the spread of the religion of Islam in the west. Muslim activists employ deceptive tactics in their attempts to polish Islam's image and make it more attractive to prospective converts. They carefully try to avoid, obscure, and omit mentioning any of the negative Islamic texts and teachings.

An example of Islamic deception is that Muslim activists always quote the passages of the Quran from the early part of Mohammed's ministry while living in Mecca. These texts are peaceful and exemplify tolerance towards those that are not followers of Islam. All the while, they are fully aware that most of these passages were abrogated (canceled and replaced) by passages that came after he migrated to Medina. **The replacement** verses reflect prejudice, intolerance, and endorse violence upon unbelievers....

In conclusion, it is imperative to **understand, the** Muslim leaders can use this loop-hole in their religion, to absolve them from any permanent commitment. It is also important to know that Muslim activists say to spread Islam **may** not always be the whole truth. **When dealing with Muslims,** what they 'say' is not the issue. The real issue **is, what** they actually mean in their hearts. "
..... Abdullah al Araby, "islamicreview.com"

THE MORALITY OF ISLAM

There is one verse in the Koran where Mohammad says or implies it's acceptable to fornicate, whore monger (solicit sexual acts for money), own slaves and prostitute your slaves out- by force if necessary;

"Let those who find not the wherewithal for marriage keep themselves **chaste, until** Allah gives them means out of his grace. And if any of your slaves ask for a deed in writing (for emancipation) give them such a deed if you know any good in them; yea, give them something yourselves out of the means which Allah has given to you. But force not your maids to prostitution when they desire chastity, in order that you may make a gain [profit] in the goods of this life. But if anyone compels them [force slaves to be prostitutes], yet, after such compulsion, is Allah oft-forgiving, most merciful [to the one forcing their slaves into prostitution]."
.... Koran, Surah 24: 33

THE GOD OF THE CHRISTIAN BIBLE AND THE GOD OF THE ISLAMIC KORAN BOTH CLAIM THAT THEY EACH CREATED THE HEAVENS, THE EARTH AND MEN.

"In the beginning, God created the heavens and the earth."
….. Bible, Genesis 1: 1

"The number of months in the sight of Allah is twelve (in a year)- So ordained by him the day he created the heavens and the earth: Of them four are sacred: That is the right religion so wrong not yourselves therein, and fight the pagans [non-Islamics] all together as they fight you all together. But know that Allah is with those who restrain themselves."
…... Koran, Surah 9: 36

"It is he [Allah] who has created you from the dust, then from a sperm-drop, then from a leech-like clot; Then does he get you out (into the light) as a child: then lets you (grow and) reach your age of full strength; then lets you become old, - Though of you there are some who die before; - And lets you reach a term appointed; in order that you may understand."
…. Koran, Surah 40: 67

These 2 Gods are not the same God so one of them is lying!
"In hope of eternal life, **which God, that cannot lie**, promised before the world began."
…... Bible, Titus 1: 2

"That by two immutable [unchangeable] things, **in which it was impossible for God [Jesus] to lie**, we might have consolation, who have fled for refuge to lay hold upon the hope set before us; which hope we have as an anchor of the soul, both sure and steadfast, and which entereth into that within the veil,"
…... Bible, Hebrews 6: 18 – 19

"Jesus said unto them, If God were your Father, ye would love me: For I proceeded forth and came from God; neither came I of myself, but he sent me. Why do you not understand my speech? Even because you cannot hear my Word. Ye are of your father the Devil, and the lusts of your father you will do. He was a murderer from the beginning, and abode not in the truth, because there is no truth in him. When he speaketh a lie, he speaketh of his own: for he is a liar, and the father of it. And because I tell you the truth you believe me not. Which of you convicts me of sin? And if I say the truth, why do ye not believe me? He that is of God heareth Gods Words, ye therefore hear them not, because ye are not of God."
…... Bible, John 8: 42– 47

The Bible -The Word of God -Jesus's thoughts are spirit and have to be spiritually discerned to be understood. Gods word is hard for a non-Christian to understand because you need the Spirit of God indwelling you so the Spirit can make it possible to understand his Word. Intellectual men have knowledge that is born from their intellect or natural mind but they are disconnected from wisdom and truth because wisdom and truth are born from God in the spirit realm and men must be led by the Holy Spirit to understand spiritually or extra-dimensionally.

Again from the book of John:
"Howbeit when he, **the Spirit of truth, is come, he will guide you into all truth**: for he shall not speak of himself; but whatsoever he shall hear, that shall he speak: and he will shew you things to come.
… John 16: 13

The God of Islam, Allah; through his prophet Mohammed; are in agreement with and promoters of :

Murder
Lies
Slavery
Adultery
Fornication
Violence
Polygamy
Intolerance
Hatred
Prostitution
Solicitation for Prostitution
etc.

These are all morally acceptable in Islam because Allah recorded these in the Koran for the use of all **Muslims, this** list is part of Allah's **Word**. This 'partial' list is completely contrary to the teachings of the Christian Bible and, according to the Bible, anyone doing these things would be unsaved, sinning and in desperate need of a Savior.
These attributes to Islamic teachings are very much in line with 'The Church of Satan' and for good reason, Satan is the God of Islam.

Below is a short list of some of the accomplishments of the followers of Islam against the United States:

Bombed the Boston Marathon
Bombed the World Trade Center in 1993
Bombed the World Trade Center again in 2001 and destroyed 2 loaded passenger jets in the process
Bombed the Marine Barracks in Lebanon
Bombed the USS Cole

Bombed the American Embassy in Africa
Bombed the Pentagon with a fully loaded passenger jet
Downed a fourth airliner in the process killing all aboard
Bombed Pan Am Flight 103
...There is a longer list of Islamic attacks and attempts of destruction against the U.S. in chapter 13 in the section titled: "Islam's Conquering of the World", page 330

Again – What is Satan's agenda for men? **Destroy – Destroy – Destroy**, steal, kill and **destroy**

"Crusader atrocities contradicted the New Testament whereas Muslim atrocities were in **accord** with the Koran."
…..Don Richardson, "Secrets of the Koran", 2003, pg. 158

In September of 2013, Bill O'Reilly from Fox News presented this commentary about Islam and terrorist activity in the world; below is an excerpt of his commentary, entitled;

"The World Failing to Confront the True Nature of Muslim Terrorism"

"Over the weekend another vicious **terror** attack, this one in Nairobi Kenya, scores of innocent people massacred, gunned down in a shopping mall. This kind of terror activity is now a growing industry throughout the world and there is a reason why.

The truth is that Muslim **Jihadists** want to kill Christians and Jews. That's what this is all about, nothing more. **The Muslim** Jihad believes that infidels do not deserve to live. But you will not hear the leaders of the world say that including President Obama. They will not tell you what is really going on here. This is simply about murder and if you are a Christian or a Jew you are a target. It is clear that Al Queda and its affiliates are now going to wage small-time terrorism all over the world...."
… Bill O'Reilly, Fox News, Sept. 2013

293.
Well Bill, it's not going to be limited to Christians and Jews, it's all religions and all people that do not convert to Islam. Islam has a mandate to deliver all of the world to Allah through death and violence if needed.

From the "World Net Daily" article entitled;

'SON OF HAMAS' WARNS ISLAMIC GROUP CAN'T BE APPEASED

August 1, 2014- "The son of a prominent Hamas leader warns that no concession by Israel will stop the Islamic organization from its stated aim to destroy Israel.

Calling Hamas a 'terrorist organization with a humanitarian face': Mosab Hussan Youseff- a convert to Christian faith and a former undercover agent for Israel- confirmed to the Fox News Channel's Sean Hannity, that the Hamas Charter calls for the obliteration of the Jews [See an excerpt from the Charter on page 323 under Hamas].

Even if Israel were to give Palestinians all of the land inside the 1967 borders, the Hamas Charter still calls for the destruction of Israel.

In an interview with CNN News Mosab Hassan Youseff continues;
…Hamas does not care about the lives of Palestinians, does not care about the lives of Israelis or Americans…The destruction of the State of Israel is not Hamas's final destination. Hamas's final destination is building an Islamic Caliphate- which means an Islamic State on the rubble of every other civilization."
…Citation, Jack Van Impe Presents, August 17th, 2014
…Original source; Sean Hannity of Fox News, CNN News, WND
…News

Chapter 12

ISRAEL DOES OWN THE LAND THEY LIVE ON TODAY!

The Jewish State and the en-grafted Christian community came from Gods promise to Abraham through Abraham's promised child – Isaac, who then had a son of his own – Jacob - whose descendants are the nation of Israel.

-Abraham's first son Ishmael; his descendants are a large part of today's Islamic world
-Abraham's second (promised) son Isaac; his seed inherited the promise and became the nation of Israel
-Isaac's son Jacob; whom God renamed Israel, makes up the Jewish world, Judaism, the nation of Israel
-Israels sons that disobeyed God set the stage for the Christian world to be grafted into Gods Kingdom through Jesus the Messiah who was a descendant of Abraham, Isaac and Jacob.

Gods original promise to Abraham was that Abraham would have a child of his own with his wife Sarai; (later Sarah), Sarah and Abraham were married and became one flesh - (flesh of my flesh, bone of my bone; who God joins together let no man separate; the 2 become 1). Hagai [Sarahs servant] was not one with Abraham; As God said to Abraham concerning Eliezer the same applies to Hagai."... This shall not be thine heir; but he that shall come forth out of thine own bowels [body] shall be thine heir."
.. Genesis 15: 4 (God speaking to Abraham)

Abraham became the father of Ishmael through his wife Sarai's servant; Hagai. Ishmael was not the promised child from God. Not only did God promise Abraham a son of his own but he also promised him and his seed (descendants) all of the land of, what is today, - Israel.

"Abram [Abraham] dwelled in the land of Canaan, and Lot dwelled in the cities of the plain, and pitched his tent toward Sodom.......And **the Lord said unto Abram**, after that Lot was separated from him, Lift up now thine eyes, and look from the place where thou art northward, and southward, and eastward, and westward: For all the land which thou seest, **to thee will I give it, and to thy seed as the dust of the earth, then shall thy seed also be numbered. Arise, walk through the land in the length of it and in the breadth of it;** for **I will give it unto thee."**
…. Genesis 13: 12, 14- 17

Esau was a deceitful man as mentioned earlier from the book of Jasher.

GODS LAND CONTRACT WITH ISRAEL

Below is an account from the Book of Jasher where the transfer of ownership of the land of Israel is written down in a "Book of Purchase" that Jacob had written:

"And all the Kings of the land of Canaan went with Jacob and Esau to bury Isaac, and all the Kings of Canaan showed Isaac great honor at his death, and the sons of Jacob and the sons of Esau went barefooted round about, walking and lamenting until they reached Kireath-arba. And Jacob and Esau buried their father Isaac in the cave of Machpelah, which is in Kireath-arba in Hebron, and they buried him with very great honor, as at the funeral of Kings. And Jacob and his sons, and Esau and his sons, and all the Kings of Canaan made a great and heavy mourning, and they buried him and mourned for him many days. And at the death of Isaac, he left his cattle and his possessions and all belonging to him to his sons; and Esau said unto Jacob, Behold, I pray thee, all that our father has left we will divide it in two parts, and I [Esau] will have the choice, and Jacob said, we will do so. And Jacob took all that Isaac had left in the land of Canaan, the cattle and the property, and he placed them in two parts before

Esau and his sons, and he [Jacob] said unto Esau, behold all this is before thee, choose thou unto thyself the half which thou wilt take. And Jacob said unto Esau, hear thou I pray thee what I will speak unto thee, saying, Abraham and Isaac, saying, unto thy seed will I give this land for an inheritance forever. Now therefore all that our father has left is before thee, and behold all the land is before thee; choose thou from them what thou desirest. If thou desirest the whole land take it for thee and thy children forever, and I will take this riches, and if thou desirest the riches take it unto thee, and I will take this land for me and for my children to inherit it forever. And Nebayoth, the son of Ishmael, was then in the land with his children, and Esau went on that day and consulted with him, saying, Thus has Jacob spoken unto me, and thus has he answered me, now give thy advice and we will hear. And Neboyoth said, What is this that Jacob hath spoken unto thee? Behold, all the children of Canaan are dwelling securely in their land, and Jacob sayeth he will inherit it with his seed all the days. Go now therefor and take all thy fathers riches and leave Jacob thy brother in the land, as he has spoken. And Esau rose up and returned to Jacob, and did all that Nebayoth the son of Ishmael had advised: And Esau took all of the riches that Isaac had left, the souls, the beasts, the cattle and the property, and all the riches; he gave nothing to his brother Jacob; And Jacob took all the land of Canaan, from the brook of Egypt unto the river Euphrates, and he took it for an everlasting possession, and for his children [Israel] and for his seed after him forever. Jacob also took from his brother Esau the cave of Machpelah, which is in Hebron, which Abraham had bought from Ephron for a possession of a burial place for him and his seed forever. And Jacob wrote all these things in the Book of Purchase, and he signed it, and he testified all this with four faithful witnesses. And these are the words which Jacob wrote in the book, saying: The land of Canaan and all the Cities of the Hittites, the Hivits, the Jebusites, the Amorites, the Perizzites, and the Gergashites, all the seven nations from the river of Egypt unto the river Euphrates. And the city of Hebron Kireath-arba, and the cave which is in it, the whole did Jacob buy from his brother Esau for value, for a

possession and for an inheritance for his seed after him forever. And Jacob took the book of purchase and the signatures, the command and the statutes and the revealed book, and he placed them in an earthen vessel in order that they should remain for a long time, and he delivered them into the hands of his children [National Israel]. Esau took all that his father had left him after his death from his brother Jacob, and he took all the property from man and beast, camel and ass, ox and lamb, silver and gold, stones and bdellium, and all the riches which had belonged to Isaac the son of Abraham; there was nothing left which Esau did not take unto himself, from all that Isaac had left after his death. And Esau took all this, and he and his children went home to the land of Seir the Horite, away from his brother Jacob and his children. And Esau had possessions amongst the children of Seir, and Esau returned not to the land of Canaan from that day forward. And the whole land of Canaan became an inheritance to the children of Israel for an everlasting inheritance, and Esau and all his children inherited the Mountain of Seir.
..... Book of Jasher 47: 11– 33, pp. 138– 140

The above account is the detailed story, with a signed contract with witnesses that Israel absolutely had ownership and all rights to the land of Israel. Israel is not nor ever has been an illegal occupant of their own land. **God promised it to them forever** and forever it shall be Israels.

Years later, after the above account in chapter 47; there is the account of Jacobs death in chapter 61 of the book of Jasher, then as today there were disputes over the ownership of the land of Israel:

"And all the Kings of Canaan heard of this thing and they all went forth, each man from his house, thirty-one Kings of Canaan, and they all came with their men to mourn and weep over Jacob. And all these Kings beheld Jacobs Bier, and behold Joseph's crown was upon it, and they also put their crowns upon the Bier, and encircled it with crowns. And all these Kings made in that place a great and heavy mourning with the sons of Jacob and Egypt over Jacob. For all the Kings of Canaan knew the valor of Jacob and his sons. And the report reached Esau, saying, Jacob died in Egypt, and his sons and all Egypt are conveying him to the land of Canaan to bury him. And Esau heard this thing, and he was dwelling in Mount Seir and he rose up with all his sons and all his people and all his household, a people exceedingly great, and they came to mourn and weep over Jacob. And it came to pass, when Esau came he mourned for his brother Jacob, and all Egypt and all Canaan again rose up and mourned a great mourning with Esau over Jacob in that place. And Joseph and his brethren brought their father Jacob from that place, and they went to Hebron to bury Jacob in the cave by his Fathers. And they came unto Kireath-arba, to the cave, and as they came Esau stood with his sons against Joseph and his brethren as a hindrance in the cave, saying, Jacob shall not be buried therein, for it belongeth to us and our Father. And Joseph and his brethren heard the words of Esau's sons, and they were exceedingly wroth, and Joseph approached unto Esau, saying, what is this thing which they have spoken? Surely my Father Jacob bought it from thee for great riches after the death of Isaac, now five and twenty years ago, and also all the land of Canaan he bought from thee and thy sons, and thy seed after thee. And Jacob bought it for his sons and his seed after him for an inheritance for ever, and why speakest thou these things this day?

And Esau answered, saying, Thou speakest falsely and utterest lies, for I sold not anything belonging to me in all this land, as thou sayest, neither did my brother Jacob buy aught belonging to me in this land. And Esau spoke these things in order to deceive Joseph with his words, for Esau knew that Joseph was not present in those days when Esau sold all belonging to him in the land of Canaan to Jacob. And Joseph said unto Esau, Surely my Father inserted these things with thee in the record of purchase, and testified the record with witnesses, and behold it is with us in Egypt. And Esau answered, saying unto him, bring the record, all that thou wilt find in the record, so will we do. And Joseph called unto Naphtali his brother, and he said, Hasten quickly, stay not, and run I pray thee to Egypt and bring all the records; the record of the purchase, the sealed record, and the open record, and also all the first records in which all the transactions of the birth-right are written, fetch thou, and thou shalt bring them unto us hither, that we may know from them all the words of Esau and his sons which they spoke this day. And Naphtali hearkened to the voice of Joseph and he hastened and ran to go down to Egypt, and Naphtali was lighter on foot than any of the stags that were upon the wilderness, for he would go upon ears of corn without crushing them. And when Esau saw that Naphtali had gone to fetch the records, he a his sons increased their resistance against the cave, and Esau and all his people rose up against Joseph and his brethren to battle. And all the sons of Jacob and the people of Egypt fought with Esau and his men, and the sons of Esau and his people were smitten before the sons of Jacob, and the sons of Jacob slew of Esau's people forty men. And Chushim the son of Dan, the son of Jacob, was at that time with Jacob's sons by Jacob's Bier to guard it. And Chushim was dumb and deaf, still he understood the voice of consternation amongst men. And he asked, saying, why do you not bury the dead, and what is this great consternation? And they answered him the words of Esau and his sons; and he ran to Esau in the midst of the battle, and he slew Esau with a sword, and he cut off his head, and it sprang to a distance, and Esau fell amongst the people of the battle. And when Chushim did this thing the sons of Jacob prevailed over the sons of Esau, and the sons of Jacob buried their father Jacob by force in the cave, and the sons of Esau beheld it. And Jacob was buried in Hebron, in the cave of Machpelah which Abraham had bought from the sons of Heth for the possession of a burial place, and he has buried in very costly garments. And no King had such honor paid him as Joseph paid unto his father at his death, for he buried him with great honor like unto the burial of Kings. And Joseph and his brethren made a mourning of seven days for their father. And it was after this that the sons of Esau waged war with the sons of Jacob, and the sons of Esau fought with the sons of Jacob in Hebron, and Esau was still lying dead and not buried.

And the battle was heavy between them, and the sons of Esau were smitten before the sons of Jacob, and the sons of Jacob slew of the sons of Esau eighty men, and not one died of the people of the sons of Jacob, and the hand of Joseph prevailed over all the people of the sons of Esau."
…..Book of Jasher 56 : 43 - 68, 57 : 1 – 2, pp. 173 – 175
Israel is forever including the land of the people of the descendants of Abraham, Isaac and Jacob.

Chapter 13

THE MUSLIM MAHDI – Mohammed's successor

"In Islamic Eschatology, the Mahdi...(English: The Guided One) is the prophesied redeemer of Islam who will rule for seven, nine or nineteen years (according to various interpretations) before the day of judgment.. and will rid the world of evil [by Islamic standards of evil: which would equate to Israel and Christianity]."
…… Mahdi, Martin, 2004, pg. 421

"Allah's apostle said, 'The hour will not be established until the son of Mayam descends amongst you as a just ruler; he will break the cross [destroy Christianity], kill the pigs [Jewish people], and abolish the jizya tax, money will be in abundance so that nobody will except it."
…. Hadith writer Sahih al-Bukhari 3: 43: 656

Islam claims that Jesus will return with their Mahdi to assist in ridding the world of evil. I believe it's another one of Satan's attempts to legitimize Islam by deceitfully hijacking the name of the Lord of Glory (Jesus) into the service of Satan, this absolutely will not happen. My theory is that the Anti-Christ is this Mahdi which is a Muslim who has no moral or ethical convictions about lying or falsely representing himself to gain a victory for Islam. 3.5 years into the Anti-Christs reign he breaks what began as a 7 year peace contract in an attempt to rule the world. He will start out peacefully at first but then switches to what Mohammed prescribes in the Koran; by deceit and violence. One of the last prophetic events that will happen pointing to the return of Jesus is the rebuilding of the Temple in Jerusalem where the Anti-Christ will reign from prior to his eviction by Jesus. This re-built Temple has to be in place during the 7 year peace contract. This will be something to watch for if you are one that does not believe in the Rapture of the church. The first one to set himself up as God in Jerusalem will be Satan's own Anti-Christ.

302.
A MUSLIM WOULD TELL YOU THE 'GODS' OF CHRISTIANITY AND ISLAM ARE NOT THE SAME GOD

The following is an excerpt from the "John Ankerburg Show" from 2003. Dr. Ankerburg is interviewing an ex-Muslim who is now a Christian educator; Dr. Ergun Caner:

Dr. Ankerburg: "My question to you [Dr. Caner] is, 'Is the God of the Bible the same as the God of Islam'?"

Dr. Caner: "If you would have said to us when we were Muslims that Allah and Jehovah are the same God, we would have been offended. As Christians, we find it blasphemous. No one who has read the Qur'an [Koran], no one who has read the Bible would ever say that it's the same God. As a matter of fact, this is, interestingly enough, this is one of those things about which we can agree on with most Muslims. We have never, we have never met a Muslim ulema who would say that the Jehovah described in the Bible is the same God as the Allah of the Qur'an. The message seems to come from our culture instead. The message comes from our syncretist, post-modern "group hug" kind of culture [in the West] that wants us all to be talking about the same God. But nothing can be further from the truth."
...... Ex-Muslim Dr. Ergun Caner, an interview from the John Ankerburg Show, 2003

The bottom line is that Islam is a religion of death to the non-Muslim; death to other people in other religions who do not convert. Death to other Muslim believers who believe **"different"** Hadiths. Death to their own family members who bring dishonor to the family according to Allah. Death to the entire world if that's what it takes to turn the world over to Allah [Satan].

Jesus speaking: "Verily, Verily, [truly, truly] I say unto you, He that heareth my word, and believeth on him that sent me[Jehovah], hath everlasting life, and shall not come into condemnation; but is passed from death unto life.".…... John 5: 24

THE FALLING AWAY

"Let no man deceive you by any means: for that day shall not come, except there come a falling away first, and that man of sin be revealed, the son of perdition; Who **opposeth** and **exalteth** himself above all that is called God, or that is worshiped; so that he as God **sitteth** in the temple of God, shewing himself that he is God."
…. 2nd Thessalonians 2: 3 – 4

The above verse is talking about a false Messiah [Anti-Christ] that's going to set himself up as Jesus- the true Messiah, the creator of the **universe.** It talks about the Anti-Christ that's coming to claim [falsely] that he is God and therefore worthy to sit on Gods throne and be worshiped as God. (Just like Satan proclaimed prior to his original fall)

This verse also talks about a "falling away first"; I believe what is happening to the Christian World, and America especially; qualifies as 'falling away'. **Our educational systems are leading people away from God by the droves through the teaching of evolution.** This 'falling away' is what sets the stage for the Anti-Christ to rise to power. Few are reading Gods Word as they should and are ignorant of the **"things** that are coming" and have no recognition or defense for **them.** People don't know there is spiritual power available to Christians and they are ignorant of what God says about not taking the mark of the beast. By taking the "mark" they instantly are bound for hell. They don't know there is this Anti-Christ figure coming "first"to set up his headquarters in Jerusalem and from what little they do know about the Bible they will think it's the true God himself, not an imposter. Add that to all of the different translations of the Bible that are so far removed and diluted from the original that a great deal of the power of God's Word is missing. Add to that the deceived Christian Pastors who are engaged in mixing the Christian Bible with the Islamic Koran just to make Christianity palatable to Muslims and thus, theoretically- easier to have them accept the Christian religion. These two religions do not blend!

"And what concord [harmony] hath Christ with Belial [a demon]? or what part hath he that believeth with an infidel [unbeliever]? And what agreement hath the temple of God with idols? For ye are the temple of the living God; as God has said, I will dwell in them, and walk in them; and I will be their God, and they shall be my people."
….. II Corinthians 6: 15 – 16

CHRISLAM

There are 30 plus pastors, led by Rick Warren and Robert Schuler, that are re-writing the Bible by taking Jesus, Jehovah and the Holy Spirit out and replacing them with Allah and Mohammed. Through the leadership of Rick Warren they are also eliminating all references to 'Heaven' and 'Hell', 'sent' and 'lost'. They suggested removing all reminders of Jesus's work on the cross by removing all crosses from churches. They also plan to eliminate all 'alter calls' and 'prayer services'.

They are eliminating:
Jesus from the church
Power through prayer from the church
The sign of hope- the cross
The hope of salvation- 'alter calls' and repentance to cleanse men through Jesus's shed blood

This new "Religion" is called Chrislam; a mixing of Christianity with Islam and **it's** as dead as Satan's future.
In this new translation the "Body of Christ" is now called "The building"
The Church is now called "The Campus"

Here is an example of what this new **"religions"** book is going to say.

The Original Bible Version:
"And Philip said, if thou **believest** with all thine heart, thou **mayest**. And he answered and **said, I** believe that Jesus Christ is the son of God."
..... Acts 8: 37

The New Chrislam Version:
"And Philip said, if thou **believest** with all thine heart, thou **mayest**. And he answered and **said, I** believe that Mohammed is the son of Allah."
.... Acts 8: 37

The Original Bible Version:
"For the husband is the head of the wife, even as Christ is the head of the **Church:** and he is the **Savior** of the body."
...... Ephesians 5: 23

The New Chrislam Version:
"For the husband is the head of the wife, even as Mohammed is the head of the Campus, and the Savior of the building."
...... Ephesians 5: 23
(.... Jesus's **tithe** dollars at work!)

...", and see thou hurt not the oil and the wine."
... Revelation 6: 6

The oil is the Holy Spirit!
The wine is the blood of Christ!
The blood flows through the body!
The body is the Church!
The Church belongs to Jesus!
The wine is inside the Church!
The oil is inside the Church!
Neither will be in the Church of Chrislam!

Rick, Robert and the other 30 Christian Pastors who are re-writing Gods word to appease Islam - **RECONSIDER**

"You will have to care enough to lovingly speak the truth, even when you would rather gloss over a problem or ignore an issue. While it is much easier to remain silent while others around us are harming themselves or others with a sinful pattern. It is not the loving thing to do. Most people have no one in their lives who loves them enough to tell them the truth (even when its painful), so they continue in self destructive ways, often we know what needs to be said to someone, but our fears prevent us from saying anything. Many fellowships have been sabotaged by fear: No one had the courage to speak up in the group while a member's life fell apart. The Bible tells us to "Speak the truth in Love" because we can't have community without candor. Solomon said, "An honest answer is a sign of true friendship. Sometimes this means caring enough to lovingly confront one who is sinning or is being tempted to sin."
…... Rick Warren, "The Purpose Driven Life", pg. 146

Words and names have meaning, Jesus is not Mohammed, Allah is not Jehovah. Mixing light and darkness is not possible. Do not compromise or adulterate the word of the one true living God. You are not mixing words in a book; you are mixing Spirit with

Spirit. You are mixing the thoughts of Spiritual entities; the Holy Spirit and a Satanic Spirit; when you mix clean water with contaminated water you end up with contaminated water.

IS THERE A SIGNIFICANT ISLAMIC COMMUNITY IN THE U.S.A.?

Remember Siraj Wahhaj from earlier? He was the Muslim speaking to a crowd of Muslims in New Jersey back in 1992, 20 + years ago.

"Take my word, If 6 – 8 million Muslims unite in America, the country will come to us."
….. Siraj Wahhaj

What is Siraj talking about; "Come to us". He is talking about 100's of thousands of Muslims moving to America, establishing a foothold, changing the laws to Sharia Law and expanding into your neighborhood, by force if necessary. Taking over for Allah. There was a bill introduced in Oklahoma in 2012 to introduce Sharia Law here but, thankfully, it failed. Muslims are not moving here because they enjoy the American lifestyle, the contrary is true, the Koran declares Christians enemies of Muslims. The following articles will bear this out:

The Rise of Islamic No Go Zones

"Three and a half years ago, one of the Church of England's most senior bishops, Pakistani-born Michael Nazir-Ali, [said] that Islamic extremists had created "no-go" areas across Britain too dangerous for non-Muslims to enter. His politically incorrect concern sparked a firestorm of denial and criticism. The Muslim Council of Britain, for example, dismissed it as the Bishop's "frantic scaremongering"and "intolerance", and scoffed,

'We wouldn't allow "no-go" areas to happen. I smell extreme intolerance when people criticize multiculturalism without proper evidence of what has gone wrong.'
[... The Muslim Council of Britain]

Well, **the evidence** of how multiculturalism "has gone wrong" is in. This week Soeren Kern at the Hudson Institute [said] 'The proliferation of such no-go zones throughout Europe-autonomous Islamic "micro-states" under Sharia rule (having rejected their host countries' legal systems), where non-Muslims must either conform to the cultural, legal, and religious norms of fundamentalist Islam or expect to be greeted with violence....a more precise name for these zones would be Dar al-Islam" - the House of Islam, or the place where Islam rules.

England, Sweden, Germany, France, Italy, the Netherlands – in every European country with a large Muslim immigrant population, the story is the same: Islamic supremacists refuse to assimilate into the Western melting pot; instead they carve out a foothold in a neighborhood, and then, through intimidation or outright violence, push out the infidels [Christians] whose failed secular values are no longer acceptable. Even **public** services such as police, firefighters and ambulances are often driven out of such neighborhoods with stones, bottles or bullets. Lacking the political and cultural will to assert control in areas that in some cases have become urban war **zones, the** authorities have simply retreated and abandoned them.
…..frontpagemag.com/2011/mark-tapson/the-rise-of-islamic-no-go-zones

Muslim Enclaves U.S.A.

"It seems almost unthinkable, but Islamist groups are, as we speak, hard at work creating Muslim states-within-states in the U.S. Indeed, this process has been unfolding for a long time across the Western world, through the creation of isolated Muslim

Enclaves in both rural and urban areas, as well as through the designation of "No-Go-Zones" where governments admit to having little authority over Muslims living there, essentially leaving them to function as autonomous religions.

Daniel Pipes has tracked numerous examples since 2004 of Muslim groups working to create communities based solely on Islam and run by Sharia law. As discussed by David Kennedy Houck in 2006, "Although such concepts are antithetical to a free society, U.S. democracy allows the internal enclave to function beyond the established boundaries of our constitutional framework."

For example, one such community, Gwynn Oak, has been created in Baltimore, Maryland, consisting of Muslim immigrants and African-American converts. The project is led by John Yahya Cason, director of the Islamic Education and Community Development Initiative. Cason explained that the neighborhood is a response to the problem that "Muslim communities are ruled by Western societal tenets, many of which clash with Islamic norms." In his opinion, there is a need for communities with "the totality of the essential components of Muslim social, economic, and political structure." As such, the Gwynn Oak Enclave follows specific moral rules based on Islam and people there speak Arabic. On September 13, 2009, the construction of its three-story mosque began. Approximately 400 Muslims now live in the vicinity.

Another example involves the Islamic Center for Human Excellence, which received funding from the United Arab Emirates. In August 2004, it was granted permission to build a Muslim neighborhood in Little Rock, Arkansas, complete with a mosque, school, and 22 homes; it would not allow the presence of alcohol. The goal was for Muslims to find an area to escape the alleged crime and depravity of American life, although the imam behind the effort said that non-Muslims are welcome to join.

Far more radical groups than these are now taking the lead in promoting and creating Islamic enclaves on U.S. soil. One such organization is As-Sabiquin, headed by Imam Abdul Alim Musa, who is very honest about his disturbing objectives. The group's website calls for installing Islamic law worldwide, fighting for "oppressed" Muslims, and "build[ing] model communities where Islam is lived." The website contains a point by point plan to assemble mini-states in America, beginning with the construction of a mosque and finishing with "establishing geographical integrity by encouraging Muslims of the community to live in close proximity to the masjid [mosque]" and "establishing social welfare institutions."
...... frontpagemagazine.com

Islam is building their own Islamic territories within the borders of the U.S. and bringing in more and more Muslims and converts to reach their objectives, not because they love the American or Western lifestyle. Why are they coming to America if our lifestyle clashes with their "norms"; they think the Western lifestyle is so depraved that they are forced to build their own communities to separate themselves from Americans inside of America. Would it not be easier if they just stayed where they were and lived the Islamic lifestyle there. Why would the Imam's encourage Muslims to live close to the Mosques? Because the Imams and clerics at the mosques are the ones that call for 'Jihad' and they are the ones that need the followers of Islam in close proximity for control purposes when they decide to provoke Muslim believers to violence.

List of the Cities with Islamic "No-Go Zones" in America:

Seattle Washington	Houston Texas
San Francisco California	Kansas City Missouri
Santa Clara California	Columbia Missouri
Los Angeles California	Cleveland Ohio
San Diego California	Boston Massachusetts
Chicago Illinois	Laurel Maryland
Plainfield Indiana	Potomac Maryland
Detroit Michigan	Washington D.C.
Philadelphia Pennsylvania	Orlando Florida
Brooklyn New York	Tampa Florida
Herndon Virginia	Boca Raton Florida
Springfield Missouri	Fort Lauderdale Florida
Charlotte North Carolina	Raleigh North Carolina
Denver Colorado	Tucson Arizona
Dallas Texas	Arlington Texas

… List compiled from "Jack Van Impe Presents"

Below is an Article from the Wall Street Journal concerning all of the "Calls to Violence" in Egypt:

"Egypt Cracks down on Radical Muslim Clerics"

"Cairo- Egypt's interim government stripped tens of thousands [40,000] of Imams, or Muslim Clerics, of their preaching licenses this week in what amounts to the most aggressive assault on religious freedom since the military deposed the country's Islamic President 10 weeks ago."
….. Matt Bradley, Leila Elmergawi, WSJ, September 11, 2013

As stated earlier, the Clerics or Imams are the ones who call for "Jihad" which is a call to commit murder or violence against their opposition.

Here is another article about the mind-set of the leaders of Islam which are the Imams and the Clerics in charge of the Mosques that they want their Muslim followers to live close to:

"American Imam Praises Fort Hood Shooter"

"The personal website for a radical American Imam living in Yemen who had contact with two Sept. 11 hijackers is praising alleged Fort Hood shooter Maj. Nidal Malik Hasan as a hero.

One U.S. official said Monday that the government had discovered electronic communications that showed Hasan had reached out to the Imam, Anwar Aulaqi, in the past. But investigators said late Monday there was no indication Hasan was directed to attack or had help in the massacre last Thursday.

The posting Monday on the website for Aulaqi, who was a spiritual leader at two mosques where three Sept. 11 hijackers worshiped, said American Muslims who condemned the attacks on the Texas military post last week are hypocrites who have committed treason against their religion.

Two U. S. intelligence officials told The Associated Press the website was Aulaqi's. They spoke on condition of anonymity of discuss intelligence collection.

Aulaqi said the only way a Muslim can justify serving in the U.S. military is if he intends to "follow in the footsteps of men like Nidal."
…... USATODAY.com, staff

Let me help clarify what Aulaqi said about Muslims serving in the U.S. military; its only acceptable if they plan on murdering as many U.S. military men as possible to strike a blow for Allah.

313.
Summer of 2014, Major Nidal Hasan, after seeing all of the brutality of ISIS in Iraq sent a letter to the head of ISIS asking him if he could become a citizen of the Caliphate that they were trying to establish.

BACKGROUND ON THE PROPHET MOHAMMED

When Mohammed was 40 years old in 609 A.D. He claims the angel Gabriel [Jibril] visited him and spoke to him. These visitations would last for 23 years and they ended when Mohammed passed away in 632 A.D. According to the Koran Chapter 7 verse 15 Mohammed could neither read nor write so he had scribes record everything spoken to him by the angel Gabriel. Mohammed himself claimed repeatedly that he was not the author of the Koran but it was given him by the angel Gabriel . My contention is that the same thing that happened to Dr. Schucman of ACIM also happened to Mohammed in that it was Satan that actually spoke to him and claimed to be Gabriel speaking for the Creator God of the universe, Jehovah, Jesus and the Holy Spirit. As mentioned earlier, Satan has an intimate knowledge of the Bible and the Torah, he knew everyone that was mentioned in the Bible and Torah and witnessed everything unfold before his eyes. There is a passage in the Koran that I believe Satan placed in the Koran to throw off the reader about who the true author really is, Satan's form of psychological warfare:

" And he [Mohammed] is not a with-holder of [the knowledge of] the unseen. And it [the Koran] is not the word of the devil, expelled [from the heavens]. So where are you going? It is nothing but a reminder to the worlds."
… Koran 81: 21- 27

Allah of the Koran is not the Creator God, he is the God of this world, Satan, he is as capable as the trinity of inspiring the written word through injected thoughts or audible communication through men who yield themselves to him. Mohammed was hearing none other than Satan as he recited the Koran in order to counter the Torah and Biblical Scriptures to create followers that would yield their lives to him and kill and destroy for him. In the end his followers would also be destroyed because they gave their allegiance to Satan and did his will on the earth.

As mentioned previously Satan has reversed the roles of some of the characters in the Bible, below is a "Bible Koran Comparison" chart that lays out what Satan has done in the Koran:

BIBLE   **KORAN**

Satan is Satan..............................The Jewish and Christian God is Satan; including their followers where Israel is Satan and the U.S. is the Great Satan

Jesus is God ....Jesus is a prophet that converted to Islam

Jesus is Creator...........................Jesus is a Created being

The Trinity is God ....Satan is God, Allah

Other details that Satan reversed:

Earth before the Sun...................Sun before the Earth

Plants before the Sun..................Sun before the Plants

Heaven still implies Heaven in the Koran but there is no Islamic Heaven, Satan wants his followers to believe there is. Hell is still Hell and evil means the same as in the Christian Bible.

The Koran took 23 years to complete
ACIM took 10 years to complete
The Bible took 1600 years to complete, History in the making

As in ACIM, in the Koran Satan has taken on the role of a guide where he has his followers call on him and subject themselves to him, and in this case Satan leads his followers to commit murder, genocide, atrocities on a scale approaching Hitlers 3rd Reich. The people of Israel and the United States both are considered "Satanic" by Islam solely due to the doctrine within the Koran. The death and destruction perpetrated by Islamic fundamentalists is not because they went rogue it's because they have a strict adherence to the teachings of the Koran and the Koran requires of it's followers to participate in world domination. If Jesus tries to inject a thought otherwise into a Muslim that would be taken as an evil suggestion from Satan and ignored.

"And if an evil suggestion comes to you from Satan [the Jesus of Christianity], then seek refuge in Allah. Indeed, he is hearing and knowing." ... Koran 7: 200

Another example, keep in mind the Koran says that Jews and Christians are the enemies of Islam;

"Do not follow the footsteps of Satan. Indeed, he is to you a clear enemy." ... Koran 2: 208

Muslims argue that the Koran was written verbatim, word for word, with no doctrinal input from Mohammed, I agree. Satan added a clause during his dictation of the Koran to Mohammed; he was not allowed to add anything of his own to the Koran. Just as in ACIM, with the exception of what Jesus told Mohammed, a.k.a. "The Satanic Verses", the entirety of the Koran are the words of Satan;

"If he [Mohammed] had dared to attribute some of [his own] sayings unto us, we would indeed have seized him by his right hand and would indeed have cut his life vein."
... Koran 69: 44-46

If Satan were writing his own version of a Holy Book to mislead men with mans destruction in mind and Jesus stepped in and spoke a few words to Mohammed in disguise, what would Jesus have said? Jesus did step in a speak to Mohammed. Now we have a situation where Jesus is imitating who Mohammed thinks is Gabriel which is really Satan pretending to be an angel speaking for the Creator of the universe. How would Jesus speak to people through Mohammed where Mohammed would not get suspicious about who was actually speaking to him?

#1.... Jesus would have to arrange a situation where what he is ……..telling Mohammed makes sense at the time.
#2.... Jesus would have to use Satan's literary or conversational ……..style.
#3 …Jesus would make a statement that would expose Satan as ……..the true author of the Koran.
#4 …Jesus would provide a way out for those trapped by Satan's ……..deceit.

The Koran is full of stories and characters that are similar to the Bible. With that being said, most of the prophets of the Koran are characters from the Bible: Those prophets are Adam, Noah, Abraham, Lot, Ismael, Isaac, Jacob, Joseph, Job, Moses, Aaron, David, Solomon, Elijah, Elisha, Jonah, Zachariah, John the Baptist and Jesus. Mohammed was the last prophet after Jesus. The next prophet coming is the one who will rule all of Islam on the earth, The Mahdi. The problem is, Islam has to destroy all other religions from the earth prior to his return. Satan used the same Biblical stories and characters to legitimize his new false religion.

To penetrate through all of the deceit, Jesus may have said something like;

We [The Trinity] would never send an apostle or prophet before you except to foretell or tell Jehovah's desires. Satan has come to you and written his desires using Jewish and Christian theology, history and scriptures and we [The Trinity] will cancel out Satan's vain desires. We will also send a sign to confirm that Satan is the author. The God of Judaism and Christianity is "omnipotent and wise" and we will take all of Satan's suggestions and turn them into mere trials for humanity. But those who follow Satan by your allegiance to him and reject my invitation, you do err and the one true God is not in you.

This is an interpretation of the "Satanic Verses" that Salman Rushdie made famous through his book of the same name back in 1989. At the time Iran's Ayatollah Khomeini issued a Fatwa (a death sentence) against Salman Rushdie for exposing what happened to Mohammed when Mohammed wrote the words of Jesus in the Koran. Islam claims that the Koran is 100% Holy and incorruptible so the exposure of its corruption ignited a firestorm in the Islamic world. The following is an excerpt from a Christian website relaying what happened after Jesus had spoken to Mohammed:

"The angel Gabriel [Satan in disguise] informed him (Mohammed) that the verses were put on his tongue by Satan [which would be Jesus]. Mohammed felt sorry and confessed his mistakes, supposing a similar fate befell preceding apostles. Later on Allah annulled these Satanic Verses with better "revelations"...So, provably, there was one occasion when Mohammed was unable to tell the difference between the voice of Satan and the voice of Allah."
…beholdthebeast.com

The Bible clearly states that Satan can and will pretend to be a Holy being or angel and attempt to deceive men into doing his will on the earth. Satan's will is certainly not Jehovah's will, Jehovah sent truth and life to the earth in the form of Jesus and Satan desires only death for all men as is clearly demonstrated in the text of the Koran and the infrastructure of Jihad: Madrases and Terrorist training camps and the dozens of terrorist organizations; (see chart on page 320.)

"For such are false apostles, deceitful workers, transforming themselves into the apostles of Christ. And no marvel; for Satan himself is transformed into an angel of light [Gabriel in this case]. Therefore it is no great thing if his ministers [Mohammed] also be transformed as the ministers of righteousness; whose end shall be according to their works."
… 2nd Corinthians 11: 13- 15

Given this revelation concerning the inspirational source of the Koran, how can it be trusted to hold the truth of the Creator God; Jehovah. Satan and the true God both spoke to Mohammed, and Mohammed, by his own admission, could not tell the difference between them. In Islam these questions have to be asked;
How much of the Koran is God and How much is Satan?
How can we trust a prophet when he can't tell who is speaking to him and both God and Satan have clearly spoken to him?
Is anything written in the Koran from God or is it all from Satan?
Could the entire Koran have been written by Satan and God tried to intervene?
The Koran is all from Satan except the following verses which have been taken out of the Koran:

THE SATANIC VERSES

"Never did we send and apostle or a prophet before thee but when he frame a desire, Satan threw some [vanity] into his desire. But God will cancel anything [vain] that Satan throws in. And God will confirm [and establish] his signs. For God is full of knowledge and wisdom, that He may make the suggestions thrown in by Satan, but a trial. For those in whose hearts is a disease and who are hardened of heart: Verily the wrong doers are in a schism far [from truth]."
… citation;
www.beholdthebeast.com/satanic_verses_in_the_Koran.html

319.

As mentioned earlier, these verses are considered to be from Satan by Islamic scholars and have been removed from the Koran.

As for Salman Rushdie, he survived for years and as of May 14, 2014 he is still alive. That was the date that Vanity Fair revisited Salman Rushdie in an article they did titled "How Salman Rushdie survived the Satanic Verses Fatwa" which was the 25th anniversary of the Fatwa. The article states that over the 25 years since the Ayatollah's declaration 60 people associated with Mr. Rushdie have died in Islamic attacks due to the Fatwa. Mostly book translators and publishers but also two Islamic Clerics that spoke out against the Fatwa were murdered. Bookstores in the U.S. and the U.K. were bombed. [Islam is not a peaceful religion] ...vanityfair.com/online/daily/2014/04/14/salman_rushdie_fatwa_satanic_verses

The Koran also has a chapter dedicated to demons, in it demons are excited about their God [Satan] and they seem really happy and they defend him. This does not agree with the demons written about in the Christian Bible.

"Say: It has been revealed to me that a company of demons listened [to the Koran]. They said, we have really heard a wonderful recital!" ... Koran 72: 1

Demons speaking in the next 2 verses:
"There are some foolish ones among us who used to utter extravagant lies against God [the God of Islam; Satan]. But we do think that no man or spirit should say ought that is untrue against God [the Muslim God; Satan]."
...Koran 72: 4- 5

The only recital that would please a demon to the point that they said it was a wonderful recital would have been an overall doctrine about death, destruction and deceit; and that would only come from Satan.

320.
MUSLIM JIHADISTS.... to Islam .... and Satan's Army or ISLAMIC TERRORIST ORGANIZATIONS...to the West

The Islamic Madrases educate and train Islamic warriors [the West call terrorists] to go out and join the Jihad or Holy War to bring about the conquest of the world for Allah. Their sole purpose of existence is Genocide (murdering people based on their religion, ethnicity or race). The U.S. has a list of 45 Militant Islamic organizations or terrorist factions that are recognized for their violence and the threat that these groups pose to the United States and the Western world. The following list is centered only on the U.S. and Canada but there are many other groups world wide that other countries have targeted as "Islamic Militant Terrorist Organizations". I have also listed the countries that have joined the U.S. in declaring them terrorist organizations along with their Jihadist objective:

ISLAMIC JIHADIST ORGANIZATIONS DECLARED TO BE TERRORIST ORGANIZATIONS BY THE UNITED STATES

Abdullah Azzam Brigades; U.S. and U.K.
...............Sunni Islamic Militants.
...............Objective: Global Jihad movement

Abu Nidal Organization, a.k.a.- Fatah, The Arab Revolutionary
...............Brigade, Black June. U.S., U.K., E.U. and Canada
...............Objective: Anti-Israel Palestinian Jihadists

Abu Sayyaf; U.S., U.K., Australia
...............Objective: Establish an Iranian-style Islamic Theocracy
...............in the Southern Philippines

Aden-Abyan Islamic Army; Canada, U.K.
...............Militant Islamists from Yemen
...............Objective: Attempting to change the outcomes of
...............elections in Yemen. (Possible U.S.S. Cole bombing)

al-Aqsa Martyrs' Brigades; U.S., Canada, E.U.
...............West Bank coalition of Palestinians
...............Objective: Launch suicide attacks against Israel

al-Gama'a al-Islamiyya; U.S., U.K., E.U., Canada, Russia
...............Egyptian Sunni Islamists
...............Objective: Overthrow the Egyptian Government and
...............install a more strict Islamic state.

al-Nusra Front; a.k.a.; al-Nusra-Sunni Islamic Mujahideen, U.S.,
...............U.K., Turkey, Australia,
...............Branch of Syrian and Lebanese al-Quaeda
...............Objective: Overthrow the Jordanian Government and
...............institute their sect of Sharia Law.

Al-Qaeda; a.k.a.; al-Quaida and al-Qa'ida, U.S., U.K., Russia,
...............Iran, India, E.U., Canada, Australia, United Nations.
...............al-Qaeda believes it is their religious right to kill
...............civilians in their attempts to conquer the world because
...............it is the command of Allah.
...............Objective: To force Sharia Law and the Islamic
...............Religion on the entire globe. They are also engaged in
...............an Islamic version of ethnic cleansing among certain
...............Muslim sects.

al-Qaeda-Arabian Peninsula; a.k.a.; Ansar al-Shari'a;
...............U.S., Canada, Australia, Saudi Arabia
...............Objective: Eliminate all Western influence that has
...............crept into "Eastern Islamic States" and replace these
..............."Westernized" governments with more strict
...............fundamentalist Islamic Regimes which are observant to
...............Sharia Law.

al-Qaeda-Islamic Maghreb; U.S., Russia, Canada, Australia,
...............Algeria.
...............Objective: To overthrow the Algerian Government and
...............install a fundamentalist Islamic State with Sharia Law.

al-Shabaab; a.k.a.; Harakat al- Shabaab al-Mujahideen;
...............U.S.,U.K., Canada, Australia
...............Objective: This Somalian Islamic Militant Group is
...............waging Jihad against the enemies of Islam in Somalia to
...............install an Islamic government.

Ansar al-Sharia, Tunisia; U.S., Tunisia
...............Objective: This Tunisian Islamic Group is engaged in
...............propaganda warfare through its campaigns on social
...............media. They are engaged in deceit and blame-shifting
...............attempting to make Muslims seem like the victims
...............when they are, in fact, the aggressors.

Ansar al-Islam; U.S.,U.K., Canada, Australia
...............Objective: Fight foreign invaders in Iraq and Syria and
...............work to institute strict Sharia Law.

Ansar Bait al-Maqdis; U.S., U.K., Egypt
...............Funded by former members of the Muslim Brotherhood
...............Objective: The disruption of the "Westernized" Muslim
...............Governments and calls for the destruction of Israel.
...............Responsible for rocket attacks into Israel and the
...............assassinations and assassination attempts of government
...............officials in Egypt.

Ansar Dine; associated with al-Qaeda Islamic Maghreb; U.S.
...............Objective: To introduce strict Sharia Law across Mali.

Ansary; U.S., U.K.
...............Islamic Jihadist Militants based in Northeast Nigeria
...............Objective: This offspring of Boka Horam was organized
...............to defend the interests of Islam and Muslims on the
...............entire continent of Africa.

Army of Islam; a.k.a.; Tawhid and Jihad Brigades [Gaza Strip]
...............U.S.
...............Objective: The destruction of Israel, the kidnapping of
...............Israeli citizens and civilian reporters
...............[most notable; Gilad Shalit, Alan Johnson]

Boco Haram; U.S., U.N., U.K., Canada, Nigeria
...............Boca Haram translation: "Western education is a sin"
...............Northeastern Nigerian Islamic Militants
...............Objective: Establish an Islamic State in Nigeria

Caucasus Emirate; U.S., U.K., Russia, Canada
...............Islamic Jihadist organization based in Russia

...............Objective: Expel the Russian presence from the
...............Northern Caucasus and establish an independent Islamic
...............Emirate in the region.

East Turkestan Islamic Movement; a.k.a.; Turkestan Islamic
...............Party or Turkestan Islamic Movement.
...............U.S., China
...............Based in Western China
...............Objective: The independence of Eastern Turkestan and
...............the institution of Islamic Sharia Law.

Hamas; U.S., E.U., Canada, Egypt, Israel
...............Pal./Sunni offshoot of the Egyptian Muslim Brotherhood
...............Objective: The destruction of Israel by launching attacks
...............on military and civilian targets including suicide
...............bombers. Marzook, the deputy chairman of Hamas
...............stated: "Hamas will not recognize Israel...this is a red
...............line that cannot be crossed"
...............Following is an excerpt from **the "Hamas" Charter**:
..............."Israel will exist and continue to exist until Islam will
...............obliterate it: Just as it obliterated others before it."
...............citation....Hamas Covenant, 1988, via Yale Law School's
...............Avalon Project.

Haqqani Network; U.S.
..............Islamic insurgent group fighting U.S. and NATO forces
..............in Afghanistan, or any foreign invaders.
..............Objective: Formed for the protection of Islamic interests
..............in Afghanistan.

Harkat-ul-Jihad-al Islami; U.S., U.K.
..............Objective: These Islamic Fundamentalists are operating
..............in Pakistan and India to create Islamic states and protect
..............Islamic strongholds already in the regions.

Harkat-al-Jihad-al Islami in Bangladesh; U.S., U.K.
..............Objective: Same as above only they are operating in
..............Bangladesh.

Harkat-ul-Mujahideen; U.S., U.K., Canada, Indonesia
..............Pakastani Islamic militants with Osama bin Laden ties
..............Objective: This Sunni Militant Organization is
..............attempting to establish Islamic rule or Sharia Law in
..............India's Jammu and Kashmir regions.

Hezbollah; translated; "The Party of Allah"
.... U.S., U.K., Turkey, Canada, Egypt
..............Shi'a Islamic Militants from Lebanon
..............Founded by Muslim Clerics and funded by Iran, Syria
..............Objective: Their original objective was to end the Israeli
..............occupation of Lebanon in 1982. Today, they are engaged
..............in the production of a Shi'a Islamic state in Lebanon
..............where they have 22 seats in the House of Parliament.
..............Won 8 seats in 1992 and 14 seats in 2005.
..............What Hezbollah has done in Lebanon is an example of
..............what they are doing all over the world. Occupy and little
..............by little turn the country to an Islamic majority and take
..............over politically; defeat from within.

Indian Mujahideen; U.S., India, New Zealand
..............Objective: To create an Islamic Caliphate, [Def; an
..............Islamic Territory/State led by a supreme religious and
..............political leader known as a Caliph who is a successor to
..............Mohammed]. The Caliphate will be across South Asia
..............and institute strict Islamic Sharia Law.

Islamic Jihad Union or Group; U.S., U.K.
..............An al-Qaeda affiliate operating in Pakistan, Germany
..............and other Western European Countries.
..............Objective: To occupy, commit Jihadist terrorist activity,
..............and eventually take over these regions for Islam and
..............introduce Islamic rule and Sharia Law.

Islamic Movement of Uzbekistan; U.S., U.K., Russia, Canada
..............and Australia.
..............Objective: A militant Islamic Group formed to
..............overthrow the government of Uzbekistan and install an
..............Islamic regime to rule with Sharia Law.

ISIL - Islamic State of Iraq and the Levant, a.k.a.;
ISIS – Islamic State of Iraq and Syria, or "Islamic State"
..............U.S., U.N., U.K., Saudi Arabia, Canada, Australia
..............The Levant is an overall region that includes parts of
..............Jordan, Israel, Lebanon, Syria, Iraq and Egypt.
..............Objective: To establish an "Islamic State" in the Levant.
..............This is a militant terrorist Jihadist Islamic
..............group that is attempting to set up a Caliphate in the
..............Levant region. If successful, they will install their own
..............Muslim leadership under strict Sharia Law even if that
..............requires the destruction of other Muslim Jihadists of
..............another sect. They also capture, attempted to destroy or
..............push out non-Muslim religious communities in the
..............region.

Jaish-e-Mohammed; translated: "The Army of Mohammed"
..............U.S., U.K., India, Canada, Australia and Pakistan.
..............Objective: These Islamic militants are attempting to
..............separate Kashmir from India and institute Islamic Sharia
..............Law.

Jemaah Islamiyah; U.S., U.K., Canada, Australia
..............Objective: These Southeast Asian militant Islamist's are
..............attempting to establish an Islamic State and Sharia Law
..............in Southeastern Asia.

Jamaah Ansharut Tauhid; U.S.
..............Indonesian based Islamic terrorist organization
..............Objective: To establish a Caliphate in Indonesia and
..............institute and Islamic state with Sharia Law; perpetrate
..............violence against the enemies of Islam: targets include
..............Indonesian Judges, prosecutors and police.

Jundallah; Translated: "Gods soldiers"
..............a.k.a.; The Peoples resistance movement of Iran.
..............U.S., Iran
..............Objective: The minority "Islamic Sunni Extremists" are
..............striking back at Iran's Shi'ite Islamic majority in Iran.

Kata'ib Hezbollah; U.S.
..............Shi'a insurgent militant Iraqi Islamists
..............Objective: Resistance to U.S. and Iraqi forces in Iraq.
.... Funded by Irans Quds Forces.

Lashkar-e-Taiba; U.S., U.K., Russia, India, Canada, Australia
..............Islamic Pakistani's operating in Southern Asia
..............Objective: To introduce an Islamic State in South Asia
..............and liberate Muslims living in Indian Kashmir.

Lashkar-e-Jhangvi; U.S., U.K., Canada, Australia
...........Pakistani Sunni's that joined forces with al-Qaeda and
...........the Taliban.
...........Objective: To destroy Shi'as and establish a Sunni
...........Caliphate in Pakistan/Afghanistan.

Libyan Islamic Fighting Group; U.S., U.K.
...........A Libyan Islamic organization affiliated with al-Qaeda
...........Objective: To introduce Islam into the government of
...........Libya and institute Sharia Law. Once attempted to
...........assassinate Qaddafi.

Moroccan Islamic Combatant Group; U.S., U.K.
...........Sunni Islamist terrorist organization with ties to the
...........Afghanistan Taliban operating in North Africa.
...........Objective: Attempting to install a fundamentalist Islamic
...........regime in Morocco, also working in Western Europe and
...........French Canada.

Muslim Brotherhood; Egypt, Saudi Arabia and Russia consider
...........them to be an Islamic Terrorist Organization but U.S.
...........President Barrack Obama does not. President Obama has
...........or had 6 ex-members of the Muslim Brotherhood working
...........in his administration.

Osbat al-Ansar; U.S., U.K., Canada and Russia
...........Sunni Fundamentalist's from Lebanon
...........Objective: Establish a radical Sunni Islamic State in
...........Lebanon with the Sunni version of Sharia Law.

Palestine Liberation Front; U.S., Canada
..........Objective: Backed by Iraq to launch attacks on Israel

Islamic Jihad Movement of Palestine;
..........U.S., U.K., E.U., Canada, Australia.
.........A Palestinian Islamic Militant Organization, backed by
..........Iranian financing, Militant Wing is the al-Quds Brigade.
..........Objective: The complete destruction of Israel. Their
..........leader, Ramadan Shalah stated: "I will never, under any
..........conditions, accept the existence of the State of Israel."

Popular Front for the Liberation of Palestine;
...........U.S., E.U., Canada
...........Objective: This Islamic terrorist organization favors a one
...........state solution in the Palestine/Israel conflict where Israel
...........is destroyed and Palestine conquers the land of Israel.

Popular Front for the Liberation of Palestine-General Command; U.S., E.U., Canada
...........Objective: Based in Syria, this Militant Islamic group and
...........its paramilitary wing; "Jihad Jibril Brigade" are actively
...........engaged in its attempt to completely destroy the nation of
...........Israel.

Tehrik-i-Taliban Pakistan; a.k.a.; Pakastani Taliban
...........U.S., Canada
...........An organization of several Islamic Militant Groups based
...........on the Afghanistan/Pakistan border.

...........Objective: The resistance of the Pakastani government, the
...........introduction of their interpretation of Sharia Law and to
...........fight all foreign invaders including U.S. and NATO forces
...........and allies.

....cited from the encyclopedia Wikipedia:

....wikipedia.org/wiki/List_of_Designated_terrorist_organizations

It's clear to see that to staff all of the above organizations they would need a constant supply of new recruits. It started in their homes, secular schools and Madrases where they learned hatred and distrust of the West. Then they went to terrorist training camps to learn how to fight and kill with firearms, bombs, traps, tactics, etc. Then they were either recruited or chose their Jihadist organization when they went to fight for Allah. It's all about the commands in the Koran to convert the entire globe to Islam even if they have to kill people to get it done.

Islam is not in full agreement as to when the Koran was actually canonized and published, some think Mohammed himself organized the Koran in book form but others believe it was left to one of his Caliphs to do. However, there was enough word of mouth about Allah's desires for his followers to fight and the conquering of Nations began prior to Mohammed's death. Mohammed himself organized Caliphates and Caliphs to run them during his lifetime. As stated earlier, the Koran wasn't finished until the day Mohammed actually died in 632 A.D. (But the fighting and/or peaceful conversion started before then). For arguments sake, I will use the day of Mohammed's passing as the beginning point or publication point of the Koran, the year 632. When Mohammed would form a Caliphate he would appoint a Caliph or leader to rule over it. In Mohammed's time they were the Umayyad Caliphates with Rashidun Caliphs.

So by now, they have had time to develop a track record of success. The chart on the following page outlines the cities or countries that were converted, attacked, overrun, laid siege to by Islam as commanded by Allah and carried out by Mohammed and Mohammed's own Caliphs and others who rose to power over the centuries.

*Edmund Burke had no idea that an evil religion would murder people to try to take over the world when he said; "All that is necessary for the triumph of evil is that good men do nothing." He is right!

Fox News; Sean Hannity interviews Dick Cheney, August 2014:

"I think the danger is enormous.... I look at things like the Rand Report that was published a couple of months ago that talked about a 58% increase in Jihadist groups...over a 3 year period."

330.
ISLAM'S CONQUERING OF THE WORLD

Year......People, Country, Region or City conquered, or attempt

630.............Mecca
(632.............Mohammed died but his followers continued)
636.............Persia [Iran]
637.............Syria
639.............Armenia
639.............Egypt
651.............Persia (again) and Mesopotamia, beginning in 633
652.............Northern Africa
654.............Cyprus
655.............The Mediterranean Sea (The Battle of Masts)
665.............North Africa (again)
670.............Maghreb (Morocco): first city founded by Muslims
674-678......1st Siege of Constantinople
711-750......Attempted to conquer the Caucasus
712.............Sindh (Pakistan Region), beginning in 664
717-718......2nd Siege of Constantinople
718.............Hispania, beginning in 711
736.............Georgia
751......Transoxiana (Afghan./Turkestan Region),beginning in 662
820.........Crete, including multiple invasions on the Isle of Patmos
827.............Southern Italy
831.............Palermo
840.............Crete, (again)

842..............Messina
846..............Rome invasion
859..............Enna
878..............Syracuse
900..............Catania
902..............Sicily
960..............Egypt (again)
965..............Cyprus (again)
975......Levant (Syria, Iraq, Egypt, Israel, Jordan, Lebanon region)
1001............Saharan West Africa, proselytized (peaceful converts)
1209............India, certain states, beginning in approximately 1000
1237............Isfahan in Iran
1258............Baghdad, Islam fought to keep control
1260............Damascus and Aleppo
1260.........Mamluk (Egyptian) army destroyed North of Jerusalem
1292............Sumatra, Proselytized during Marco Polo's expedition
13th Century...The Mongols converted to Islam and Syria, Persia, ...Mesopotamia and the Eastern territories converted to Islam.
1413............attempted Venice, Ottoman Islamic Navy
1413............attempted the Balkans
1453............Constantinople, Ottomans captured, renamed Istanbul
1492............Grenada
1490's.........Philippines, Borneo, Java
1511............Iran region, beginning in 1501
1517............Egyptian Mamluk Territories
1526............Delhi India, Bangladesh

1526..........Baghdad (again), beginning in 1517

1606.......Nubia (Sudan region), beginning in 700, took 906 years

1857..........Bengal, Hyderabad, Gujarat (States in India)

1948..........Israels War of Independence attempt by Syria, Iraq,
..................Egypt, Lebanon and Jordan

1967..........Israel, attempt by Egypt, Syria and Jordan

1973..........Israel, attempt by Egypt and Syria, (Yom Kippur War)

The following are attacks perpetrated within or against the United States of America:

1973..........Maryland, IDF Air Force attache assassinated, Islamic
.................Palestinian group Black September suspected.

1980..........Maryland, Iranian exile assassinated, sanctioned by the
.................Iranian Government.

1989..........New York, Bronx, Muslim extremists firebombed the
.................Riverdale press newspaper for defending Salman
.................Rushdie's book questioning Islams creation.

1993..........New York City, al-Qaeda extremists bombed the
.................World Trade Center.

1994..........New York, Brooklyn, Lebanese Islamist ambushed
.................Jewish students killing one, wounding three.

1997..........New York, Empire State Building, Islamic Palestinian
.................opened fire on the observation deck killing one and
.................injuring at least four others. His motive according to
.................his daughter: "To punish the U.S. for its support of
.................Israel."

2000..........California, Los Angeles.
..................Millinneum Plot, or, Y2K attack, A series of terrorist
..................attacks were stopped by law enforcement. The 2 U.S.
..................targets were the Los Angeles International Airport and
..................the U.S. Naval ship USS The Sullivans (DDG-68).
..................Law enforcement did not capture the attackers of the
..................USS Sullivan, the boat that had the bomb sank before
..................it made it to the Sullivan.

2000..........USS Cole, bombed by what is believed to be the same
..................Yemeni Islamic group who attempted to bomb the USS
..................Sullivan earlier.

2000..........New York, Bronx, 3 Islamic terrorists threw Molotov
..................cocktails at a synagogue in the Bronx.
..................Motive: according to authorities; "Strike a blow in
..................the Middle East conflict between Israel and Palestine."

2001..........New York City, World Trade Center Twin Towers and
..................Building #7. Destroyed by Islam, al-Qaeda, taking
..................almost 3000 lives.

2001..........New York, Maryland, Pennsylvania, 4 fully loaded
..................passenger airliners were used by Islamists as missiles
..................to attack targets in the aforementioned states.

2001..........Maryland, Pentagon, one of the above airliners was
..................used to try to destroy the U.S. Militaries Central
..................Command.

2002..........New York, Buffalo, "The Buffalo 6" or the
..................Lackawanna 6 cell, 6 Yemeni-American al-Qaeda
..................operatives who unsuccessfully planned to detonate
..................brief-cased size dirty bombs in Western New York.

2002..........Washington D.C., Baltimore, Virginia and other states,
..................The Beltway Sniper attacks, killed 10, injured 3.
..................Evidence presented at trial showed an affinity to the
..................cause of Islamic Jihad.

2002..........Los Angeles California Airport, the El Al ticket
................counter, Egyptian Islamic assassin kills 2 Israeli's and
................wounds 4 others.

2004..........New York, Washington D.C., New Jersey. Law
................enforcement stopped a bomb plot which had al-Qaeda
................backing. Islamists attempted an attack on the nations
................financial institutions. Targets included the
................International Monetary Fund, World Bank, Prudential
................in New Jersey, The New York Stock Exchange and
................Citigroup.

2005..........California, Los Angeles, a radical Islamic group
................unsuccessfully plotted to bomb several U.S. Military
................Bases, numerous synagogues and an Israeli Consulate
................in California.

2006.........North Carolina, A Muslim terrorist injured 6 when he
................drove his SUV into a crowd of pedestrians at U.N.C.-
................Chapel Hill. Investigators say his motive was to
................"Avenge the deaths or murders of Muslims around the
................world."

2006.........Washington, Seattle, The Seattle Jewish Federation
................Shooting. A Pakistani Muslim terrorist killed one,
................injured 5. His motive according to Law enforcement;
................"He was angry with American foreign policy in the
................Middle East."

2007.........New York, Queens, an unsuccessful Islamic terrorist
................plot to bomb jet fuel supply tanks and lines at the John
................F. Kennedy International Airport.

2007.........New Jersey, Fort Dix, 6 radical Muslim Islamists
................conspired to attack U.S. Military personnel at Fort Dix.
................Their goal according to investigators was; "To kill as
................many soldiers as possible."

2008.........New York City, U.S. Military recruiting office was
...............bombed. Investigators said the bombs used had the
...............same components as those used in the Iraq and
...............Afghanistan war zones implying that they were likely
...............made by Islamic terrorists in the U.S. with the same
...............type of explosives that the terrorists use while fighting
...............the U.S. forces and our allies abroad.

2009.........New York City, Subway, Several Afghani Islamic
...............terrorists plotted to bomb the New York City Subway
...............System and another target in the U.K. The authorities
...............caught them before they acted.

2009.........New York, Bronx, 4 Muslim terrorists plotted to shoot
...............down U.S. Military aircraft in Newburgh New York
...............and also bomb 2 Synagogues in Riverdale New York.
.... U.S. Law enforcement caught them before they
...............acted.

2009.........Texas, Fort Hood, U.S. Army. A Muslim terrorist
...............infiltrated the U.S. Military and killed 13 and wounded
...............29 U.S. soldiers. Major Hassan explained his motive as
...............Jihad claiming "Illegal and immoral aggression against
...............Muslims."

2009.........Arkansas, Little Rock, an al-Qaeda affiliated Islamic
...............terrorist killed one and wounded one at a U.S. Military
...............recruiting office. Investigators said he was part of
...............al-Qaeda in the Arabian Peninsula and his motive;
..............."Upset over U.S. killing of Muslims in Iraq and
...............Afghanistan."

2010.........New York City, Times Square car bomb plot, an
...............Islamic Pakistani terrorist who trained at a Pakistani
...............terrorist training camp created the bomb, placed it in
...............the car and parked it in Time Square, then he lit the
...............fuse but it did not explode. 2 street venders saw the car
...............smoking and alerted authorities. His motive according
...............to U.S. officials was; "To Kill American's"

2011.........New York, Manhattan, 2 Muslim terrorist extremists
...............plotted to bomb and unspecified synagogue, a church
...............and the Empire State Building. The were caught by
...............U.S. authorities prior to its execution and authorities
...............said they were motivated by "politics and
...............anti-semitism."

2013.........Kansas, Wichita, a bomb plot to destroy the airport
...............terminal at the Wichita Mid-Continent Airport and "kill
...............as many Americans as possible" was stopped by the
...............F.B.I. -This terrorist, an Osama bin Laden supporter of
...............al-Qaeda in the Arabian Peninsula made a car bomb and
...............was plotting to blow the terminal and himself up.
...............He claimed; "Brothers like Osama bin Laden and Anwar
...............al Awlaki are a great inspiration to me, but I must be
...............willing to give up everything to truly feel like a obedient
...............slave to Allah."

2013........Massachusetts, The Boston Marathon, 2 Islamic brothers
...............used 2 bombs that killed 3 and injured 180 people.
...............Authorities said that in a note left by the surviving
...............brother he stated the reason for the bombing; "The
...............bombings were retaliation for U.S. actions in Iraq and
...............Afghanistan against Muslims."

4 Sources for the compilation of the above list:

...en.wikipedia.org/wiki/muslim_conquests,

...wikipedia.org/wiki/History_of_Islam,

...wikipedia.org/wiki/Terrorism-in-the-United-States,

...jewishvirtuallibrary.org/jsource/History/1948_War.html

According to "Jack Van Impe Presents", Islam has slaughtered 45,000,000 Christian's worldwide in the 19th century alone. That doesn't include any of the other religions that are also targets of Islam.

When Mohammed first began the Islamic Holy Wars back in the 600's they were not known as terrorists and they probably did not make any governmental list as radicals. They were Jihadists which meant then as it does today "fighters of Holy Wars" only the wars are not Holy nor is the God that calls Islam to fight a Holy God. Only Satan would call a man to murder another man and call that Holiness, the Western World calls it Genocide. When a Muslim speaks of "peace" he is looking forward to the peace Islam will have after they conquer the world and the command of Allah is satisfied. Until they conquer the world, they will always be required to fight to convert the world to Islam.

Early Islamic fighters were known as "Religious Invaders" and they were, and still are, relentless in their conquests. In the above list Nubia in the Sudan region took 906 years before the region finally fell, from 700 to 1606 they fought for that region. As long as there are Muslims who follow the Koran there will never be "man made" peace in the world. No Peace-Talks will ever amount to anything permanent as long as Islam is given the go-ahead to lie so they can win in a negotiation with an infidel. Islamists are only buying time so they can reorganize and rebuild their ammunition and bomb supplies. They will re-staff and develop a new plan of attack then eventually launch their attack. Just look at Israel and Gaza since Israel handed over Gaza to the Palestinians. The original contract stated that there would be no attacks out of Gaza against Israel if Israel agreed to the exchange. Israel agreed and Islam has been organizing and launching attacks ever since. Peace talks entered into with an Islamic State or terrorist organization have always failed at some point, broken by Islam. The Koran calls Jews and Christians infidels. The Koran says not to make friends with infidels which are the followers of Satan according to the Koran, they call Israel and America Satan and "The Great Satan". Is a Christian a Satanist? Is a Jewish person a Satanist? No to both of the above questions, they both call upon Jesus. Jesus is the Messiah of Israel and the Savior of the Western world. Satan wants his Islamic followers to think the West is Satanic so they will think they are fighting evil.

In the year 630 there was one Muslim town, Mecca, conquered for Allah, as of 2010 there are 49 Muslim majority countries. In

1378 years Islam went from 0 countries to 49 countries where Islam has rule.

"Islam is the dominant religion in the middle east, North Africa, the Horn of Africa, the Sahel (Saharan Desert/Sudanese Savanna region), and some parts of Asia. Large communities of Muslims are also found in China, the Balkans, India and Russia...The study found more Muslims in the United Kingdom than in Lebanon and more in China than in Syria."

...wikipedia.org/wiki/Islam_by_country

With all of the above in mind, lets read one more time what Siraj Wahhaj said, who was standing on U.S. soil when he said it, to a group of Muslims in the U.S.

"Take my word, If 6-8 million Muslims unite in America, the country will come to us."

....Siraj Wahhaj

Here is one addition that no Christian American wants to see on "Islam's Conquering of the World" list:

2024........The United States of America, beginning in 1948, after
...............infiltrating the U.S. for decades and running for
...............political offices nationwide, Islam established a
...............foothold in the U.S. by bringing millions of Muslims
...............from abroad and converting U.S. citizens to Islam. By
...............shear force of numbers, they elected an Islamic
...............President who immediately began working to populate
...............Congress with Democratic Muslims in order to abolish
...............the Constitution and institute Sharia Law. Islam
...............reversed centuries of Christian based Laws and enacted
...............Sharia Law so quickly that most were left scratching
...............their heads and asking themselves "What Happened".
...............When members of the New Islamic America were asked
...............to comment on the U.S.'s rapid conversion one replied
..............."The country just came to us, it was time for a change"

If Islam has its way! After Sharia Law is established in the U.S. then the Muslim leaders can legally force everyone to convert to Islam by choice or threat of death, or, as will probably happen, many Christians will flee the country. Any President in the United States will have the full force and cooperation of the U.S. Military to achieve the objectives of the administration. Since this will be enacted as Law then the Police forces around the Country will also be bound in their duty to uphold the Law to carry out all new legislation no matter if they agree with it or not. It would be an extremely turbulent time in U.S. history, Civil unrest, hundreds of what would normally have been law abiding citizens in the "Christian" America would be marked as "Anarchists" in the "Islamic" America and the courts would be jammed for years hearing cases against Sharia Law. As for any Christian who refuses to convert to Islam, death, by Sharia Law. Women may legally be beaten by their husbands for disobedience, Homosexuals and Lesbians will be put to death according to Sharia Law. The same Marriage documents that Homosexuals fought for to declare themselves as legally married will probably be the same legal documents that an Islamic court will use to obtain a pair of convictions.

With all of the checks and balances in Washington, what real effect would an Islamic President have during his presidency?

If elected, an Islamic American President would cut our armed forces, raise taxes, spend the U.S. into trillions of dollars of debt. He would favor Islamic causes in the U.S. and abroad while at the same time try to suppress Christian freedom of expression. He would not work to secure our borders as they should be. He would not impede the flow of Islamists entering the U.S. He would stand by while Rome is burning to the ground around him and do nothing that would have a substantial long-term effect. Since lying is acceptable in Islam, he and his administration would consistently lie to and misdirect the American public and the world. He would implement his own agenda on the American public with or without Congressional approval. He would have x-members of Islamic Terrorist Organizations working in his administration. He would cancel the Christian National Day of prayer at the White House yet invite Islamic clerics to the White House for prayer. He would strive to keep his true religion from the American people to the point of forbidding News Agencies from running clips of him professing to groups of Muslims that he is a Muslim. He would remove or cover-up all symbols of Christianity from the White House press room and other televised speaking engagements. He would feign being appalled at terrorist activities around the world but then do nothing substantive about it. Inaction or little action would be the rule rather than the exception concerning Islamic organizations. My hope would be that any U.S. President who is a Muslim would be an apostate Muslim, the non-violent, non-take-over-the-world variety as opposed to the fundamentalists that want to destroy everything in sight for Allah. A Muslim President would be looking out for future Islamic American interests rather than the present Christian American interests.

The only way for America to survive as a Christian nation is for our **government** to recognize that Islam is a clear and present danger to the western way of life. If for no other reason than "National Security" we need to shut down these No-Go Zones and suspend all immigration from Muslim countries. Put a halt to Muslim enclaves and cease the construction of all Mosques nationwide. Our **nation** is in danger, our families are in danger, our very lives are in **danger**. According to Islam, America is an enemy of the Muslim world and, as an enemy, should be destroyed or taken over.

Islam relies heavily on what western countries call "tolerance"and "intolerance"; our **society** has become "tolerant" to a fault especially when Islam is using it against us and most American's aren't aware of it. Islam cries "foul" every time someone speaks out against a Muslim or the Islamic religion or a person of **Middle-Eastern descent.** They use our own "Political correctness" to their advantage to deceive unwitting Americans and westerners into thinking that Islam is being 'victimized' while, all along, planning our destruction and take-over as a **country**. Our **fathers** fought and died for the American Christian way of life, so many have made the "**Supreme Sacrifice**" so their children could live free in a **country** founded on Biblical values and mo**ralities**. We owe it to our veterans and our grand-children to not give away the sacrifices of the past and allow a doctrinally hostile religion to walk right into America and take our freedoms away from us without so much as a **challenge**. The citizens of Germany held Adolf Hitlers book in their hands and read what Adolf **planned** to do. They had an opportunity to challenge his ideology and change the course of **history** but they choose to do nothing and remain ignorant and that choice cost millions **upon** millions of innocent civilian **lives.** Today the entire 'Western **world**' is wearing the shoes of 1930's Germany. We can choose to do nothing as they did or we can change our laws to stop any future hostility that may arise from Islamic Imams who want to strike a blow **for** Allah. We need our Congressmen and Senators to understand the truth of Islam and the true intent of the Islamic agenda on American soil. Our lawmakers are the first line of defense in turning back the Islamic tide which is attempting to undermine the American way of life from within **the** borders of the United **States.** Islams plot to take over the United States and the **World** for Allah needs to be on the minds of every American citizen in the **country.** Would America have tolerated Adolf Hitler sending a couple of hundred thousand or millions of Germans to the United States during World War II. We need legislation that prohibits a hostile people from amassing an Islamic stronghold within the borders of the United States right under the noses of the very citizens they plan to conquer. Write your Congressmen and Senators and voice your concerns, let them know that you are expecting some sort of legislation that insures the protection of the American people, the Country and the American way of life, urge them to educate themselves about the Islamic agenda for the world and to do something about it.

One of the unfortunate by products of challenging Islam in America **are** the people of Middle Eastern descent that have truly escaped Islamic **oppression** and are living peaceful productive lives in America. My question for them would be; Can you blame an American for the concerns they have about a religion that calls for their destruction? We don't know what is actually in the heart of a Muslim, only your actions tell us that. America needs an assurance of truth and peace and safety and none of those things are in the doctrine that Islam adheres to in the Koran. Unfortunately, your religion makes it acceptable for you to lie to us so how can we believe you when you tell us you are a peaceful Muslim or even a non- Muslim? Everyone involved is in a catch-22, but the side that has the most to lose is America and the rest of the Western world.

When Japan bombed the United States the U.S. government rounded up every citizen of Japanese descent that lived in the U.S. and housed them together in compounds until after the war was over. The government had legitimate concerns that our National Security would be compromised if we left potential enemy combatants on the streets within the U.S.A.. The thinking was that they may launch attacks on our citizens or attack our infrastructure. Now, as then, we should have legitimate concerns about the well being and the safety of our country and its citizens. As you can see from the list of Islamic attacks on the U.S. that is exactly what Islam is doing right now. If you think treating an ethnic people differently than everyone else in America would be politically incorrect, look at what we do to the Mexican people from South of the border. If they are entering the country illegally then we send them back to Mexico against their will. It's not a new concept, we need some sort of control over who is entering our country and why they are entering. If nothing else, create a National Registry for Islamic nations and force the citizens of those nations to apply to enter into the United States and limit their stay; that's if they have a legitimate reason for being here in the first place.

Today there are over 7 billion people in the world, of which; between 1 and 2 billion are currently Muslim. Five billion non-Muslims have been targeted for conversion or destruction by the teachings of the Koran.

"Son of Man, I have made thee a watchman unto the house of Israel: Therefore hear the word at my mouth, and give them warning from me."
..... Ezekiel 3: 17

"America will never be destroyed by a foreign power. If we fail we will **fail** from within."
.... Abraham Lincoln

Fox News, Oliver North was speaking about the tactics and objectives of radical Islam to the entire Western World;
"If we don't do more (to stop Islam) our children will indict us on willful indifference and I don't want that to happen."
...Col. Oliver North, Fox News, Aug. 2014

Islam could never defeat the U.S. **militarily, the** only way they can achieve their objectives would be to occupy and tear us apart piece by piece, and for that they would need our cooperation. As it stands today, they have our full cooperation and that cooperation needs to end.

Jesus extends an invitation to all who follow Islam or any other religion for that matter;

"But all things that are reproved [disapproved of] are made manifest by the light: for whatsoever does make manifest is light. Wherefore he saith, Awake thou that sleepest, and arise from the dead, and Christ shall give thee light." ... Ephesians 5: 13- 14

"If thou shall confess with thy mouth the Lord Jesus, and shalt believe in thine heart that God has raised Him from the dead, thou shalt be saved. For with the heart man believes unto righteousness; and with the mouth confession is made unto salvation... For whosoever [all people from all nations or religions] shall call upon the name of the Lord [Jesus] shall be saved." ... Romans 10: 9- 10, 13

Hopefully, in the end, Islams attempt to take-over may turn out to be a moot point since we have ended the 6th day or 6000th year of earth history. Jesus is due to return for his Church and rapture them off of the planet while God sends his judgment upon the earth as described in the book of Revelation.
The Church Age is the time between Jesus's two appearances on the earth – he was born and had his 33 year life and ministry about 2000 years ago. He is coming back to 'Rapture' (snatch away) all those that believe in him and received him as their Lord (any day). Christians will be off of the earth for 7 years only to return again with Jesus to rule and reign with him for 1000 year's – beginning after the 7 year tribulation period.

Islamic scholars made room for a "Coming 'Guided One'"; patterned after Jesus in the Christian Bible; The Islamic Mahdi is not in the Koran, he was added later by the Islamic scholars who wrote the Hadiths. The one that Islam is calling their "Mahdi" is, in my opinion, going to be the Christian Anti-Christ. As mentioned earlier, everything recorded in the Bible Satan has turned around backwards for Islam's use. Some Hadith writers place their Mahdi back on earth for 7 years; exactly the length of the tribulation as recorded in the Bible. He's the one that uses the Temple in Jerusalem as a headquarters. Islam also records Jesus as only a prophet; not God, and Jesus converts to Islam and actually helps the Mahdi to destroy Christians that will not convert to Islam!

ABSOLUTELY NOT GOING TO HAPPEN: Yet another Satanic Lie! Jesus is God, He will always be God and as God he will never bow down to Satan or the Mahdi as the Islamic end times prophecies proclaim: Jesus is going to destroy the Unholy Trinity including the Islamic Mahdi, if he is in fact the Anti-Christ, at the end of the seven year Tribulation as described in the book of Revelation.

The Islamic Hadith writers, like Mohammed, made up claims that were inspired by Satan that pervert the characters and ideologies in the Bible to create doubt in the minds of the unwary or just outright misguide those who don't know the truth.. Jesus and the rest of the Trinity created the universe and everything in it. All power was given to Jesus in heaven and in earth before Mohammed was ever born. If Mohammed were alive today and just starting the Islamic religion in the U.S.; He would be ranked amongst the occultists such as David Koresh, Anton Lavey or Jim Jones. Unfortunately, he was born in a place and time where his Satanic ideologies could take hold and spread through an unsuspecting country where Christianity had not been preached sufficiently and the people did not know what (lying) spirit they were dealing with.

ALL MEN HAVE ETERNAL CONSCIOUSNESS IN HEAVEN OR HELL

We need to recognize who our enemies really are- 'We do not fight against men but spiritual wickedness that Satan oppresses men with. Our true wars are fought Spirit against Spirit, who's side are you on?
We, as the human race have an eternal destiny ahead of us with or without the God that created us, that all depends on the choices we each make in this life.
Evolutionists are hoping that they are correct and when they die their consciousness just fades to black and that's the end of them. There is a price to pay for being wrong! There is a price to pay for

teaching others the "wrong way"! **My desire is that** God reveals himself to evolutionists and those who have rejected Christ because of the evolutionary teaching and they find their way back into a relationship with God before its to late. I hope God reveals himself to everyone else on the planet that doesn't know him. I can't prove Heaven exists just as you can't prove it doesn't exist, if I could prove it I would be touring the nations showing everyone the proof but again, that would exclude the faith required to receive God.

SATAN AND ISRAEL

Satan launched his plans for mans destruction on the earth: Evolution through Darwin, World War II through Hitler, Islam through Mohammed, the Satanic Church through Anton Lavey and this list is by no means complete and it continues to grow. There is a common thread throughout all of Satan's attempts to deceive men: Death – Destruction – Deceit - Loss. As mentioned earlier, Satan is against everything that God holds dear, especially men. God declared Israel to be his chosen people to represent him on the earth. Satan is especially interested in harming Israel and because of this up to 20,000,000 Jewish people died in Hitlers holocaust. In Genesis, Satan told the Israeli spies that they were grasshoppers in the eyes of the sons of Anak and those "thoughts from Satan" and Israels lack of faith in God caused 40 years worth of the resistance that the Jewish people suffered through in the wilderness between Egypt and the promised land. Today, the nation's that surround Israel hold conferences on the destruction of Israel and are outspoken about their plans to destroy Israel. Islam's sworn enemies are Israel and America- 70% of Americans claim to be Christian and the second largest population of Jewish people on earth live in America. America has supported Israel militarily in the past and hopefully we will continue to do so in the future. Satan is currently the God of this world and he is being held in check by Christians who recognize his presence and pray against his attempts to destroy. **Christians are not against men who are trapped in Satan's false religious systems, we are**

347.

100% in favor of your deliverance from all of Satan's false religions. Christianity needs more spiritually minded souls to help combat what Satan has deployed against men on the earth. As it stands, men who are not part of Jesus's Church and are overtly speaking out against Christianity are helping Satan's agenda by destroying mans faith in the one true God and we have no choice but to resist.

The U.S. Military and our allies went on a mission to liberate the countries that were invaded by the Nazis and the Russians during World War II. Our militaries defeated the men involved in the invasions but did not defeat the root cause which was a Satanic ideology; the evolution religion. Today, men still think they are better, smarter, more advanced than other men as Hitler did and that is seen in the forced teaching of a failed religious theory every day in our schools world-wide; Satan is still pushing for men to expel God from the minds of our children. And along with God goes all true morality which, when absent, allows Satan to walk in and plant 'immorality' into the minds of our children. In the earliest days of the United States, during the Indian Wars, this ideology was present in America. The U.S. government forced the Indian tribes from their lands based on the assumption that the Indians were less evolved, advanced or intelligent. Indians were viewed as 'Uncivilized', 'Red-skins' or 'Savages' all of which implied a less evolved or less civilized state. After all, the "civilized" white man needed to bring civilization and settle the West. This was not a case of evolutionary advancement, it was just a culture clash and the government used the Indian's "supposed" inferiority as an excuse to take their land from them. The same goes for the black community, any early artwork done depicting cavemen as "less advanced" people all had dark skin. Most depictions in museums or Zoo's had dark skinned models for the lesser 'advanced' peoples, evolutionarily speaking. The implication being if you have black skin or brown skin you are less evolved which was the exact reasoning of Adolf Hitler and Haeckel and Darwin.

The "Black Slave Trade" would never have happened if it were not that some men thought themselves more evolved, intelligent or capable than black men and thus it was acceptable to take ships to Africa and forcefully load the black native people onto those ships and sail them to the U.S. or Europe to sell them. Black skinned people were viewed as commodities by white skinned traders.

Two Christian men: Abraham Lincoln in America and William Wilberforce in Great Britain worked for and were successful in abolishing the Black Slave Trade off of the American and European continents. Lincoln was successful in 1862 and the Evangelical Christian William Wilberforce in 1833.

These are examples of two men that Jesus used personally to destroy the works of Satan.

Christians worldwide need to launch a campaign to eliminate evolution from our school systems and re-introduce Christianity and Gods creation model along with daily prayer back into our schools. America was founded as a Christian country with Christian moral values. At the very least teach nothing **in our science classes** about how the earth or creatures came to be; neither evolution or the Christian models of creation. Leave evolution and Gods creation model for classes on religion in our public schools and Churches to teach. Since evolution has not been proven and **is being taught as a fact** then our school systems are teaching a blatant falsehood, it should be taught as what it is, a religion, nothing but an unproven alternative to Christianity.

Evolution is like Madame Curry's radium drinks; on the surface it all seemed reasonable and most people thought the "experts" knew what they were talking about. Then the true effects began to surface but when those effects were revealed the damage was already done and the effect was catastrophic and today both evolution and radium drinks are clearly proven to be detrimental to man's well being.

Are you on Satan's short list of people he can use to deceive men? Does Satan view you as he does men like Lyell, Darwin, Lavey, Schucman, Haeckel, Hitler, Stalin, Mohammed and others. If your name is on Satan's "Go To" list and **if you have a desire to live a truthful life,** God can help you!

"For all have sinned and fallen short of the glory of God."
….. Romans 3: 23

There is an open door for all men to become Christians; from all religions; Hindus, Islam, Buddhists, **evolutionists,** Satanists, **atheists,** Rick Warren's and Robert **Schuler's** Chrislam or any other religion.

"For whosoever shall call upon the name of the Lord [Jesus] shall be saved……
That if thou shalt **confess with thy mouth the Lord Jesus,** and shalt **believe in thine heart that God hath raised him from the dead, thou shalt be saved.** "
….. Romans 10: 13, 9

Definition of "Whosoever" - Any man or woman in a physical body, any age, living upon the earth.

Definition of "**Saved**" - When you 'the spirit' dwelling inside your body is sealed with an eternal seal by Gods **Holy** Spirit as belonging to the 'Triune' God. The Kingdom of Heaven now belongs to you. At that instance God will never leave you or forsake you, you are his forever. ------ Hebrews 13: 5

"Behold, I [Jesus] stand at the door and knock: If any man **hears** my voice, and **opens** the door, I will come in to him, and will sup [eat] with him, and he with me.
…. Revelation 3: 20

"To open their eyes [give them an understanding], and to turn them from darkness to light, and from the power of Satan unto God, that they may receive forgiveness of sins, and inheritance

among them which are sanctified by faith which is in me [Jesus]."
.... Acts 26: 18

"And I [Jesus] say unto you, ask and it shall be given you, seek, and you shall find; knock, and it shall be opened unto you. For everyone that asketh receiveth; and he that seeketh findeth; and to him that knocketh it shall be opened."
.... Luke 11: 9

The Kingdom of Heaven is a free gift and it's there for the asking!

"Then Peter said unto them, Repent, and be baptized every one of you in the name of Jesus Christ for the remission of sins, and you shall receive the gift of the Holy Ghost. " (The 'Gift' is the Holy Ghost)
..... Acts 2: 38

When you receive the gift of the Holy Ghost it's called the Baptism where he moves inside of your body alongside your spirit and seals your spirit blameless. He guides you through life to help you in any righteous endeavor you undertake.

"These things have I written unto you that believe on the name of the son of God [Jesus]; that ye may know that ye have eternal life, and that ye may believe on the name of the son of God."
.....1 John 5: 13

"For God so loved the world, that he gave his only begotten son [Jesus], that whosoever believeth in him should not perish, but have everlasting life."
..... John 3: 16

Chapter 14

THE TESTIMONY OF A BELIEVER
My witness that Gods Word is True

What is the importance of a Christian's testimony, the telling of the things that God has done in his, **a believer's life**?
The short answer is - **Other** people who are currently going through the same sort of thing will hear the testimony of Gods deliverance and they may develop the faith that the same deliverance can happen to them and pursue their own deliverance from God.

If you are suffering from something that Satan has bound you with and someone tells about how Jesus delivered them from the same sort of oppression then God gets the **glory** when you develop **faith for and receive** your deliverance. **Men develop** faith in God through hearing testimonies because "faith comes by hearing" and God gets the **glory** from men because of their deliverance after hearing the testimonies of believers. There is no doubt from where the deliverance came from.

"And they overcame him [Satan] by the blood of the Lamb [Jesus], **and by** the word of their testimony; and they loved not their lives unto the death."
….. Revelation 12: 11

Part of my personal testimony:
The **'back story'** – I had gone to church as a child, I attended church for **about** 4 or 5 years during grade school but quit. It had been 26 years since I regularly attended **church, I** was living by my own will and ignoring any prompting [conscience: voice of Gods Spirit] that I would feel inside concerning the things of God. I was 44 years old when this series of events happened. In the beginning, I thought this story would go to my grave with me. I thought I would never tell another living soul this part of my

testimony because of the embarrassment that would go with it. Today, it's been ten years since this series of incidents, I believe this can serve as a way to show people how Satan can take a person that was a confessed Christian (but at the time carnal, walking after the flesh) and turn him into a murderer --- almost. I certainly was not walking after the Spirit as God desires for us, I was walking after my selfish, carnal flesh and that almost cost me and at least 3 others everything. God intervened and changed my life forever, he set me on a new path and led me to an understanding of his kingdom I didn't realize I could ever know. God literally revealed himself and his kingdom to me!

God knows what we are going through in our everyday lives. As recorded earlier, God's omnipresence and omniscience allows God to know everything that's happening in our lives. An example of the way God sees our heart condition (what's happening in our souls) is recorded in the book of Mathew -Chapter 5:

"Ye have heard that it was said by them of old time, Thou shalt not commit adultery: But I say unto you, That whosoever looketh on a woman to lust after her hath committed adultery with her already in his heart."
….. Mathew 5: 27 – 28

Even though Mathew 5: 27- 28 is talking about adultery it is essentially saying that through God's omnipotence God knows every sin that we keep to ourselves in our heart or soul and if we just think about it with desire it's the same as committing the sin since we have an internal law that tells us not to sin. At the time murder was definitely in my heart and I could feel myself going down a path that could not have had a desirable ending yet I felt compelled to follow it. At the time, I was a physical fitness fanatic and spent 5 or 6 days a week in a gym working out. It was while I was in the gym that a certain group of men and I did not get along and it escalated out of control. I finally reached my breaking point and decided that I was going to take matters into my own hands and resolve our differences once and for all. I planned on taking a pair of loaded handguns into the gym concealed in a gym bag while these men were present and pull them out and have a one sided shoot out with them. I had been planning this for a few months and I had the handguns, I had a gym bag that I was going to conceal the guns in, I had the plan and was getting ready to execute my plan – until one evening in the gym. I was there exercising and during a rest period between sets I was mentally rehearsing my assault on these men in my mind. I remember looking down and I saw my trigger finger going back and forth like I was pulling the trigger of a gun. I was not consciously pulling the **trigger**, it was as if something else was using my finger to pull the trigger. The sight of that shocked me, I was startled awake, so to speak, and it dawned on me that I was really planning on shooting these guys, the thought shifted from my carnal flesh into my Spirit and my Spirit took over, prior to that it was like a fantasy only it wasn't a fantasy any longer - I had the guns and I had the bag and the plan was ready to go. I was getting ready to murder at least three unarmed men. I knew all along that what I was planning was against Gods law -'Thou shall not **murder**', I knew that but was ignoring the Holy Spirit – until then! I got up and left the gym and on the drive home I remember **being** mentally tormented and in anguish; I said out loud "God - just kill me, don't let me hurt **anyone**." At the time I was really hoping that God would put an end to me and my torment since I was powerless to do anything about it **myself**.

Two days after-wards I returned home from work to an empty house. I went into the living room, turned on the ceiling fan and sat in my recliner to cool off from working in the heat all day. I was sitting there in my recliner just staring at the wall with my hands folded behind my head. I blinked! Normally, blinking is **not unusual** or even worth mentioning only on this particular blink when my eyes re-opened there were 3 beings in my living room right in front of me. Two were standing, facing me, right at my feet in what looked like a **military** 'parade rest' position. They were dressed in dark slacks with their hands behind their backs and their feet were shoulder width apart. I never looked up at their faces to see what they looked like because I was really focusing most of my attention on the gentleman (or Spirit) sitting on the floor just in front of me to my right side. He was engaged in conversation with the two that were standing directly in front of me. They looked exactly like men, I mentioned the slacks that I saw on the two who were standing in front of me, I could not see below their knees to see their shoes because they were covered up by my legs and the recliner I was sitting in. The gentleman sitting on the floor was a different story. The biggest feature the stood out about him were his eyes, he had the most intense looking eyes I have ever seen. The whole time I was observing their visit, which lasted between 15 and 20 seconds, I kept thinking "I hope he doesn't look at me", his eyes were intimidating. I didn't know if they knew that I was looking at them because my head was back and my eyes were barely open but open enough to see everything. The best way I know to explain his eyes would be to take the bone structure of an eagle or hawk, enlarge them to man size, graft them onto a man where a mans eyes would be. Cover the new bone structure with human skin and eye brows. His hair was as white as snow, literally, and as mentioned he looked like a man, somewhere between 60 – 65 years old. He had a few very slight or minor wrinkles, he had a couple of what most people refer to as 'liver spots' on his skin, just small dark spots, larger than freckles. He was wearing blue jeans with a red plaid lumberjack style shirt with a white t-shirt underneath. I would guess he was about 5 foot 5 inches tall and about 135 pounds.

I heard absolutely nothing; it was like turning on the television and pressing the mute button, no sound at all yet he was making casual hand gestures and speaking to the two that were standing the entire time. I blinked again, and they were gone.

Now you know why I had so much trepidation about telling

anyone about these events but hopefully the Lord can use my past and turn it into a message of hope for someone, God did deliver me from Satan's grip and torment. He led me back to church where I have been attending faithfully ever since. This happened when I was 44 years old and today I am 54, (late 2013) and I am still going strong for the Lord and the men in the gym are still safe and sound and never knew what I had planned for them.

To cap this story off, the very next day I came home from work and there was a dead bat on the street right in front of the mailbox. In my mind, all of my life the symbol of evil has always been a bat. That was the first dead bat that I had ever seen. I believe that was Gods way of saying 'evil will never be an issue in your life again.'

Not even a year after the first series of events I had another event happen. It was 2 or 3 o'clock in the morning and I awoke in another dimension but I was still in my same bed. Normally, my bedroom has blue and white wallpaper with lots of items hanging on the walls around the room. I also have a 125 gallon aquarium and 2 dresser drawers and a huge antique storage chest. When I woke on this particular night, there was no wallpaper, no aquarium, nor dressers or antique storage chest. The walls were painted a buckskin color with very sparse decorations hanging on them. There was a hallway in this other dimensional bedroom leading out of the room, it was lit up and looked like a normal everyday room and hallway except it wasn't my "normal" room. Immediately to my right, there was a sofa with its back facing my bed and the sofa was facing a tall chest with a television sitting on top of it. The sofa was not mine, the television was not mine, my room isn't arranged anything like this extra dimensional room was arranged. The television was 'on' and all I could see was a fuzzy static, no sound, nothing identifiable. There was a man with his back to me sitting on the sofa watching the television and eating something occasionally, I had a friend that ate sunflower seeds and then he would use a cup to spit the hulls into, that's what it looked like this man was doing as he watched the television. I thought I would try to get this gentleman's attention and say something to him. That's when I realized that I really could not move as freely as I am accustomed to moving. It took a great deal of effort to lift myself up and wave my hand to get his attention. I could hardly speak, he finally noticed me behind him when he turned his head slightly and he had a surprised look on his face until I managed to say hello. He relaxed and smiled, he didn't say anything. I would estimate that he would have been around 30 years old and his skin was like the skin of a baby and he looked more angelic than human by his complexion and countenance. He was white skinned but he had hair that looked like the hair of a black person, very tight and curly. After our midnight greeting I laid back down and closed my eyes trying to understand what I had been shown. About 10 seconds later I re-opened my eyes and my normal room was back and the only visible part of the vision that I witnessed was the gentleman on the sofa. He was now a glowing white cloud in the outline of the gentleman, no details of his face or hair or anything identifiable. I laid back down again and about 10 seconds later I opened my eyes and he was fading away from my sight, he was now a see-through wispy white cloud form and about 5 or 10 seconds later he completely vanished from view. I believe God let me see my guardian angel.

"The Angel of the Lord encampeth round about them that fear him, and delivereth them."
…. Psalms 34: 7

THE DOWNLOADS FROM HEAVEN!

During 2004-5-6 I also experienced what I can only describe as downloads out of the blue. Similar to what Sgt. Pinniston experienced in the United Kingdom UFO incident only without the presence of a craft that I could see. These events occurred on several occasions without warning at different times of the day and night and after-wards I would be left with an intense headache. I would estimate that they occurred about once every 3 months on average for about 2 and half years. If they occurred at night I could easily see letters, numbers, words and symbols flashing by extremely fast in front of my eyes and they would be superimposed over anything I happened to be looking at. It wasn't just one column of symbols or numbers streaming by one after the other it was the whole panorama flashing by in different directions. Everywhere I looked left or right, up or down, my peripheral vision, eyes open or eyes closed they were there. This part would last from 3 to 5 minutes then it changed to what I would describe as a car racing on a lit racetrack at night only not lit up from above but only these small lights comparable to 60 watt bulbs. The only things visible were colored lights that looked as if they were mounted on roadside poles only you couldn't see the poles, just the lights going by. Imagine you are racing a car and the road you are on is winding back and forth and its hilly terrain so you are going up and down and back and forth. Your car is going 150 miles an hour at night with no headlights; all you see are these aforementioned seemingly suspended lights zooming by one after the other. These brilliantly colored vivid lights were red, green, blue and yellow and there were hundreds of them lined up along the raceway and they flashed by extremely fast. That part lasted about 2 to 4 minutes and was actually a beautiful thing to see. If it happened in daylight I would put my hand over my eyes so I could watch it. At first, I thought I was having ocular migraines but what I was seeing didn't match any of the symptoms other than the headaches after-wards.

THERE IS NOTHING TO SMALL FOR THE LORD
That's why he sent the Holy Spirit – to help men

There are many men today that believe God set the world in motion and just left us to fend for ourselves, either that or they think God just does not exist or they don't want to acknowledge his existence. This incident will show that God is working in and around his people today, up close and personally as the Bible records. Gods word says he will help us in every endeavor that a Christian undertakes. Even if it's a task that seems small and insignificant, God will help you if you ask him to.

This happened during a two week vacation back in the summer of 2004. I was remodeling my Florida room on the back of the house. It was only screened in at the time but the weather blew through year round so I decided to frame it in and put windows in. I was about half way into the build and was using a nail punch to counter-sink the finishing nails on the trim of the windows to give it a more finished look. I had been working for a few hours and went in for lunch. I returned to the porch afterward and was going to continue counter-sinking nails and could not find my nail punch (counter-sinking tool). I began my search; I went and looked on all of the framing that I had done, not there. I looked on the floor in the Florida room – not there, then I went inside thinking I took it in when I went in for lunch, not there. I re-searched the framing, my pockets, the shelving over and over again. I had just used it earlier, now it was nowhere to be found. An hour later I was ready to go jump in my truck and drive to the hardware store when I thought about asking the Holy Spirit if he could tell me or show me where my nail punch was. I did ask him and this was what I heard inside my mind as a series of thoughts in return. It sounded like my own 'thinking' or 'inner voice' that I always hear when I think to myself, but I followed the instructions that I heard:
Walk outside ------I walked outside (I was standing in the Florida room when I originally asked)
Stop ----------------I stopped
Face Left ----------I faced left
Walk Straight -----I walked straight
Stop ----------------I stopped
Face Left ----------I faced left
Walk Straight -----I walked straight
Stop ----------------I stopped
Face Left ----------I faced left

359.

Now I'm outside on the side of the house facing the Florida room so I'm thinking "**It's on** the framing right in front of me somewhere" I looked all over the framing **and** I was, of course, **wrong.**

Continuing:
Take **a** ½ Step **Back** – I took a half step **back.**
Look Down ------------I looked down
-----That nail punch was buried in the grass exactly between my 2 feet.
It didn't take 2 or 3 attempts; this happened on the 1st attempt on the first and only set of instructions.

I was an hour looking for something that the Holy Spirit was aware of the whole time. Ask God for help even if it seems insignificant and **listen** to that still small inner voice.
Satan uses what sounds like the same inner voice and that's how he deceives men, they think **it's** their own thoughts but its Satan shooting fiery darts into our minds. Yet another reason to read and know Gods word so you may recognize who is speaking to you.

A situational example: **Let's** say you are a woman and you are at work and you go into the supply room. You see a package of new pens sitting on the shelf and this thought emerges in your mind "No one will notice if I slip these into my purse." Then this thought emerges in your mind "Thou shall not **steal**"

The **first** thought was from Satan, the second thought was from God. The Holy Spirit uses the scriptures and brings them to your remembrance at times when Satan is tempting you. **The more** scriptures you know the more detailed the communication from God can be.

"And I will pray the Father, and he shall give you another **Comforter, that** he may abide with you for ever;.... But the

360.

Comforter, which is the Holy Ghost, whom the Father will send in my name, he shall teach you all things, **and bring all things to your remembrance**, whatsoever I have said unto you."
..... Jesus speaking, John 14: 16, 26

The above verse Jesus said **"Whatsoever I have said unto you"**, for today's man Jesus speaks through the Bible; the Bible, along with Gods law written on our hearts, is the way we know; in 'Word' form what Jesus says to us and desires for us. Gods law written on our hearts is a sense of right and wrong but his word, the Bible, is a detailed understanding of right and wrong and the more of the Bible that we accumulate in our souls the more the Holy Spirit can 'bring Gods Word up' to us when we need it and the less we fail in life.

"Even the Spirit of Truth; whom the world [those without Jesus] cannot receive [without first receiving Jesus], because it seeth him not, neither knoweth him: but ye know him: for he dwelleth with you, and shall be in you."
...... Jesus speaking, John 14: 17

Chapter 15

SPEAKING IN AN UNKNOWN LANGUAGE or TONGUES

There are **pastors** today that believe 'Speaking in Tongues' have ceased because they have passed away with the **apostles** and they do not teach the use of it to their congregations. These **pastors** are in error, speaking to God in an unknown language is still very useful and in full operation today reserved for those who believe. Speaking **an** "unknown language" is bypassing our intellect and allowing our **spirit** inside to speak directly to God on a myriad of subjects, persons or organizations around the world. The Bible says that knowledge is imparted to us by **speaking** in **tongues** so, in a sense, we are educating ourselves and building ourselves up by allowing the Holy **Spirit** to reveal information to us that is not readily available elsewhere. Example, this book. **It's** not limited to our own personal **needs, this** revealed knowledge can help men worldwide. In a sense, it allows God to operate through men who do not know where God needs the authority of a man's prayer directed; God uses this heavenly prayer language, (an unknown tongue), and the Holy Spirit conveys information that the Spirit world can use to aid men and destroy Satan's works. Speaking in **an** unknown tongue aids men in doing a work for God by allowing the Spirit to pray through them even when the men do not know what to pray for. The mystery is that you don't know what you are praying for or who you are praying for. You could be **praying** for a specific person in Zimbabwe or a **Church** in Argentina. God will use your prayers anywhere he needs them at the time. You could be **praying** for your next job or yours or someone else's child's protection from a bully at school. The whole world may benefit from one believer who prays in an **unknown** tongue. God speaks his own word in the Spirit through the authority of a mans **physical** body to benefit men. Why would God want that to cease? Who would want that to cease? Satan

"But you shall receive power after that the Holy Ghost is come upon you: and you shall be witnesses."
.... Acts 1: 8

"For he that speaketh in an unknown tongue speaketh not unto men, but unto God: for no man understandeth him; howbeit in the Spirit he speaketh mysteries. I thank my God, I [Paul the Apostle] speak with tongues more than ye all."
....1 Corinthians 14: 2, 18

"He that speaketh in an unknown tongue edifieth [builds up] himself; "...
....1 Corinthians 14: 4

"And when the day of Pentecost was fully come, they were all with one accord in one place. And suddenly there came a sound from heaven as of a rushing mighty wind, and it filled all the house where they were sitting. And there appeared unto them cloven tongues like as of fire, and it sat upon each of them. And they were all filled with the Holy Ghost, **and began to speak with other tongues, as the Spirit gave them utterance."**
..... Acts 2: 1- 4

Why would the Holy Spirit stop praying through the very men that he was sent here to help? Gods power is released through prayer!

"And these signs shall follow **them that believe**; In my name shall they cast out devils; **they shall speak with new tongues**;"....
......Mark 16 : 17*

*Mark 16: 17 is reserved for a specific group of believers; it's only available for an exclusive group - "Them that believe". There is great power available for those who believe God. If you believe you will receive, if you don't believe you will not receive.

"For the eyes of the Lord run to and from throughout the whole earth, to show himself strong in the behalf of them whose heart is perfect toward him..."
..... 2 Chronicles 16: 9

ARE THERE CONTRADICTIONS IN THE BIBLE OR IS IT A COMPREHENSION ISSUE?

As recorded in the 1st chapter about Gods separate creation of our spirits and our bodies some viewed this as an error and a contradiction in Gods Word. They discounted the truth of God's Word which, in their minds, made the Bible not worth looking further into. God desires his people to study his word that he sent to us. Some of the word of God takes time to understand. What people think they know about what the Bible says and what the Bible actually says could in reality be two separate things. Also, be aware of modern watered down translations because some of these are missing up to 200 verses and others have built-in errors due to copyright issues.

"Study to shew thyself approved unto God, a workman that needeth not to be ashamed, rightly dividing the word of truth."
.... 2 Timothy 2: 15

Another example that requires study is how Judas actually died; did he hang himself or did he fall off of a cliff and burst asunder? The answer is in the parallel versions of these accounts in the books of Acts and Mathew:

"Men and brethren, this scripture must needs have been fulfilled, which the Holy Ghost by the mouth of David spake before concerning Judas, which was guide to them that took Jesus."
... **Acts 1: 16**

"For he [Judas] was numbered with us, and had obtained part of this ministry."
... **Acts 1: 17**
"And he [Judas] cast down the pieces of silver in the Temple, and departed, and went and hanged himself."
... **Mathew 27: 5**
"And the Chief priests took the silver pieces, and said, it is not lawful for to put them into the treasury, because it is the price of blood."
... **Mathew 27: 6**
"And they [priests] took counsel and bought with them the potter's field to bury strangers in."
... **Mathew 27: 7**
"Now this man [Priest from the Temple] purchased a field with the reward of iniquity; and falling headlong, he burst asunder in the midst, and all his bowels gushed out."
... **Acts 1: 18**

Judas died by hanging and a priest from the Temple died when he went to buy the field.

Chapter 16

THE HEALING SCRIPTURES AND HINDRANCES TO SCRIPTURAL HEALING

Pastor Kenneth Copeland taught from Proverbs 4: 20- 23 about receiving scriptural healing and in that teaching he said that the memory of a baked potato will not nourish you but if you eat a freshly baked potato that will nourish you. What was Kenneth saying? He's saying that it's good to have healing scriptures memorized and down in your heart but the real power for healing by these scriptures comes from actually reading them again and again from print.

"My son, attend to my words; incline thine ear to my sayings. <u>Let them not depart from thine eyes</u>; keep them in the midst of thine heart. <u>For they are life unto those that find them, and health to all their flesh.</u>"
… Proverbs 4: 20- 23

The above verses say that in order to have health for our bodies we need to read the word of God continually, especially the scriptures that talk about healing. Where it says to 'incline your ear to Gods sayings' implies that they need to be read out-loud so you can hear the scriptures as you read the scriptures. Why? The Bible says that we build our faith by hearing the scriptures. If you read out-loud you will build your faith in the healing that is provided inside of Gods word.

"So then faith comes by hearing and hearing by the word of God."
… Romans 10: 17

There are, however, 4 hindrances to receiving this healing power through the scriptures:

1. You must be born again
2. Harboring Unforgiveness
3. Unconfessed Sins
4. Faithlessness or unbelief

Hindrance #1; To receive anything from the Lord you must be born again. Gods promises are reserved for those who are heirs of salvation.

"According as his divine power hath given unto us all things that pertain unto life and godliness, through the knowledge of him that hath called us to glory and virtue: whereby are given unto us exceeding great and precious promises: that by these you might be partakers of the divine nature, having escaped the corruption that is in the world through lust; [By the new birth]"
... 2 Peter 1: 3- 4

Hindrance #2; If you harbor unforgiveness God will not hear your prayers or requests.

"And when ye stand praying; forgive, if ye have ought against any: that your Father also which is in heaven may forgive you your trespasses. But if you do not forgive, neither will your Father which is in heaven forgive your trespasses."
... Mark 11:25- 26

"For if you forgive men their trespasses, your heavenly Father will also forgive you: But if ye forgive not men their trespasses, neither will your Father forgive your trespasses."
... Mathew 6: 14- 15

Jesus speaking; "For which is easier, to say, Thy sins be forgiven thee; or to say, Arise, and walk? But that you may know that the Son of man hath power on earth to forgive sins,... Arise, take up

thy bed, and go unto thine house."
... Mathew 9: 5- 6

Hindrance #3; Unconfessed sins; If you don't repent for your sins God cannot hear your prayers.

"If I regard wickedness in my heart, the Lord will not hear."
... Psalms 66: 18

"Now we know that God heareth not sinners: but if any man be a worshiper of God, and doeth his will, him he heareth."
... John 9: 31

"But your iniquities have separated you from your God; and your sins have hidden his face from you, so that he will not hear."
... Isaiah 59: 2

"The Lord is far from the wicked, but he hears the prayers of the righteous."
... Proverbs 15: 29

"And whatever we ask we receive from him, because we keep his commandments and do those things that are pleasing in his sight."
... John 3: 22

Hindrance #4; Faithlessness and unbelief. We believe God by faith in his word, then we receive from him.

"For unto us was the gospel preached, as well as unto them: but the word preached did not profit them, not being mixed with faith in them that heard it."
... Hebrews 4: 2

"So we see that they could not enter in because of unbelief."
... Hebrews 3: 19

"And He [Jesus] did not many mighty works there because of their unbelief."
… Mathew 14: 58

"And these signs shall follow them that believe; In my name [Jesus] shall they cast out devils; they shall speak with new tongues; They shall take up serpents; and if they drink any deadly thing, it shall not hurt them; they shall lay hands on the sick and they shall recover."
… Mark 16: 17- 18

The Bible records that when we pray we are to direct our prayers to Father Jehovah in the name of Jesus.

Jesus speaking: "And in that day you shall ask me nothing. Verily, verily, I say unto you, Whatsoever you shall ask the Father in my name, he will give it you. Hitherto have you asked nothing in my name: ask, and you shall receive, that your joy may be full."
… John 16: 23- 24

The Bible records that as born again Christians we have the authority on the earth to imprison any and all of Satan's works or attacks (which would include sickness and disease). We also have the authority to release righteous works over our lives.
Jesus speaking; "And I will give unto thee the keys of the Kingdom of Heaven and whatsoever thou shalt bind on earth will be bound in heaven: and whatsoever thou shalt loose on earth shall be loosed in heaven."
… Mathew 16: 19

Jesus came to the earth to destroy the works of Satan. That destruction of Satan's ruler-ship over the earth happened when Jesus went to the cross and just prior. Jesus was beaten and bruised to pay for our sins and iniquities. Jesus was wounded because man continually broke Gods laws which is the act of transgressing Gods law. Jesus was beaten with a cat of nine tails whip that is a whip with 9 strips of leather. These whips have pieces of metal tied to the ends for traumatic impact on the body. Jesus suffered an extremely painful death so that all of mankind could be restored to right standing with God the Father. As men receive Jesus as their Lord and Savior they are declared sinless and they become the body of Jesus on the earth and as such they are given authority over Satan's works.

"He that commiteth sin is of the devil; for the devil sinneth from the beginning. For this purpose the son of God was manifested, that he might destroy the works of the devil. Whosoever is born of God doth not commit sin; for his seed remaineth in him; and he cannot sin because he is born of God."
… 1 John 3: 8- 9

Even if you wanted to sin in your spirit you absolutely cannot sin. Its impossible for you, the born again believer, to sin according to the above verse. As mentioned earlier; you are a spirit, you have a soul and you live inside of a temporary home called a body. Your spirit is sealed against the corruption of this world when saved. Your body is not part of salvation, it remains earthly, fleshly and corrupt as it was prior to you being born again. Your flesh is capable of sinning and does as often as you allow it to. Its nature is to lust after worldly things and disregard the things of God. Your job as a born again believer is to rule over your flesh and keep it under subjection to your spirit.

"This I say then, walk in the spirit and ye shall not fulfill the lust of the flesh. For the flesh lusteth against the spirit, and the spirit against the flesh: and these are contrary the one to the other: so that you cannot do the things that ye would."
… Galatians 5: 16- 17

The following is a scriptural confession that, when read out-loud, will build your faith for healing. It will also deal with all of the hindrances to receiving your healing and place you on a scripturally sound footing to receive your healing from the Lord. Pages 370 – 376 are the healing confession:

HEALING SCRIPTURES CONFESSION. to be read out-loud

Jesus, my Lord and Savior, receive my into your Kingdom. I repent of my sins and I receive your Holy Spirit to guide me through life. Thank you Jesus for making me an heir of salvation and an heir of eternal life.

Father Jehova, your word says that I should not harbor unforgiveness in my heart towards anyone. I release all unforgiveness right now. I forgive everyone that ever sinned against me and I am free from unforgiveness as your word says; ..."Forgive, and you shall be forgiven."....Luke 6: 37

Father, your word says that I should confess repent for my sins so you will hear my prayers. I do repent for all of my sins, known and unknown,m sins of commission and sins of omission. Thank you Father for removing my sins from me as is recorded in Psalms 103: 12 "As far as the east is from the west, so far hath He removed our transgressions from us."

Father, your word says that if we read the scriptures our flesh would be healed according to Proverbs 4: 23; "Let them [the scriptures] not depart from thine eyes; ... For they are life... and health to all their flesh" Father, as I read, help me to believe and build my faith for my own healing according to your word; Thank you Father.

"Surely He [Jesus] hath borne our griefs, and carried our sorrows: yet we did esteem him stricken, smitten of God, and afflicted. But He was wounded for our transgressions. He was bruised for our iniquities: The chastisement of our peace was upon Him; and with His stripes we are healed."
... Isaiah 53: 4- 5

"So you shall serve the Lord your God, and He will bless your bread and water. And I will take sickness away from the midst of

you. No one shall suffer miscarriage or be barren in your land; I will fulfill the number of your days."
… Exodus 23: 25

"He sent His word and healed them, and delivered them from their destruction's."
… Psalms 107: 20

"He heals the brokenhearted and binds up their wounds...Great is our Lord and mighty in power..."
… Psalms 147: 3

"O Lord my God, I cried out to You, and You have healed me."
… Psalm 30: 2

"Many are the afflictions of the righteous, but the Lord delivers him out of them all. He guards all his bones; not one of them is broken."
… Psalms 34: 19

"...Who came to hear Him and be healed of their diseases, as well as those who were tormented with unclean spirits. And they were healed,. And the whole multitude sought to touch Him, for power went out from Him and healed them all."
...Luke 6: 17

"Now it happened on a certain day, as He was teaching, that there were Pharisees and teachers of the law sitting by, who had come out of every town of Galilee, Judea, and Jerusalem. And the power of the Lord was present to heal them."
… Luke 5: 17

"And when Jesus went out He saw a great multitude; and He was moved with compassion for them, and healed their sick."
...Mathew 14: 14

"Then Jesus returned in the power of the Spirit to Galilee... "The Spirit of the Lord us upon Me, because He has anointed Me to preach the gospel to the poor. He has sent Me to heal the brokenhearted, to preach deliverance to the captives and recovery of sight to the blind, to set at liberty those who are oppressed, to preach the acceptable year of the Lord."
...Luke 4: 14, 18

"Now Jesus went about all Galilee, teaching in their synagogues, preaching the gospel of the Kingdom and healing all kinds of sickness and all kinds of diseases among the people."
... Mathew 4: 23

"... And these signs shall follow those who believe: In My name they will cast out demons; they will speak with new tongues; they will take up serpents; and if they drink anything deadly, it will by no means hurt them; they will lay hands on the sick, and they will recover."
... Mark 16: 15

"And the multitudes with one accord heeded the things spoken by Philip, hearing and seeing the miracles which he did. For unclean spirits, crying with a loud voice, came out of many who were possessed; and many who were paralyzed and lame were healed."
... Acts 8: 6

"But go rather to the lost sheep of the house of Israel. And as you go, preach saying, 'The Kingdom of Heaven is at hand.' Heal the sick, cleanse the lepers, raise the dead, cast out demons. Freely you have received, freely give."
...Mathew 10: 6

"Therefore I say to you, whatever things you ask when you pray, believe that you receive them, and you will have them"
... Mark 11: 24

"Is anyone among you suffering? Let him pray. Is anyone among you sick? Let him call for the elders of the Church, and let them pray over him, anointing him with oil in the name of the Lord. And the prayer of faith will save the sick, and the Lord will raise him up. And if he has committed sins, he will be forgiven."
… James 5: 13- 14

"Then Jesus answered and said to her, "O woman, great is your faith! Let it be to you as you desire". And her daughter was healed from that very hour."
Mathew 15: 28

"...the blind men came to Him. And Jesus said to them, "Do you believe that I am able to do this?" They said to Him, "Yes, Lord." Then He touched their eyes, saying, "According to your faith let it be to you." And their eyes were opened."
….Mathew 9: 28

"And His name, through faith in His name, has made this man strong...Yes, the faith which comes through Him has given him this perfect soundness in the presence of you all."
… Acts 3: 16

"A merry heart does good, like medicine, but a broken spirit dries the bones."
… Proverbs 17: 22

"Hope deferred makes the heart sick, but when the desire comes, it is a tree of life."
… Proverbs 13: 12

"My son, do not forget My law, but let your heart keep My commands; for length of days and long life and peace they will add to you."
… Proverbs 3: 1

"Now to Him who is able to do exceedingly abundantly above all that we ask or think, according to the power that works in us."
...Ephesians 3: 20

"For with God nothing will be impossible"
... Luke 18: 27

"Bless the Lord, O my soul, and forget not all His benefits: who forgives all your iniquities; who heals all you diseases..."
...Psalm 103: 2

"For I will restore health to you and heal you of your wounds, " Says the Lord."
... Jeremiah 30: 17

"But those who seek the Lord shall not lack any good thing."
...Psalm 34: 10

"And my God shall supply all your need according to His riches in glory by Christ Jesus."
... Philippians 4: 19

"But when the multitudes knew it, they followed Him; and He received them and spoke to them about the kingdom of God, and healed those who had need of healing."
... Luke 9: 11

"And it happened that the father of Publius lay sick of a fever and dysentery. Paul went in to him and prayed, and laid hands on him and healed him."
... Acts 28: 8

"And when He had called His twelve disciples to Him He gave them power over unclean spirits, to cast them out, and to heal all kinds of sickness and all kinds of disease."
... Mathew 10: 1

"Now God worked unusual miracles by the hands of Paul, so that even handkerchiefs or aprons were brought from his body to the sick,, and the diseases left them and the evil spirits went out of them."
… Acts 19: 11

"And He called the twelve to Him, and began to send them out two by two, and gave them power over unclean spirits... And they cast out many demons, and anointed with oil many who were sick, and healed them."
...Mark 6: 7, 13

"Now there are diversities of gifts, but the same spirit. There are differences of ministries, but he same Lord. And there are diversities of activities, but it is the same God who works all in all. But the manifestation of the Spirit is given to each one for the profit of all: For to one is given the word of wisdom through the Spirit, to another the word of knowledge through the same Spirit, to another faith by the same Spirit, to another gifts of healings by the same Spirit, to another the working of miracles, to another prophecy, to another discerning of spirits, to another different kinds of tongues, to another the interpretation of tongues. But one and the same Spirit works all these things, distributing to each one individually and He wills."
… 1 Corinthians 12: 4

"Let us therefore come boldly to the throne of grace, that we may obtain mercy and find grace to help in time of need."
… Hebrews 4: 16

"And Jesus answered and said to him, "What do you want Me to do for you?" The blind man said to Him, "Rabboni, that I may receive my sight." Then Jesus said to him, "Go your way; your faith has made you well." And immediately he received his sight..."
… Mark 10: 51

376.

"Then Jesus said to the centurion, "Go your way; and as you have believed, so let it be done for you." And his servant was healed that same hour."
...Mathew 8: 13

"... for she said within herself, "If only I may touch His garment, I shall be made well." But Jesus turned around, and when He saw her He said, "Be of good cheer, daughter; your faith has made you well"
... Mathew 9: 21

"Jesus Christ is the same yesterday, today, and forever."
... Hebrews 13: 8

Thank you Father for building my faith for healing in my body. I bind all demonic spirits and I bind all sickness and diseases that have entered into my body. I curse those demonic spirits and all sickness and disease and I command that they dry up and die in the name of Jesus and I cast them out of my body right now. I plead the stripes and the blood of Jesus over my physical body because the scriptures proclaim that Jesus paid the price for my healing by the stripes he took on his body for us. I loose and release health, wholeness, soundness and complete restoration of my mind and body right now in the name of Jesus of Nazareth. According to the scriptures if I receive Jesus as my Lord and Savior, repent of my sins, forgive all who have sinned against me, and believe in faith that I am healed then sin cannot exist in my body just as it does not exist in my spirit. My spirit is sinless, my body is now sinless and I believe in faith that I am healed by the stripes of Jesus and I receive my healing right now in Jesus name. All of my organs function the way God designed them to function. My circulatory system, respiratory system and immune system all function in the perfection that God designed them to function. I am healed of my infirmities. Thank you Father Jehovah, I praise you, I glorify you Father.
In the name of Jesus I pray, Amen

Read this confession over and over again until the manifestation comes. It may take longer than you think it should but stay in faith until you receive your healing. God provided through his word multiple avenues of healing; The laying on of hands, Elders in the Church anointing the sick with oil mixed with the prayer of faith, intercessory prayer and the healing scriptures. All of these require men to take their authority over Satan's works to restore the sick. God has already healed us at the cross and it is our responsibility to release our authority and our faith as born again believer's to tap into what God has provided for us by faith. We recognize that the power comes from the righteousness of Jesus and nothing that we provide or do will amount to anything. The Bible says that mans self righteousness are as filthy rags and not worthy of comparison to the righteousness of Jesus. Gods healing for our bodies was bought and paid for and delivered to us through Jesus alone. His grace is sufficient for us, His mercy is everlasting, His love for us is beyond comprehension, there is nothing that a born again believer can do to separate himself from the love of Christ. The same goes for those who think that they are not worthy of the kingdom of heaven, Jesus would say to you "All have sinned and come short of the glory of God". In Gods economy there are no sins greater or lesser than other sins, sin is sin and every man was born a sinner and every man will be declared sinless upon their day of salvation. After salvation its the Holy Spirits job to teach you and guide you through the Kingdom.

CONCLUSION

The Spirits of two kingdoms are operating on the earth- good and evil, light and darkness- both are present with mankind. The manifestations of Satan have all led to death and destruction. The manifestations of the Holy Spirit have all led to prosperity and eternal life for those that believe. By default, a person who does not make a choice of his own free will to serve Jesus will end up with Satan. The choice of good or evil is built into every man and the choice is left for each to decide. Which side did Hitler, Stalin or Darwin choose? Which side did Billy Graham, Oral Roberts or Paul Crouch choose? God says that he has set before us "Life and Death" and then tells us which one to choose- "Choose Life".

In my mind, Jesus and the Kingdom of Heaven are a fact, I have absolutely no doubts about the Kingdom of Heaven or the prison called Hell. I have seen into the Spirit world, I have had experiences with the Spirit world, I have heard 100's of testimonies as to what the Lord Jesus has done for other people on the earth. I have seen and heard testimonies of what Satan has done to people on the earth and not one was a good report. I know people that the medical profession has given up on because they had no cure for them but through prayer and faith they were miraculously healed and are still going strong today- including my own mother for a season.

The evolution religion has been shown to be much less than the "Science" that the academic community hopes you will continue to believe. There is sufficient evidence to conclude that it is not a viable theory and, according to the Scientific Method should be replaced with a new theory. At the very least it should be relegated to an elective course on World Religions. Christian's are being taxed and thus being forced to pay for a religion that they have been deceived into accepting as proven science. American's still have the right to their own religious freedoms and beliefs. For most of us those freedoms and beliefs do not include being forced to financially support and learn a government sponsored false religion. The evolution religion stands in direct opposition to my religion, don't force me to pay you to teach my children your religion when I already have my own. In the United States, you have a right to exercise your religion and I have a right to exercise my religion, I don't have a right to force my religion on you just as you don't have the right to force your religion on me, your rights end where mine begin. Even though the 'Separation of Church and State' was never a Constitutional law of the land everyone seems to use it to separate Christianity from the U.S. government. If it's true for Christianities separation then its also true for evolutions separation. One woman decided to expel God from school because she had the right to keep her child from hearing a public prayer to God. Why are the 30 percentiles [anti-Christians] ruling 100% of the population of America, this is a democracy and normally the majority rules.

Jesus is about to call his **church** off of the earth and when that happens its going to be a living nightmare for anyone that is left behind. The anti-Christ is going to make Hitler look like a choir boy- the death toll could possibly be in the billions. If you are reading this after the 'Rapture' of the Church – DO NOT TAKE THE MARK – this mark will be **from a worldwide** ruler and it allows men to buy and sell and this ruler can track men through this mark. The Bible says the mark will be the mark of the number of a man '666' and placed somewhere on the body. That will be **instant** Hell for anyone that takes it. There will be angels present on the earth preaching the Gospel of Jesus and saving souls for the **Lord. Live** off of the land if you have to and barter for anything you need. If you are reading this before the **Rapture** I strongly urge you to find a good Christian **church** and confess Jesus as your Lord and Savior to keep yourself from going through what is getting ready to beset the earth. If you were a child and brought up in church as I was but then lost your faith in the Lord as I did because a deceived evolution teacher taught you something different- then, by all means come back and renew your relationship with the Lord and avoid the Tribulation that is coming. As mentioned earlier the 6000 year predestination of earths history is up, he's coming very soon!

Finally, I know many Islamic followers have been faithful to the words of Mohammed all of their lives. Your families before you, for centuries, were also followers of Mohammed and having to tell you the truth about your religion is not something I take lightly by any means. The only way you are going to see Heaven is through Jesus Christ and that is my hope for you and your families, that is what my God commands of me, to tell you the truth. As long as you have breath in your body and can speak you can ask Jesus to be your savior and He will. The same goes for all of the "Religions" of the world, Jesus will deliver you all if you ask him to.

"And the servant of the Lord must not strive; but be gentle unto all men, apt to teach, patient, in meekness instructing those that oppose themselves; if God peradventure will give them repentance to the acknowledging of he truth; and that **they may recover themselves out of the snare of the devil, who are taken captive by him [Satan] at his will.**"
... 2 Timothy 2: 24- 26

"I call heaven and earth to record this day against you, that I have set before you life [Jesus] and death [Satan], blessing and cursing: **therefore choose life,** that both thou and thy seed [children] may live!"
.... Deuteronomy 30: 19

"Let us hear the conclusion of the whole matter: Fear God, and keep his commandments: for this is the whole duty of man. For God shall bring every work unto judgment, with every secret thing, whether it be good, or whether it be evil."
... Ecclesiastes 12: 13- 14

REFERENCES

The Christian Bible or Holy Bible; containing the old and new testaments in the King James Version (any or all of the 66 books contained within the Holy Bible) The Assurance Analytical Study Edition, Assurance Publishers, Inc. 2000 Cleveland TN

The Islamic Koran or Quaran; The Custodian of the Two Holy Mosques: King Faud Complex: The Kingdom of Saudi Arabia, predominantly from an English Ali Translation.

Dr. Kent Hovind Seminar; 2005, DVD, 16 hour seminar comparing evolution to creation.

The Book of Jasher; translated from Hebrew to English in 1840, considered a lost book up until 1840, originally published by J.H. Parry and Company in Salt Lake City, Utah in 1877. Today's exact lithographic reprints are published by Artisan Publishers, a subsidiary of Hoffman Printing Co., Inc. Muskogee, Oklahoma.

All other references; in line.

Alphabetical Reference Guide

Abel, Arthur ("Talks with Great Composers") Pg. 95

Adams, John Quincy (Quote) Pg.57

Ager, Derek ("Fossil Frustrations") Pg. 86

Ahmnadinejad, Mahmoud (Quotes) Pg. 285

Al Araby, Abdullah (Muslims may lie!) Pgs. 286, 287, 288

Al-Bukhari, Sahih (Hadith writer) Pg. 301

Alfan, Hannes ("Cellular Structure of Space, Cosmic Plasma") Pgs. 140, 141

Ankerburg, Dr. John (John Ankerburg Show, The 2 Gods) Pg. 302

answersingenesis/articles (Age of the earth) Pgs. 66, 204

Barnabus (Epistle of) Pgs. 63,67

beholdthebeast.com (The Satanic Verses) Pgs. 317, 318

Behrensmeyer, Kay (Geologist) Pg. 202

B.F.R.O. - (Big Foot Research Organization) Pgs. 157, 184, 185

Birch, L.C. (Nature Magazine, April 1967) Pg. 91

Birnes, Dr. Bill (U.F.O. Investigator) pg. 114

Bonaparte, Napoleon (Quote) Pg. 56

Boornazian, Aram (The Shrinking Sun) Pgs. 196, 197

Bormann, Martin (Head of the Nazi Party Chancellery) Pg. 13

Bounoure, Professor Louis (Director of the Strasbourg Zoological Museum) Pg. 85

Bradley, Matt (Wall Street Journal – Radical Muslim Clerics) Pg. 311

Brahms, Dr. Johannes (Music Composer) Pg. 95, 96, 97

Braun, Werner Von (N.A.S.A.) Pg. 92

Brooks, Michael ("Earths Magnetic Field Boosts Gravity") Pg. 173

Burke, Edmond (Quote) Pg. 329

Burton ("The Human Side of the Physiologist: Prejudice and Poetry") Pg. 91

Bush, George (Quote) Pg. 56

Cameron, Playfair, Wellum ("The Longevity of Homosexuals: Before and After the AIDS Epidemic") Pg. 234

Caner, Dr. Ergun (Muslim turned Christian speaks about the 2 Gods of Christianity and Islam) Pg. 302

Cheney, Dick (Former U.S. V.P. Interview concerning Islamic Terrorist Organizations - Quote) Pg. 329

CNN News Pgs. 285, 293

Copeland, Kenneth (Scriptural Healing) Pg. 365

Curie, Madamme (Radiation Poisoning) Pgs. 225, 226

dailypaul.com (World-Wide Incarceration Rates) Pgs. 233, 234

Darwin, Charles ("The Origin Of Species" - Quotes) Pgs. 4, 9, 87, 88, 89

Darquera, Dr. Javier Cabrera (Ica Stones depicting dinosaurs) Pgs. 147, 148

Da Vinci, Leonardo (Quote) Pg. 55

Dawkins, Richard (Biologist) Pg. 86

Death by Medicine; A Research Paper done by: Gary Null PhD, Carolyn Dean MD ND, Martin Feldman MD, Debora Rasio MD, Dorothy Smith PhD Pgs. 227, 228, 229

Derbyshire, David (Weekly Telegraph News; Mankind dates back to 5353 B.C.) Pgs. 221, 222

Dickens, Charles (Quote) Pg. 57

Drosnin, Michael (Bible Code) Pgs. 183, 184

Eddy, Dr. John "Jack" (The Shrinking Sun) Pgs. 196, 197, 201

Ehrich, (Nature, 1967) Pg. 91

Einstein, Albert (Quote) Pgs. 55, 58

Faulkner, Dr. Danny ("Universe by Design") Pg. 201

Fedduccia, Alan (U.N.C.- Chapel Hill, leading authority on birds) Pg. 85

Fisher, Albert (Grolier Encyclopedia) Pg. 84

Fleishman, Albert ("The Doctrine of Organic Evolution in the Light of Modern Research") Pg. 90

Fox News Pgs. 293, 329, 342

Freeman, Alan (Economist) Pgs. 234, 235

frontpagemagazine.com (article on Islamic No-Go Zones, Enclaves) Pgs. 307, 308, 310

Gentile Nations List Pgs. 72, 73, 74

Glanz, James (New York Times article – Light) Pg. 136

Gould, Stephen (Harvard University) Pgs. 84, 85

Graham, Billy (Quote) Pg. 246

Gunter, Dan (Chevron Oil Company) Pg. 143

Haeckel, Earnst ("Ontogeny Recapitulates Phylogeny") Pgs. 204, 205, 206, 207

Hannity, Sean (Fox News) Pgs. 293, 329, 342

Hapgood, Charles ("Mystery in Acambaro") Pgs. 149, 150

Hardy, G. W. (Cambridge University Mathematician) Pg. 99

Hasan, Major Nidal (Fort Hood Shooter) Pgs. 312 - 313

Henry, Patrick (Quote) Pg. 57

Hillary, Sir Edmond (First to climb Mt. Everest) Pgs. 143, 144

Hitler, Adolf (Quotes) Pg. 11, 12

Holt, Lt. Col. Charles (Bentwaters AFB Deputy Base Commander) Pg. 118

Hovind, Dr. Kent (Quotes and Citations) Pgs. 87, 132, 136, 143, 145, 195, 196, 200, 203, 206, 218, 219, 220, 221, 232, 233, 242

Hoyle, Sir Frederick (Cambridge University) Pg. 90

Jasher, The Book (Another account of the events in the Christian Bible and Jewish Talmud, spoken of by the Prophet Samuel and mentioned in the book of Joshua) Pgs. 150, 151, 152, 154, 155, 156, 157, 159, 161, 164, 165, 176, 177, 178, 179, 222, 223, 296, 297, 298, 299, 300

Jeffery, Grant ("The Signature of God") Pg. 88

jewishvirtuallibrary.org/jsource/History/1948-_War Pg. 336

Kass, Robert (Bible Code Statistics) Pgs. 181, 182

Keith, Sir Arthur (Quotes) Pgs. 10, 52

kgov.com/carbon_14_and_dinosaur_bone's (Carbon 14 results in error) Pg. 216

Lavay, Anton (Founder of the Church of Satan) Pgs. 240, 241

Lee, Robert ("Radiocarbon: Ages in Error") Pg. 89

Leedskalnin, Ed (Coral Castle builder) Pgs. 169 – 173

Lessum, Don (OMNI Magazine; Fresh Dinosaur Bones) Pg. 220

Lewin, Roger ("Bones of Contention") Pgs. 202 – 203

Lewis, C. S. (Quote) Pg. 246

Lincoln, Abraham (Quotes) Pgs. 54, 342, 347

Lipson, H. S. ("A Physicist Look at Evolution) Pg. 92

Lyell, Charles ("Principles of Geology") Pgs. 2, 3, 8

Maddox, Dr. Barney (Human Genome Project) Pg. 132

Martin (Mahdi: Islamic Eschatology) pg. 301

Matritiano, Carol ("Let My Children Go") Pg. 21

Mayyam.com (Ramanujan) Pg. 98 – 99

McDougle, Dr. Duncan (Weight of Souls) Pgs. 27 – 28

Mongolia State University (Fossil Radioactivity should not exist, but it does exist today) Pg. 217

Moorbath, Dr. Stephen (Oxford University) Pgs. 219, 220

Mozart, Wolfgang Amadeus (Quote) Pg. 57

MUFON (Mutual Unidentified Flying Objects Network) Pg. 111

Muggeridge, Malcolm ("Something Beautiful From God") Pg. 86

Nature Magazine (Kay Behrensmeyer Article) Pg. 202

ncsu.edu/news/press-releases (Dr. Mary Schweitzer) Pg. 211

New Realities Magazine (Dr. William Thetford interview) Pg. 250

Newton, Sir Isaac (Quote) Pg. 55

New York Times, (Scientists Break the Speed of Light) Pg. 136

North, Colonel Oliver (Fox News Quote) Pg. 343

nsf.gov (National Science Foundation News) Pg. 214

O'Reilly, Bill (Fox News report on Muslim Jihadists) Pg. 293

Patterson, Dr. Colin (Darwins Inigma) Pg. 84

Payne, Thomas ("Common Sense") Preface

Perloff, James ("Tornado in a Junkyard") Pg. 92

Peterson, Freya (Global Post News; Israeli Genocide) Pgs. 15, 16

Pewe, Troy L. (Vollosovitch Mammoth) Pg. 201

Popper, Dr. Karl (Quote) Pg. 87

Quora.com (Radioactive fossils) Pg. 217

Ramanujan, Srinivas (Mathematician) Pg. 98

Rambsel, Yakov (Bible Code author "His name is Jesus") Pgs. 180, 182, 183

Raup, David (Evolution and the Fossil Record) Pg. 84

Reagan, Ronald (Quote) Pg. 54

Rhodes, James ("The Hitler Movement") Pg. 11

Richardson, Don ("Secrets of the Koran") Pgs. 277, 282. 293,

Ripps, Dr. Eliyahu (Bible Code) Pgs. 183 – 184

Roosevelt, Theodore (Quote) Pg. 56

Ruse, Dr. Michael (University of Guelph) Pg. 85

Rushdie, Salman ("The Satanic Verses") Pgs. 317 - 320

Sanhedrin 97 (Age of the Earth) Pg. 68

Satanic Verses (The words of Jesus to Mohammed) Pgs. 317, 318

Satinover, Dr. Jeffrey (Bible Code) Pg. 182

Schucman, Dr. Helen ("A Course in Miracles") Pgs. 247 – 251, 271

Schuller, Dr. Robert (Proponent of "A Course in Miracles" and Chrislam) Pg. 254

Schweitzer, Dr. Mary (N.C. Museum of Natural Science) Pgs. 209 – 214

Seifer, Marc (Wizard: The life and times of Nicola Tesla") Pg. 94

Setterfield, Barry (Astronomer) Pg. 136

Sitchen, Zachariah (Anunnaki) Pgs. 153, 154, 159, 160, 165

southfloridaonline.com/article-coral-castle (Leedskalnin) Pg. 170

stangrist.com/giants (Giant Human Skeletons) Pg. 219

Swift, Dennis (Ica Stones and Moche Pottery depicting dinosaurs) Pgs. 146 – 149

Swinton, W. E. (British Museum of Natural History) Pg. 85

Tahmisian, Dr. T. (Atomic Energy Commission) Pg. 90

Tesla, Nicola (Electrical Engineer) Pgs. 55, 93 – 95

Thetford, Dr. William ("A Course in Miracles") Pgs. 250, 251, 271

Thornhill, Wallace ("Electric Universe") Pg. 59

tisfortrex.com: Thomas, B. (Dinosaur soft tissue) Pgs. 208, 209

United Kingdom Sunday Times (Scientist breaks the speed of light) Pg. 136

universe.com ("On the hunt for high speed Sprites") Pg. 139

USAToday (article on Fort Hood Texas Shooter) Pg. 312

Vanityfair.com (Salman Rushdie article) Pg. 319

Van Beethoven, Ludwig (Quote) Pg. 57

Van Gogh, Vincent (Quote) Pg. 56

Van Impe, Jack (Islam in America) Pgs. 293, 311, 336

Von Braun, Wernher (Quote) Pg. 92

Wahhaj, Siraj (Islamic Leader) Pgs. 284, 307, 316, 338

Wall Street Journal, (Radical Muslim Clerics) Pg. 311

Warren, Rick ("The Purpose Driven Life"- Chrislam proponent) Pg. 306

Washington, George (Quote) Pg. 54

West, Dr. Ronald R. (Kansas State University) Pg. 89

Wikipedia encyclopedia:
(List of designated terrorist organizations) Pg. 328
(Muslim Conquests) Pg. 336
(History of Islam) Pg. 336
(Terrorism in the United States) Pg. 336
(Islam by Country) Pg. 338

Wilberforce, William (Abolished slave-trade in Europe) Pg. 347

Winfrey, Oprah (Proponent of "A Course in Miracles") Pg. 254

WND News (News affecting the world-wide Christian community) Pg. 293

Wopnick, Dr. Kenneth (Editor: "A Course in Miracles") Pg. 248

Wysong, R. L. ("The Creation-Evolution Controversy") Pg. 91

Made in the USA
Middletown, DE
17 December 2018